Changing Minds or Changing Channels?

CHICAGO STUDIES IN AMERICAN POLITICS

A series edited by Benjamin I. Page, Susan Herbst, Lawrence R. Jacobs,
and Adam Berinsky

Changing Minds or Changing Channels?

Partisan News in an Age of Choice

KEVIN ARCENEAUX AND
MARTIN JOHNSON

THE UNIVERSITY OF CHICAGO PRESS   CHICAGO AND LONDON

KEVIN ARCENEAUX is associate professor of political science and an affiliate of the Institute for Public Affairs at Temple University. MARTIN JOHNSON is associate professor
in the Department of Political Science, the Survey Research Center, and the Media and
Research Lab at the University of California, Riverside.

The University of Chicago Press, Chicago 60637
The University of Chicago Press, Ltd., London
© 2013 by The University of Chicago
All rights reserved. Published 2013.
Printed in the United States of America

22 21 20 19 18 17 16 15 14 13   1 2 3 4 5

ISBN-13: 978-0-226-04727-0 (cloth)
ISBN-13: 978-0-226-04730-0 (paper)
ISBN-13: 978-0-226-04744-7 (e-book)

Library of Congress Cataloging-in-Publication Data

Arceneaux, Kevin.
   Changing minds or changing channels? : partisan news in an age of choice / Kevin
Arceneaux and Martin Johnson.
      pages ; cm. — (Chicago studies in American politics)
   Includes bibliographical references and index.
   ISBN 978-0-226-04727-0 (alk. paper) — ISBN 978-0-226-04730-0 (pbk. : alk paper) —
ISBN 978-0-226-04744-7 (e-book)   1. Television broadcasting of news—Political
aspects—United States.   2. Television and politics—United States.   3. Television in
politics—United States.   4. Mass media and public opinion—United States.   5. Mass
media—United States—Influence.   6. Television viewers—United States—Attitudes.
7. United States—Politics and government—21st century—In mass media.   8. United
States—Politics and government—21st century—Public opinion.   I. Johnson, Martin,
1970 March 10–   II. Title.   III. Series: Chicago studies in American poltics.
   PN1992.6.A695 2013
   384.55—dc23
                                                                    2012046143

To Juliet and Sherri

Contents

Acknowledgments

We began this project during the summer of 2005. Martin was an assistant professor at the University California, Riverside, and made the cross-country trip to New Haven to visit Kevin, who was finishing up a two-year postdoctoral fellowship at Yale University and preparing to join the faculty at Temple University as an assistant professor. We intended to work on an ultimately less promising conference paper but found ourselves discussing recent developments in political communication research. We were taken with how far some of our colleagues were willing to overstate the implications of laboratory experiments and assume that large treatment effects observed in such experiments translate to similarly sized effects in more natural viewing environments.

We began an extended conversation that blossomed from a narrowly focused methods paper into a reconsideration of media effects in general. The media environment was in flux and called out for a rethinking of media effects. In our lifetimes, we had witnessed an explosion of choices in television programming and realized that most of what we thought we knew about the influence of television news came from a time when there were few choices on the television dial, relatively speaking.

In this endeavor, we owe a considerable intellectual debt to Shanto Iyengar and Don Kinder, who taught us the value of experimental research for studying the effects of news media and also supplied the theoretical foundation for describing and cataloging those effects. These are big shoes to try on, and we do not pretend to fill them. But, if nothing else, we think we have shed light on where scholars should go next. We set ourselves to building on Iyengar and Kinder's work and the work of the experimentalists who followed in their footsteps by figuring out how to distinguish which sorts of people are inclined to view which sorts of programs, political or otherwise. We hoped to learn more about how media influence people and how extensive media influence is. This book represents a preliminary effort in that direction, an investigation of what happens when people are allowed to sort themselves into audiences for political and entertainment television programming.

It is fortuitous that our professional path passed through Yale in the early years of the twenty-first century. The Institution for Social and Policy Studies (ISPS), where Kevin was a postdoc, has been at the vanguard of the experimental movement in political science. Our work is heavily indebted to the field experimental approach in which ISPS scholars innovated. Our central insight that choice can be embedded in the laboratory environment comes from our experience with and understanding of noncompliance in randomized field experiments. What many laboratory-trained experimentalists saw as a nuisance we saw as an opportunity. It is also fitting that the seeds of our project were planted at Yale, which coincidentally happened to be the site of the *News That Matters* studies and Carl Hovland's pathbreaking randomized experiments on mediated communication and persuasion.

We are deeply indebted to Don Green, who was director of ISPS and the first person with whom we discussed the ideas that inform this book. As always, Don was generous with his time, supportive, and helpful as we worked through our initial ideas about the experimental design and what would become the selective exposure protocol. We are especially grateful to David Nickerson, who completed his doctoral work at Yale under Don's mentorship and was the first person to befriend a newly arrived and somewhat bewildered postdoc who felt very much out of his element. With David's help, we refined our formal model of selective exposure, and it was his quick mind that conceived of the participant preference protocol—an experimental design that unbeknownst to all of us had been a staple of randomized control trials in medicine for years. We would not have gotten as far along with this project as we did without David's unselfish willingness to help others think through a research question, experimental design, methodological approach, and more.

We could not have successfully executed our research plan without the help of colleagues at UC Riverside, who provided useful insights along the way and gave us access to their students and, thus, a subject pool for many of our experiments. We thank Juliann Allison, Ben Bishin, Bruce Bordner, Shaun Bowler, David Crow, Kevin Esterling, Vanesa Estrada

Correa, Indridi Indridason, Masa Omae, Yuhki Tajima, and Antoine Yoshinaka.

Our project has also benefitted immensely from the support of many colleagues along the way. We thank Jamie Druckman, whose enthusiasm for the project early on inspired and motivated us to stick with it. His close read of the manuscript and incisive comments were invaluable as we revised the book. Shanto Iyengar deserves many thanks for his encouragement and support. In addition to setting in motion the broad literature to which we hope our book speaks, he helped refine our thinking about selective exposure and introduced us to John Tryneski and the University of Chicago Press. Markus Prior was an essential adviser for the project. Much of our understanding of how entertainment seeking shapes media influence comes from his work and our many discussions with him. Markus never shies away from asking pertinent but difficult questions. Our book is all the better for it.

Megan Mullin deserves our gratitude for reading many chapters of our manuscript draft. Her careful eye and sharp intellect helped us turn limp, turgid prose into something less so. Kevin Esterling and Shaun Bowler have been especially helpful as sounding boards. So many others contributed to this project, at various stages. For providing helpful and insightful advice, we thank Jason Barabas, Michael Bailey, Larry Bartels, Toby Bolsen, John Bullock, Michael Delli Carpini, Johanna Dunaway, Jim Endersby, Henry Farrell, Kelley Garrett, Andy Gelman, Alan Gerber, Marty Gilens, Mike Hooper, Dan Hopkins, Greg Huber, Jenn Jerit, Jon Ladd, Rick Lau, Regina Lawrence, Matt Levendusky, Diana Mutz, Betsy Levy Paluck, Neil Malhotra, Marc Meredith, Russ Neumann, Costas Panagopoulos, John Barry Ryan, John Sides, Talia Stroud, and Chris Wlezien. Our thinking and writing were also clarified along the way by seminar participants at the Annenberg School of Communication, Columbia University, Florida State University, Princeton University, Temple University, Texas A&M University, UC Riverside, the University of Pennsylvania, and Yale University.

We are delighted that our book found its way to the University of Chicago Press. We are humbled to share a place in a catalog with so many important works, including *News That Matters*. We are also fortunate to have worked with John Tryneski, who ably guided two first-time book authors through the process. Rodney Powell, an assistant editor at the Press, was also exceptionally helpful.

We could not have completed this research without the aid of an army of research assistants at UC Riverside and Temple. We specifically thank John Cryderman and Chad Murphy as coauthors who contribute to chapters 5 and 7, respectively, in addition to playing vital roles on our research team. We are also in the debt of the other graduate research assistants without whom the Media and Communication Research Lab (MCLab) would have ceased operation: Jackie Filla, Byran Martin, and Justin Nelson, who worked on the project early on, as well as Nic Boushee, Andrew Flores, Chris Haynes, Tom Hayes, Anwar Hijaz, Glenn Loveall, Andrea Silva, Carrie Skulley, and Amber Tierney. A number of undergraduate students were also essential to the operation of the lab, and we thank Arash Aalem, Hemant Bajaj, Caleb Cavazos, Jennifer Dubé, Rachelle Jung, Jennifer Kanjana, Rinata Krel, Phillip Lee, Renee Manson, Lauren Menor, Kyla Persons, Joel Ruvalcaba, Daniel Sanchez, Roxanna Sanchez, Rebecca Tekeian, and Brandon Vaters.

Cindy Fraley and the staff of AppleOne employment agency (Riverside, California, location) enabled us to expand the subject pool and include nonstudent adults. We also would have had difficulty competently attending to the more mundane but essential matters of running a lab and securing the necessary funding without the administrative support of Gina Barnes and Kim Fahey at Temple University and Monique Davis-Brooks and Tanya Wine at Riverside. Dannette Bock helped us copyedit and ready the manuscript for final submission. Joe H. Brown copyedited the manuscript during the production phase for the University of Chicago Press. We appreciate their thoroughness and keen attention to detail.

This research would not have been possible at all without the generous support of the National Science Foundation (SES-0752354, SES-0752546), the Committee on Research, UC Riverside, Academic Senate, and Temple University. We owe a debt of gratitude to Glenn Stanley and colleagues in the Department of Psychology at UC Riverside, who have been gracious landlords for the MCLab, as well as Steve Cullenberg, dean of the College of Humanities, Arts, and Social Sciences, and Paul Richardson, the facilities manager. We also thank the Pew Research Center for the People and the Press for providing access to the June 2010 Media Consumption Survey. The Pew Research Center bears no responsibility for interpretations and insights informed by the use of these data in chapter 3.

Our journey began many years before our 2005 meeting in New Haven. We entered in the same graduate school cohort at Rice University and quickly established a strong rapport. We have been friends and kindred intellects ever since. We count ourselves lucky that Cary Funk led our first-semester graduate seminar on research design. Not only did she teach us the value of experimental methods, but she also introduced us to *News That Matters* as an exemplar of what experiments could achieve in generating knowledge about politics. It was the late 1990s, and few political scientists employed randomized experiments in their work. We were set, however, for the resurgence in experimental political science that followed in the first decade of the new millennium.

We would be remiss for not thanking our advisers at Rice University for shaping us into the scholars we have become. John Alford's quick wit and deep intellect inspired us to ask big questions and think beyond the confines of convention. Throughout graduate school and well beyond, Bob Stein has been an insightful mentor, an enthusiastic advocate, and a great friend. We learned to be reflective and critical of our own work from Rick Wilson, who was highly influential in setting us on the path to being experimentalists. Paul Brace provided us with guidance and camaraderie. Randy Stevenson sparked our interest in advanced methods. Each of these individuals believed in us as students, nurtured us, and has been a constant supporter ever since graduate school. We are fortunate for having them in our lives.

The love and support of our parents and family is responsible for sustaining us, giving us confidence and strength. Without the devotion and encouragement of Carolyn and Karl Arceneaux, it is doubtful that Kevin would have sought a college education. They demonstrated the value of working hard in their words and deeds and sacrificed so that their children could succeed. When Martin was in high school, Guy Johnson provided him an introduction to hypothesis testing and experimental design, sharing his first copy of Campbell and Stanley's indispensable *Experimental and Quasi-Experimental Designs for Research*. Vivian Johnson was an assiduous teacher to Martin and others. She remains an inspiration and would have gotten a kick out of Rachel Maddow.

Finally, we thank our partners, Juliet Whelan and Sherri Franks Johnson, who fill our lives with love and happiness. An architect and a historian, respectively, they have generously discussed this research with us over the years. They tolerated our time away from home as we visited each other to work on the project, and they took time out of their busy days to be hospitable on our many visits. They have celebrated our achievements and commiserated over our setbacks. Juliet and Sherri deserve a great deal of credit for this enterprise coming to fruition.

*   *   *

Parts of chapter 5 are drawn from Arceneaux, Johnson, and Cryderman (in press). Parts of chapter 7 are drawn from Arceneaux, Johnson, and Murphy (2012). All material is used with permission.

CHAPTER ONE

The Expansion of Choice

Walk into the average American home, turn on the television, and enter a variegated world of news and entertainment. The old standbys of the broadcast networks are in the lineup, with serious news programs at the appointed hour and soap operas, game shows, sitcoms, and dramas the rest of the time. Venture into the channels available through most cable packages and find ever more, specialized viewing choices. A half dozen channels or more are devoted to the news twenty-four hours a day, seven days a week. The shows on these networks range from the sedate anchor-behind-a-desk format to lively opinionated talk shows on which the hosts and guests lob invective and unsubstantiated claims without compunction.

Keep flipping the channel, and happen on all sorts of diversions from the worries and cares of the day. On MTV, to take one example of many, cameras follow *Jersey Shore* star Mike "The Situation" Sorrentino to the gym, tanning salon, laundromat, nightclubs, and back home. Elsewhere on cable television, viewers can find endless depictions of more interesting things like people building unique motorcycles, decorating impossibly elaborate cakes, crafting beautiful tattoos, rescuing endangered animals, and catching catfish with their bare hands. Of course, there are also stations devoted to second-run movies and fresh scripted dramas like *Mad Men* on the AMC channel.

It is not an exaggeration to say that the emergence of cable television has been revolutionary. Devised as a technology for bringing television to areas where broadcast signals founder, cable television also expanded the number of channels available for programming. In the 1970s, the average household in America had six or so channels from which to choose. Many of these were of poor broadcast quality on the UHF spectrum. By the end of 2010, the majority of homes—over 90 percent—have access to either cable or satellite television, giving the average home in the United States access to more than 130 channels (Nielsen Co. 2008).[1]

More channels translate into more choices, and the expansion of choice afforded by cable television has not only changed the face of television news and entertainment but also had profound implications for the reach and effect of news media.[2] Before the rise of cable television, viewers could watch news programming a few times a day at fixed intervals and had little in the way of televised entertainment options during those newscasts (Prior 2007). In contrast, today's cable television provides something for almost everybody (Webster 2005). The array of choices is vast, and the content itself is more varied and increasingly specialized as television programmers seek audience niches (Mullen 2003).

Four decades ago, when cable television was a far less developed resource, the trustees of the Alfred P. Sloan Foundation commissioned respected political leaders and scholars to assess the cable television industry of the day and forecast its harms and benefits in the future.[3] The report that emerged from the Sloan Commission saw much potential in the new medium and the potential viewing options that it might eventually offer (Parsons 2008; Mullen 2003). It viewed cable television as a boon to viewers, particularly the possibility that the expansion of programming it afforded would help edify the public:

> [Cable television] cannot, of itself, create a politically aware citizenry, for no one can be forced to twist the dial to the channel carrying political information or political news. But cable television can serve, as perhaps no medium before it has been able, those who wish to be part of the political process, and skillfully used it might very well be able to augment their number. . . . Politics, whatever opprobrium may sometimes be attached to the word, is important. The cable can literally bring that fact home, and in doing so help the entire political process function efficiently and effectively in the public interest. (Sloan Commission 1971, 122)

As with many other innovations, however, cable television has seen its promise give way to disappointment. Instead of supplying the public with the informative and edifying content envisioned by the Sloan Commission, cable news outlets have become purveyors of pitched, partisan discourse. Many see the news channels that have emerged on cable television as a nuisance at best and more likely a destructive force in the American polity.

In particular, the emergence of partisan news options on cable television has led many observers to fret that the expansion of choice has enabled people to live in a world where facts neatly fit their ideological preconceptions, enabling them to wall themselves off from reality (Manjoo 2008; Sunstein 2007). We agree that the partisan news offered by cable television makes this possible, but it is only one aspect of the new media environment. The choices available to viewers today go well beyond public affairs programming. There is a world of far less meaningful programming being issued on entertainment channels. Although it receives less attention from scholars who study news media, the expansion of entertainment choices is just as important a phenomenon as the rise of partisan news shows because it alters the reach and influence of news media. If we wish to understand how partisan news media shape people's political views and behavior, we cannot study them in a vacuum. At the same time, Rachel Maddow (MSNBC) and Sean Hannity (Fox News) have become household names in certain, distinct households; so have people like "The Situation" (MTV), Kim Kardashian (E! Entertainment Television), and Cesar Milan, the Dog Whisperer (National Geographic Channel).

In this book, we investigate media effects in the context of choice. The television landscape has changed dramatically in the types of programs it offers viewers and the sheer number of them. We are most interested in the political implications of this expansion of viewing options—in particular, the claims that the new cable news, featuring the expression of politically ideological reporting, polarizes the public, affects distinct partisan issue agendas, and diminishes confidence in political and social institutions. We argue that television viewers are active participants in the media they consume. They are not, as many scholars and media observers implicitly assume, an inert mass, passively and unquestioningly soaking in the content to which they are exposed. They make choices about what to watch on television—be it partisan news or something else—and those choices shape how they react to the content they view.

Placing Partisan News Media in the Context of Choice

Ideologically slanted news is certainly available today, primarily on Fox News and MSNBC. If the presence of these partisan news shows is not bad enough, many scholars and public intellectuals worry that "the inclination to seek out or selectively expose oneself to one-sided information" creates a public that is increasingly encouraged to view the world from only one's own point of view and that, as a result, adopts more extreme and polarized political attitudes (Jamieson and Cappella 2008, 214; see also Stroud 2008, 2010). As people are "exposed largely to louder echoes of their own voices," the result is likely to be "misunderstandings and enmity" (Sunstein 2007, 73) as well as the creation of "parallel realities" in which liberals and conservatives no longer share even the same facts (Manjoo 2008, 25). These worries coalesce into the broader concern that the rise of partisan news on cable television threatens the functioning of American democracy as politics increasingly becomes two strongly opposed ideological camps talking past each other rather than deliberating toward sound public policies on matters of collective, and not particular, concerns.

The partisan news media may indeed have a deleterious effect on democracy, but we doubt that partisan news shows are *directly* responsible for polarizing the mass public. For one, partisan news shows attract small audiences. The week of January 16–20, 2012, offers a more or less representative snapshot of broadcast and cable news audiences. According to the Nielsen Media Research Group, which rates television programs, the top-rated prime-time partisan news programs drew in anywhere from 0.8 million (*Hardball with Chris Matthews*) to 3.4 million (*The O'Reilly Factor*) viewers, on average. In contrast, the broadcast evening news programs drew 7.4 million (NBC) to 10.2 million (CBS) viewers, on average. This broadcast news audience is smaller than it was in the past (Webster 2005), but it is more than three times the size of the partisan news audience. Even if we assume that there is no overlap in partisan news audiences, the four top-rated shows draw roughly 7.5 million viewers on any given day. This is a large number of people to be sure, but, as figure 1.1

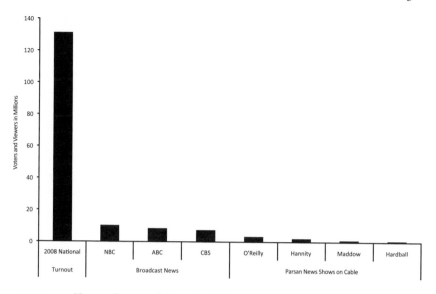

FIGURE I.I. News audiences and the national electorate.
Source: Nielsen Media Research Group as reported by TV by the Numbers (2012a, 2012b).
Note: Bars represent average viewers per day (in millions) during the week January 16–20, 2012.

shows, it pales in comparison to the 130 million individuals who vote in national elections.

Not too long ago, things were different. In the 1970s, most people got their news from one of the three major broadcast networks (ABC, CBS, or NBC). The news shows on these networks were nearly identical: an anchor sitting behind a desk reading the news and showing video footage of events. Reporting followed shared standards of objective journalism. Remove, balance, fairness to all sides, and impartiality were the goal in network reportage. The reporter and the news anchor were cast in the role of Joe Friday, the fictional police detective on the hit 1950s television show *Dragnet*: "All we know are the facts, ma'am." What is more, many Americans watched the news simply because *there was little else to watch* (Prior 2007).

Today, television programming is so diverse that it can precisely map to the interests of its viewers. The vast array of choices viewers have at their disposal allow Americans to watch only news by tuning in to twenty-four-hour cable news channels or to avoid watching any news at all (Bennett and Iyengar 2008; Prior 2007). Analyses that draw a straight

line from the content of partisan news shows to normatively undesirable
political outcomes, such as polarization or declining trust, often fail to
appreciate that the availability of so many viewing options gives people unprecedented control over the content they consume on television.
People do not have to watch the news because they lack other alternatives. There is a plethora of entertainment options, which should limit
the reach of partisan news and substantially blunt its direct effects on
American society.

Some may consider the limited reach of partisan news a good thing,
and others may consider it too good to be true. However, the downside
we suggest is that this abundant choice also means that the capacity of
television to educate its viewers and to engage them in public life is *also*
limited. Television informs the informed who want to learn more. It provides specialized knowledge to particular people—information about
partisan politics to partisans, home-improvement training to people who
like that sort of thing, and so on. The partisan media must be placed in
this context of expanded choice if we are to understand their effects.

Partisan News Media Require a New Kind of Media Effects Research

In the early years of the twentieth century, the seemingly successful use
of mass communication to rally the country behind World War I led
many scholars to worry that their expansive reach would give media un-
paralleled power to shape and mold mass attitudes (Lasswell 1938/1972;
Lippmann 1922/1965). The rise of the Nazi Party in Germany and its
masterful use of propaganda to maintain power and motivate unspeak-
able acts of violence and genocide only fueled such concerns. In these
early models of media effects, consumers of mass media were characterized as easily manipulated victims. Subsequent scholars derisively described these models as treating the mass media like a "hypodermic needle" that injected propaganda into the veins of consumers who could not
resist its effects (Berelson, Lazarsfeld, and McPhee 1954). By midcentury, the pendulum had swung in the opposite direction. Failure to find
consistent and lasting media effects through quantitative empirical research (e.g., Hovland 1954; Lazarsfeld, Berelson, and Gaudet 1948) led
Joseph Klapper (1960) to declare in *The Effects of Mass Communication*, his influential meta-analysis: "Mass communication *ordinarily* does

not serve as necessary and sufficient cause of audience effects, but rather functions among and through a nexus of mediating factors and influences" (8). Communication designed to persuade, in particular, "functions more frequently as an agent of reinforcement than as an agent of change" (15).

Soon after the "minimal effects paradigm" became the dominant framework, scholars began to consider the more subtle and nuanced ways in which the media could influence mass attitudes. They eschewed the early fascination with persuasion, focusing instead on the ways in which news media can set the agenda by reporting on some issues at the expense of others (Cohen 1963; McCombs and Shaw 1972). By setting the agenda, news media are capable of influencing the criteria by which citizens evaluate public officials (Iyengar and Kinder 1987). Moreover, in the process of creating a narrative, even news stories that attempt to be balanced end up defining issues in particular ways. The "frame" of a news story has the ability to shape how people think about an issue and, in turn, conceptualize the solution (Iyengar 1991).

Research on the effects of partisan media brings the study of persuasion effects back into focus. Unlike mainstream media news, the ostensible goal of partisan news *is* to persuade. Recently, scholars offer evidence that exposure to partisan media does persuade (Feldman 2011), polarize attitudes (Jamieson and Cappella 2008; Stroud 2011), and misinform (Fairleigh Dickinson University 2011; Ramsay, Kull, Lewis, and Subias 2010). Besides being designed to persuade, partisan media are also designed to bolster and reinforce the preexisting attitudes of like-minded viewers, suggesting that attitude reinforcement, which was seen by Klapper as evidence of the media's minimal effects, should be reconceptualized as a media effect (Holbert, Garrett, and Gleason 2010; Levendusky 2012). Evaluating the potential for the partisan media to create insular worlds in which Manjoo's "parallel realities" exist requires that we reconsider the nature of agenda-setting effects in a media environment that features multiple conversations rather than a common one (Mutz and Martin 2001). The content of partisan media is also in direct contrast to the genteel world of mainstream news. Hosts yell at guests, their absent opponents, and the audience. Pundits make dramatic and histrionic claims. Heated arguments are frequent. These displays of hostility and aggression may serve only to damage viewers' trust in news media (Coe et al. 2008; Ladd 2010) and the political system (Mutz and Reeves 2005).

Competing Models of Viewing Behavior and Reception

In much the same way as scholars in the mid-twentieth century found, how we conceptualize viewers shapes how we think about and, ultimately, investigate partisan media effects. In this section, we contrast the model implicit in many current accounts of partisan media effects with the theoretical model we offer in this book.

Passive Reception

In the pursuit of cataloging the effects of partisan media, previous scholarship has implicitly adopted a *hypodermic needle* model of reception in three important respects. First, these researchers ignore political avoidance and proceed as if exposure to partisan news is ubiquitous. Second, they implicitly assume that exposure to news has strong direct effects on political attitudes. Third, they treat viewers as passive recipients of partisan news media. Take Jamieson and Cappella's (2008, 216) argument as a representative example: "In circumstances in which an audience is exposed regularly to a single, coherent, and consistent point of view and the voices championing that in-group view identify alternative points of view as suspect, the audience's dispositions would be expected to be reinforced or made more extreme." Partisan news is like a powerful, addictive drug that people are powerless to resist once exposed to it.

Interestingly, while research in this vein implicitly characterizes reception as passive, many scholars view the decision to seek out attitude-consistent information as a facilitator of media effects rather than a foil, as those in the minimal effects tradition saw it. Part of the difference in interpretation lies in the fact that the partisan media wish to reinforce preexisting attitudes through selective exposure, whereas the persuasive communication that Klapper considered was designed to convert mass audiences (e.g., campaign propaganda). Consequently, scholars today are more likely to view selective exposure as a key mechanism through which partisan media are able to bolster and polarize the attitudes of their audience members. Selective exposure to like-minded news creates a "reinforcing spiral" wherein the viewer's attitudes become more extreme, which in turn feeds their desire to consume more like-minded media (Slater 2007).

Nonetheless, many models of partisan media effects do not character-ize audiences as active beyond their decision to consume partisan news, and even here an individual's decision to watch partisan media, like-minded sources in particular, is treated almost like a moth's attraction to the flame. The passive audience assumption is all the more obvious when we consider that the antidote to the reinforcing spiral is exposure to al-ternative viewpoints (e.g., Jamieson and Cappella 2008, 83–84; Sunstein 2007, 158). If only people exposed themselves to news media that pre-sent ideas contrary to their predispositions, the argument goes, the ef-fects would go in the opposite direction and moderate their attitudes in the process.

Agency, Learning, and Motivation: The Active Audience

In contrast to previous approaches, our model of media effects em-phasizes the role of human agency in selecting what to watch on televi-sion. Put simply, audiences are not passive; they are active. People tend to watch shows that they enjoy (Bowman 1975) and use media to sat-isfy a variety of gratifications and needs (Katz, Blumler, and Gurevitch 1973–74). We highlight people's motivations to seek information and di-version. When choosing among news channels, partisan selectivity re-flects a learning process. With time, consumers learn about qualities of products, including television programming (Chan-Olmstead and Cha 2007; Sung and Park 2011). Morris (2005) has shown that, at the advent of Fox News, many viewers were not aware of its partisan tilt but that, since that time, partisanship has increasingly predicted who tunes in, suggest-ing that news consumers have learned where the channel stands relative to other cable channels. In a more recent study, Baum and Gussin (2008) presented individuals with the same news transcript but randomly var-ied whether it was attributed to CNN, Fox News, or a fictional television station. Even though the content remained the same, study participants perceived a liberal bias if it was attributed to CNN and a conservative bias if it was attributed to Fox News (see also Stroud 2011, chap. 4).

Cable news programs are not fooling many people. Viewers gener-ally know where the political news networks stand, and they must be mo-tivated to watch them. As such, our theoretical model considers more than just the motivation to seek out partisan news; it also considers the motivation to avoid news. Individuals who are not motivated to watch partisan news will tune it out and watch entertainment instead. Furthermore, we posit that individuals are active consumers of the information they view, accepting some messages and rejecting others (Zaller 1992).

Our Argument

We advance our own *active audience theory*, conceptually associated with but distinct from the uses and gratifications approach (Ruggiero 2000). We argue, and hope to demonstrate in the pages that follow, that understanding the effects of the partisan media requires treating television viewers as active participants and not inert, passive receivers. People have agency over what they watch, and they exercise this agency when given a choice. More important, the act of choosing has implications for the extent to which the media influence people.

Two central propositions form the core of our book. First, an active audience brings some level of scrutiny to the messages it receives. Like-minded news shows are able to reinforce and strengthen preexisting attitudes because people are motivated to maintain those preexisting attitudes (e.g., Kunda 1990) and not simply because they are easily persuaded. Furthermore, when individuals are confronted with oppositional news programs—either by choice (Garrett 2009a, 2009b) or by accident—"motivated skepticism" (Taber and Lodge 2006) should lead them to be more critical and dismissive of the opposing viewpoints they encounter. Consequently, exposure to alternative opinions on partisan news channels should not lead to attitude moderation, as many of our contemporaries hope. Instead, oppositional news shows should behave much like like-minded news shows, reinforcing and perhaps even strengthening preexisting attitudes.

Second, an active audience makes purposive viewing decisions.[4] The presence of both entertainment seekers and entertainment options should mute the reach and overall effect of the partisan news media as entertainment seekers select themselves out of news audiences. This will include some viewers with partisan inclinations who would rather watch an old episode of *Friends* than the six o'clock news. We argue that two important forces blunt the effects of partisan news in a hyperchoice media environment: dilution and differences in effects.

At the most elementary level, the availability of entertainment choices leads to the *dilution* of partisan news effects. To understand how dilu-

tion works, imagine that we still live in a time of little choice and that, at
6:00 P.M., television viewers can choose among only partisan news shows
instead of mainstream news. For lack of anything else better to do, a large
"inadvertent audience" tunes in to the partisan news each day just as they
would have watched mainstream news twenty-five years ago. Because
many scholars have not updated their conception of the news audience—
the presence of a large inadvertent news audience in particular—this is essentially the world envisioned by those who worry that partisan sorting
destroys reasoned debate and comity (e.g., Jamieson and Cappella 2008;
Mutz and Reeves 2005; Slater 2007; Sunstein 2007, 2009; Manjoo 2008).
Our contention is that simply offering individuals the choice to not watch
partisan news shows means that many will choose to watch something
else, shrinking the size of the inadvertent news audience, and diluting
the overall direct impact of the partisan news media. As we explain below, our empirical studies seek to simulate both this imagined world with
a large inadvertent audience and one in which individuals have some freedom to engage in entertainment seeking.

The second force constitutes a more subtle implication of our active
audience framework. People do not simply react to media content, as
many theories and studies of media effects implicitly assume. They make
choices about what to watch, and their choices may influence how they
react to media content. The presence of an active audience makes exposure to partisan news endogenous to the viewer's preferences and goals.
Consequently, we cannot make the assumption that the media effects we
would observe in a media environment that includes a large inadvertent
audience would be the same, but simply smaller, than the ones we would
observe in a media environment that empowers audiences to sort by interest. We must entertain the possibility that partisan news shows have a
different effect on news seekers than they do on entertainment seekers.
Because news seekers tend to have stronger predispositions and a larger
store of considerations regarding controversial political issues, they are
less likely to experience massive media effects, on average (Zaller 1992),
leading us to expect that entertainment seekers are more susceptible to
partisan news effects than are news seekers.

While we argue that the current media environment should attenuate the effects of partisan media by both diluting their reach, as people
sort out of the news audience, and having a smaller effect on those who
sort into the news audience, we are *not* arguing that the partisan media *do not matter*. It is important to keep in mind that we are talking

about the overall *direct* effect of partisan news media; that is, the effect of partisan news media has on those who watch them. The direct effect may be smaller than the one we would observe in a media environment with a large inadvertent audience, but we do not argue that this effect is zero. Furthermore, in diminishing the argument that partisan news media have massive direct effects, our research underscores the need to rethink the ways in which news media are relevant in the current media environment.

Our Approach

In addition to reshaping how we think about the effects of news media, the hyperchoice media environment complicates how we study media effects empirically. It has always been difficult to study media effects using observational data because the self-selection of research subjects into news audiences vitiates our ability to disentangle cause from effect. By expanding the dimensions among which television viewers can sort themselves, the current media environment only exacerbates this problem.

Twenty-five years ago, Shanto Iyengar and Donald Kinder (1987) reinvigorated media effects research by reminding scholars that randomized experiments offer one way to circumvent the selection bias problem and gauge the potential effects of news media. In the updated edition of their seminal work, they note that, while the rise in the profile of experimental research has been a boon to political communication research, they worry that their own "experiments erase a distinction that looms important in natural settings" (Iyengar and Kinder 2010, 143)—the fact that in natural settings people can opt out. This concern, of course, is more pressing now than it was twenty-five years ago because the inadvertent news audience is smaller. Increased opportunities to engage in selective exposure led Iyengar and W. Lance Bennett to counsel: "It is important that experimental researchers use designs that combine manipulation with self-selection of exposure" (Bennett and Iyengar 2008, 724).

Our research offers two contributions in this direction. We theorize the effect of media, given self-selection, and employ experimental designs that explicitly recognize and allow for the choices people make. The standard experimental design used by Iyengar and Kinder and many other media researchers randomly assigns subjects to forced exposure conditions. While this design is quite strong at estimating the effects of exposure to news media, it does so by *assuming that everyone watches.* As Iyengar and Kinder (1987, 61) explain, the treatment effects observed in forced experimental protocols "pertain primarily to the *capacity* of television news to influence opinion among different sorts of people, should those people be tuning in with roughly equal attention."

We employ two experimental protocols that augment the standard forced experimental design. The first is the *selective-exposure protocol*, which adds a choice condition to the forced exposure design. In the choice condition, participants are given a remote control that allows them to flip the channel among all the stimuli featured in the forced exposure conditions. Just as is the case in natural settings, participants in the choice condition can watch as much or as little of partisan news shows as they like. The selective-exposure protocol allows us to simulate a media environment in which there is a large inadvertent partisan news audience using the forced exposure conditions as well as a media environment in which participants have a minimal amount of choice. As we explain in chapter 3, we give participants a minimal amount of choice in order to estimate the *maximal* effects of partisan news media in an environment that allows for limited sorting of news seekers and entertainment seekers.

While the selective-exposure design allows us to demonstrate that even a modicum of choice can significantly attenuate the effects of partisan news media, it does not tell us why. In this regard, we employ a design used in randomized drug trials called the *patient preference protocol* (Macias et al. 2009; Torgerson and Sibbald 1998). This design also builds on the forced exposure design by assigning subjects at random to conditions in which they have no choice over what to watch. However, before participants watch the assigned program, we asked them what they would want to watch of the possible alternative if given a choice. As a result, we are able to divide the sample into news seekers and entertainment seekers prior to their exposure to the stimuli, allowing us to investigate the differential effects of the partisan news media.

Plan of the Book

Before we launch into our theoretical model and empirical findings, it is necessary to place the study of partisan news effects in contemporary and historical context. Chapter 2 provides an intellectual history of media effects research. It also describes the historical events that gave rise to the explosion of choices on cable television and the rise of ideologically oriented cable news networks. It concludes with a discussion of how this media fragmentation has influenced recent media effects research.

With the recent changes in the media environment placed in historical context, we devote chapter 3 to making the case that partisan news audiences, and television viewers in general, are active rather than passive. Individuals select into partisan news *because* they have political opinions. Other people, with less established political views or interests, choose to watch other kinds of programs. Next, we lay out our theoretical model of selective exposure, differentiating between partisan motivation to watch cable news, which has received a great deal of attention from extant research, and the motivation to be entertained, which has received less attention. We conclude chapter 3 with an argument for experimental research and a description of our experimental designs and studies.

Chapters 4–7 constitute the empirical core of our book. Across these chapters, we analyze eleven experimental studies that collectively draw on nearly seventeen hundred participants. Many of these studies go beyond the typical college student sample by including nonstudent adults drawn from broader community populations. We investigate the potentially polarizing effects of partisan news media in chapter 4. There, we show that exposure to proattitudinal news shows has the same capacity to polarize attitudes as exposure to counterattitudinal news shows. When participants are given the option to select out of partisan news shows, we discover a substantial attenuation in the polarizing effect of partisan news programs. We go on to demonstrate that many of the polarization effects that we do observe are among the inadvertent audience, as news seekers are generally less affected by exposure to partisan news than entertainment seekers.

In chapter 5, we consider whether the partisan news media can polarize political attitudes through a subtler route. If the partisan news media strengthen preexisting attitudes, viewers may be made more resistant to opposing arguments. We find evidence that the partisan news media can do just this—though mostly among those who enjoy thinking about arguments. Once again, we find that choice attenuates reinforcement effects and tends to have more powerful reinforcement effects on the inadvertent audience (i.e., those who would seek out entertainment if given the option).

Next, we go beyond the persuasive power of partisan news and consider the ways in which the partisan news media shape viewers' understanding of the more nuanced media effects developed during the broadcast news era. In chapter 6, we entertain the possibility that partisan news shows may be able to influence the public agenda. We show that, like the mainstream news media, partisan news shows can transfer salience to issues simply by discussing them. We also show that, when the partisan news media talk about different issues, they potentially diminish the common conversation taken for granted during the broadcast news era. Nonetheless, we also demonstrate that choice attenuates the agenda-setting effects of partisan news media. Interestingly, we find conflicting evidence about the differential effects of partisan news shows on agenda setting. In some instances, they have a stronger agenda-setting effect on entertainment seekers, while, in others, they have the same effect on both entertainment seekers and news seekers. Notably, however, we find that, even though partisan news media can shape the agenda for news seekers, they are less likely to have success in framing those issues.

In chapter 7, we consider how the partisan news media shape perceptions of media bias and trust in the political system. We show that, while the partisan news media can increase hostility toward oppositional news media and decrease trust in the political system, a media environment with choice attenuates these effects. Moreover, we demonstrate that the negative effects of partisan news media are largely driven by those who would typically avoid watching cable news shows.

Finally, we summarize our findings in chapter 8 with the help of a meta-analysis that statistically aggregates the findings of our many studies. This is particularly instructive in part because it shows that viewer choice blunts, rather than erases, media effects associated with partisan news. In this chapter, we also consider an array of other potential explanations for mass polarization and perceived mass polarization in the United States. Here, we present a final study showing that the availability of partisan news choices accentuates concerns about extremism and the voice that partisans have in U.S. politics. We find that the availability of partisan news in a broad choice environment is not the driver of polarization that many think it is but that these options being available alongside each other heightens concerns that partisan news divides Americans. Taking stock of what we have learned, we discuss fruitful paths forward in media research, particularly the need to study the possible *indirect* effects of the partisan news media.

Changes in Media Technology and Content

News media have changed dramatically over the last twenty years, bringing audiences both a massive expansion in content choice as well as a variety of highly specialized options that allow the tailoring of viewing to individuals' own interests and demands. Amid these changes, we recognize an important constant. While Americans are eager for information and diversion, they have a tendency to be suspicious of their news media, journalism, and public discourse regardless of the technology of the day. We argue that this suspicion is driven in part by a common and pervasive folk understanding of massive media effects. Groups of Americans can be found that think that the dissemination, and perhaps the very existence, of almost all kinds of news and entertainment represents a source of undue influence on their neighbors. The proliferation of options provides each viewer with as many opportunities for suspicion and concern as it does for diversion and edification.

Independent of the findings of whatever the most current research on the effects of mass media happens to be, political leaders and members of the public express fears of an influential mass media distorting public opinion and warping the minds of those most vulnerable. From a free speech perspective, the rhetoric asserting the political implications of these direct media effects has a particularly ignominious history, usually providing the rationale for muzzling dissent and censoring "dangerous" media content, from the founding era onward. In this chapter, we review understandings of media effects informed by twentieth-century research on the topic and discuss the constantly lurking concerns about the direct effects of offending speech, especially the expression of political opinions in the public sphere. We also review important technological changes that give rise to our own focus on the role of selective exposure. These changes have implications for media effects.

Media Effects in Theory: From Hypodermic to Minimal to Contingent Effects

The conventional narrative of the study of media effects, at least among political communication researchers, describes a pendulum swinging between understandings.[1] An era of scholarship expecting direct effects in the early twentieth century gave way to a period of hypothesized minimal effects at midcentury. By the 1980s, however, scholars were reconsidering minimal effects and identifying more nuanced but pervasive ones, like agenda setting and framing. We review the major shifts in these understandings here.

The Hypodermic Needle

Scholars of early twentieth-century propaganda, led by Harold Lasswell, focused on the dramatic content of films, radio broadcasts, pamphlets, and other public communication efforts and inferred that mass media had massive effects on the beliefs and opinions people expressed, both domestically and internationally. Writing about the communication skills of Woodrow Wilson, both at home and abroad, in the context of World War I, Lasswell developed the metaphor for this understanding of media effects, the hypodermic needle model: "From a propaganda point of view it was a matchless performance, for Wilson brewed the subtle poison, which industrious men injected into the veins of a staggering people, until the smashing powers of the Allied armies knocked them into submission. While he fomented discord abroad, Wilson fostered unity at home" (Lasswell 1938/1972, 217).

Lasswell had been struck by the techniques of the U.S. Committee on Public Information and its foreign counterparts during the Great War. The "injection" metaphor suggests that information has the medicinal or infectious properties of a liquid. As a conceptual metaphor (Lakoff and

Johnson 1980), this is quite appealing. A mind can allow an idea to "soak in"; once out of its container, information can flow where it is and is not wanted. However, the metaphor is more complex to be sure. There is the additional dimension that ideas have natural and unavoidable effects on those treated with them—whether to harm or to help. The analogy casts people as victims or at least patients and, thus, diminished or vulnerable. With relative ease, leaders and their "industrious" political operatives, like Committee on Public Information chief George Creel, could treat or infect people with those ideas directly and completely. Lasswell saw the Allies' efforts to demoralize their enemies (the Germans in particular) as effective—techniques like the spreading in the trenches of cards and tracts with such presumably powerful messages as: "To-day we are in retreat. Next year we shall be destroyed" (Lasswell 1938/1972, 165).

A classic case from this period of inferred direct effects is the panic set off by the Orson Welles radio play of H. G. Wells's *War of the Worlds*. The broadcast aired October 30, 1938, and controversially set the narrative of an extraterrestrial attack on Grover's Mill, New Jersey, as a series of reports mimicking news broadcasts interrupting a musical concert. Many listeners—especially those who turned to the broadcast while it was in progress—assumed that what they were hearing was in fact a set of news reports. Reactions ranged from mere discomfort and resignation to paralyzing fear (Cantril, Gaudet, and Herzog 1940, 96). Many frightened listeners called broadcast stations in a panic and wrote letters to newspapers in response to the radio play. As most seem to recall it, the story of the *War of the Worlds* broadcast is one about *direct* media effects inducing mass hysteria by means of a fictional Martian invasion.

Minimal Effects

Just a few decades later, political communication research conducted by the likes of Paul Lazarsfeld, Bernard Berelson, Hazel Gaudet, and their Columbia colleagues and informed by interviews with panels of voters suggested that people were far less influenced by mass media, especially electioneering, than one would have expected given analyses by Lasswell and others steeped in the direct effects framework. One of these researchers' most compelling inferences was that most voters make up their mind about which presidential candidate they will support long before the homestretch of campaign efforts of both major party candidates, appearing to be guided by their identification with political parties and other reference groups, and often interpreting events and information through those lenses. Famously, in *Voting*, Berelson, Lazarsfeld, and McPhee (1954, 234) criticize direct media effects, turning Lasswell's metaphor into a pejorative aimed at researchers rather than politicians: "Typical debates about the role of the media too often imply a simple, direct 'influence'—like a hypodermic stimulus on an inert subject—and that is a naïve formulation of the political effects of mass communications."

These insights ushered in an era of inferred minimal effects celebrated in the 1960 publication of Joseph Klapper's *The Effects of Mass Communication*. Klapper reviewed relevant research on a number of substantive potential effects (e.g., issue opinions in politics, portrayals of violence, escapist fare, and the effects of adult programs on children) and, building on work by Lazarsfeld and many others, offered the generalization that mass communication is not usually a necessary or sufficient cause of audience effects (Klapper 1960, 8). Importantly, the influence of media is limited by the behavior of members of the audience. For example, Lazarsfeld, Berelson, and Gaudet (1948) and Katz and Lazarsfeld (1955) highlight the importance of social interaction as a mediator between mass communication and many potential audience members who do not experience the messages directly but rather hear about them from family, friends, and others. More important to the present investigation, people choose what to watch, actively interpret the information they encounter, and have biased memories of the communication. Selective exposure, attention, and perception make reinforcement more prevalent than attitude *change* (Klapper 1960, 19). However, this does not entirely foreclose the possibility of media effects, which can happen when there is an alignment among media messages and these mediating influences.

Contingent Effects

Research in the 1970s and 1980s revived the specter of quite substantial, if subtle, media effects. In their elaboration of Cohen's (1963) observation that the press excels at telling audiences what to think *about*, McCombs and Shaw (1972) identified the role news media play in setting social and political agendas by associating newspaper content with variation in the stated priorities of readers. Iyengar and Kinder (1987) cemented the agenda-setting model of media effects by demonstrating that exposure to broadcast news shows has a substantial effect on what issues people believe to be important and, therefore, what issues they use to evaluate elected leaders. In subsequent work, Iyengar (1991) notes that, even in the production of supposedly objective news, journalists and editors exercise discretion in how issues are framed and contextualized. He shows that the framing of an issue substantially influences how people think about it and, therefore, what solutions they deem appropriate. Perse (2001) characterizes agenda setting and framing as examples of the *cumulative effects* of mass media because they operate over time and perhaps across media sources. A single exposure to a broadcast that indicates an issue is important may not shift the salience or rated importance of that issue, but, if people are exposed to news that gives priority to an issue across several days, as they were in the *News That Matters* studies, they accord more importance to it.

Furthermore, the nature of elite discourse as reflected in news reports can have a powerful influence on the opinions that people construct of the controversies of the day. When people experience high levels of political agreement in the media environment, they can even experience attitude change akin to persuasion (Zaller 1992; see also Chong and Druckman 2007). For example, at the outset of the Vietnam War, the high level of support for the war among liberals and conservatives in the mass public echoed the broad agreement among liberals and conservatives in Congress that a military invasion was the best course of action. As the bloody contest dragged on, however, liberal politicians became increasingly opposed to the war while conservative politicians stayed steadfast in their support, and, by 1972, such ideologically polarized attitudes were reflected in mass opinion as well. At least one element of framing could operate in a similar way—specifically, the effect of broad agreement on the definition of a problem. For example, the regularity with which the news media cast poverty and social programs meant to address it as relevant primarily to minority communities (Gilens 2003) effectively racializes these programs. Importantly, much work on contingent media influences portrays them as ubiquitous, even as those effects are moderated by social interaction.

Taking a Step Back

Although this received view of a progression through eras in how scholars understand media effects is "not a realistic account" (Perse 2001, 27), there is value in recognizing that these eras represent ebbs and flows between an emphasis on the extent to which content is considered compelling enough, effectively on its very transmission, to affect people's views or behavior and an emphasis on people's resistance to these kinds of influence. Scholars expecting direct and cumulative effects foresee little room for resistance, while research in the conditional-minimal and cognitive-transactional schools offer more hope that people are more capable of usefully interpreting or filtering what they are presented with by the mass media.

Klapper (1960, 8), for example, recognized "residual situations in which mass communication seems to produce direct effects." Even during the early period of direct effects research, some scholars recognized at least a limited role for audience agency. Wartella and Reeves (1985) point out the fact that early studies of the effects of motion pictures on children identified the moderating role of predispositions and other individual differences and were conducted between 1929 and 1932, not long after Lasswell distilled his hypodermic metaphor. Similarly, even as the *War of the Worlds* broadcast is often remembered as a parable of massive media influence, the Cantril, Gaudet, and Herzog (1940) report is far more nuanced.

Drawing on in-depth interviews with 135 listeners and two sample surveys conducted in the wake of the panic, Cantril, Gaudet, and Herzog identify five distinct reactions to the broadcast:

- People who heard it from the beginning recognized that it was a fictional radio play and were far less likely to have been frightened by it.
- Some people who tuned in late thought that it might be a newscast, but recognized something in the broadcast that was internally inconsistent, and decided that it was the work of fiction they planned to hear.
- Some conducted an "external test" and debunked it as a newscast (e.g., they turned to a different radio station and heard no similar news reports).
- Some tried to conduct this same kind of test, but effectively misinterpreted what they learned, and continued to think that the Welles program was a news broadcast.
- A fraction of listeners found the broadcast so compelling that they did not even question whether it was a news broadcast.

The panic was largely situated among the last two groups of listeners.

The reactions to the broadcast that Cantril, Gaudet, and Herzog catalog emphasize several lessons that remain relevant today, perhaps even more so given the expansion of media choice. First, only a fraction of the potential listening audience tuned in to the *War of the Worlds* broadcast at all—between 5 and 12 percent of the potential audience, a figure based on survey research and program ratings data compiled in the wake of the broadcast (Cantril, Gaudet, and Herzog 1940, 55–56). Second, the heterogeneity of responses to the program among those who heard it was dramatically affected by the choices listeners made and the availability of other radio stations for comparison. People who selected the show from the beginning tended to interpret it as entertainment. Among those who tuned in late, a large number had the idea to compare what they heard on CBS's *Mercury Theatre on the Air* with other programming available on their radio dial—selecting a different broadcast and returning to CBS for the entertaining science fiction drama. The process of selecting among programming options dramatically reduced the tendency to panic over the Welles broadcast.

In addition, the individual characteristics of listeners were also associated with their reactions to the program. Cantril, Gaudet, and Herzog (1940) identified the most important correlate of interpreting the broadcast as entertainment rather than news—beyond the time at which the listener tuned in to the program—as "critical ability" (111), a latent characteristic exemplifying formal education as well as "intelligence, general interests, personality traits, or special information" (121). Using data from a CBS-commissioned survey and education level as an indicator for critical ability, they show that, among those listening to the broadcast, about one-quarter (28 percent) with a college education but almost half (46 percent) with less than a high school education thought that it was a news program. Their interviews with listeners suggested that individual panic was associated with personal insecurity, including economic insecurity, lack of self-confidence, and religiosity, among other personality and psychological characteristics (Cantril, Gaudet, and Herzog 1940, 131–34).

We recognize that panic as the result of direct media influence is the most interesting way to interpret the story of the *War of the Worlds* broadcast; however, this is not quite consistent with the evidence. By far, the most likely reaction of listeners was to not panic. This was first and foremost because most people did not even hear the broadcast. Of those who did, most interpreted the program as entertainment because they were seeking entertainment in the first place or were able to assess the content of the Welles broadcast through comparisons with other programming. Even in the context of vivid cases like this, many researchers identify evidence of selective attention, exposure, and perception, while other scholars have enduring memories of massive media effects. We think this is due, in part, to the intuitive appeal of the hypodermic needle model. Americans, including scholars, have a strong contemporary and historical understanding of media effects as direct and extensive, largely driven by their impression of their fellows as ill informed, somewhat incompetent, and easily led, a subject to which we turn next.

Contemporary Expectations about Media Influence

The idea that individuals are susceptible to the sway of harmful ideas is still quite common in U.S. political discourse and public understandings of the role of mass media in political and social processes. In contemporary U.S. politics, most people appear to subscribe to a version of concern about media influence commonly referred to as the *third-person effect*. In the mid-1980s, the sociologist and communication scholar W. Phillips Davison (1983, 3) identified the third-person effect hypothesis: "Individuals who are members of an audience that is exposed to a persuasive communication (whether or not this communication is intended to be persuasive) will expect the communication to have a greater effect on others than on themselves."

Davison speculated that partisans in controversies often see media as biased because they assume these communications cause other people to have mistaken views—persuaded by the information the partisans perceive as false, inaccurate, or misrepresentative. Perloff (1989) experimentally confirmed this expectation, showing that partisans from different sides of a controversy exposed to the same stimulus—here, a televised news report on the war in Lebanon (ca. 1982), similar to the stimulus Vallone, Ross, and Lepper (1985) used in their famous study of hostile media perceptions—will both perceive bias and perceive that neutral audiences react to the newscast with less favorable opinions toward their own side. Issue importance or salience—having stronger feelings about an issue—also appears to augment the third-person effect, with people who consider the issue an important one expressing a greater difference between the potential effect of communication on them as opposed to others (Mutz 1989).

In a particularly interesting empirical demonstration of third-person effects, Cohen, Mutz, Price, and Gunther (1988) show that undergraduate students exposed to news reports libeling public figures (here, the California Supreme Court chief justice and a college football coach) thought that the articles would hurt the reputations of the targets among others more than it would affect their own perceptions of the targets.[2] Importantly, if the article was attributed to a biased source of information (like a partisan news organization or the newspaper of a rival university), readers thought that the effect on others, relative to themselves, would be even greater. The perceived bias of the source made the potential for third-person influence a bigger problem for the research participants.

If other people are susceptible to influence, the corollary must be that the media are unduly influential. This is itself a widely expressed concern in U.S. politics. A 2007 study conducted by the Center for Public Leadership of the John F. Kennedy School of Government and *U.S. News and World Report* asked respondents: "Thinking more about the news media's coverage of presidential campaigns, please tell me whether you strongly agree, somewhat agree, somewhat disagree, or strongly disagree with the following statement: Media coverage has too much influence on who Americans vote for." The vast majority of respondents (84 percent) agreed that news media have too much influence on voter decision-making, 56 percent indicating that they strongly agreed, and 28 percent indicating that they somewhat agreed. Only 15 percent disagreed with the premise of massive media influence, 10 percent expressing that they somewhat disagreed, and 5 percent expressing that they strongly disagreed (Center for Public Leadership 2007).

Respondents to surveys conducted by the Pew Research Center for the People and Press over more than the last decade reveal a similar sentiment. Pew interviewers frequently present their respondents with the question: "I'm going to read you some pairs of opposite phrases. After I read each pair, tell me which one phrase you feel better describes news organizations generally. If you think that neither phrase applies, please say so. . . . Would you say news organizations are growing in influence, or declining in influence?" Note that this is a subtly different question than one asking about the extent of media effects, in part because the question *assumes* the existence of a media influence that is either waning or waxing. Given that as many as eight in ten Americans subscribe to the premise, this seems not to represent a major limitation. Figure 2.1 shows that, since at least 1999, a majority of Americans perceive media influ-

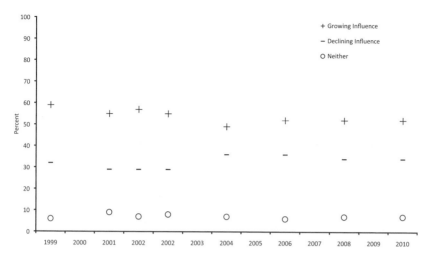

FIGURE 2.1. Perceived media influence, U.S. public.
Source: Pew Research Center for the People and the Press (2011).

ence as growing. In this dramatic period of change during the last decade of the twentieth century and the first decade of the twenty-first, including a vast expansion of television programming options and of the
Internet as well as the precipitous decline of print media, a constant appears to be that most people believe that the mass media substantially
influence *other* Americans and the nation's politics.

Historical Understandings of Direct Media Effects

Contemporary expectations of large direct effects are pervasive, but this
is a relatively old idea in Anglo-American politics. Given the importance
of voters—masses of these *other* people—to the democratic politics that
affects each of us, the social and individual harm of even these potential
effects has implications for the lives of communities and even the stability of governments. From the founding of the United States, the idea that
regular people were vulnerable to substantial harm from the ideas and
information they encountered in mass media had a great deal of reso-
nance with American elites.

   More than 125 years before Lasswell cautioned readers about Wilson's
"subtle poison" uniting allies and demoralizing enemies, the Federalist

judge Alexander Addison beat him to the metaphoric punch: "Presses established to run down the government are the most destructive of all treasons. . . . Every one who reads their productions with approbation, sucks in disease upon his mind; and every one who repeats them to others, spreads the infection" (Addison 1798, 22–23). Addison's legal thinking on the threat of radical publishers was influenced by the British jurist William Blackstone, whose *Commentaries* informed much of early U.S. legal thought. Blackstone had developed the poison metaphor even earlier in justifying a broad interpretation of libel. He had reasoned that the difference between potentially dangerous private thoughts and public expressions of them was the prospective harm on the unsuspecting. Thus, a person "may be allowed to keep poisons in his closet, but not publicly to vend them as cordials" (Blackstone 1769, 152, quoted in Rosenberg 1986).

For a decade prior to the passage of the Sedition Act in 1798, the Federalists and their opponents debated just how much freedom the press should have and how the young nation should interpret the First Amendment (Rosenberg 1984, 1986). While Addison and other Federalist judges discouraged *prior* restraint on publication, they sought aggressive punishment against publishers whose writing represented a perceived threat to the state, its officers, or their reputations (Pasley 2001). They wanted to dissuade criticism of the government by holding publishers accountable for their slights against officials. Addison used his instructions to the grand jury of Pennsylvania's Fifth Circuit Court of Common Pleas to expound on theories of republican government and his views on topics including libel and freedom of speech. In September 1798, he crafted a grand jury charge articulating "the Federalist faction's most spirited and sophisticated effort to justify libel prosecutions" under the Sedition Act, passed that year in July (Rosenberg 1984, 400). The charge was reprinted as a pamphlet, *Liberty of Speech and of the Press* (Addison 1798), and broadly circulated.

Addison used the poison metaphor for media messages but went well beyond it to articulate a domineering role for the presses of the day in directing government action via the people. Poison may infect individuals, but the power of the press had broader political ramifications: "Give to any set of men the command of the press, and you give them the command of the country; for you give them the command of public opinion, which commands every thing" (Addison 1798, 19). Addison associated this power with the words or ideas themselves because "speech, writing, and printing are the great directors of public opinion, and the public opinion is the great director of human action" (18). Much like Lasswell's understanding of the power of speech, which was deeply influenced by the experience of World War I, Addison's was informed by the then recent example of the French Revolution, which he identified as having begun with attacks on the state by French publishers.

Many observers of the day, including Benjamin Franklin, promoted the marketplace of ideas, the notion that truth would win out as people discussed a variety of different perspectives on a given controversy (Rosenberg 1986; Schmuhl and Picard 2005). Addison expressed a Federalist position denying such a notion: "But you will say, *We desire to hear both sides, that we may know truth.* My friends, truth has but one side: and listening to error and falsehood is indeed a strange way to discover truth" (Addison 1798, 23). We speculate that this may be related to his characterization of the communication of dissent as dangerous to individuals and communities. Reflecting a healthy belief in the third-person effect, his own political convictions were sufficiently strong to urge him to reject alternatives as particularly damaging, but his concern was about the ease with which others are misled: "Be assured, no matter is of greater importance, than a just confidence in government. The men, who endeavour to rob you of this, are the worst enemies of your peace. If they can succeed in robbing your minds of this confidence, they rob you of your liberty; for they deprive government of its authority; and government without authority is anarchy; and anarchy is the worst tyranny" (24).

Assumptions about Media Effects Affect Requirements for Journalism

The sense that other people are easily swayed by information has informed an idealized normative vision of what the news and journalism should look like. Walter Lippmann (1922/1965) is well-known for his skepticism regarding the capacities of democratic citizens. To many observers, the fear of ignorance among and manipulation of the masses— both then and now—suggests that news *must* be objective. This view holds that, without the certainty that the media are objective, people's views and democracy itself are imperiled. It is this vision for the press that Lippmann articulates in *Liberty and the News* (1920).[3] He argues that "the most destructive form of untruth is sophistry and propaganda by those whose profession is to report the news" (10)—an argument that could come from almost any contemporary observer wringing his or her hands about the existence of Fox News, MSNBC, or both. So the logic goes, not only is the mixing of opinion with news untruthful; it also exhibits the same kinds of threats that Addison associated with revolutionary printers in France and the anti-Federalist presses in the United States.

A common reflection on the partisan television environment created by contemporary cable systems suggests that viewers of Fox News Channel and MSNBC are provided with, not only different perspectives on the news, but different facts as well. Lippmann sounded the same caution almost a century ago, insisting: "True opinions can prevail only if the facts to which they refer are known; if they are not known, false ideas are just as effective as true ones, if not a little more effective" (Lippmann 1920, 71). He further called for a rigorous, independent, objective journalism, staffed by professional, "patient and fearless men of science who have labored to see what the world really is" (82). Again, this proposal reflects an underlying ideology itself, assuming both that people are easily swayed and, thus, that the only way to protect them from themselves and partisans is to ensure restrictions on opinionated content self-imposed by the news industry: "We shall accomplish more by fighting for truth than by fighting for our theories" (98).

The idealized professional-scientific journalism that Lippmann envisioned did not come to pass, although the value of objectivity was certainly enshrined in the journalism training curriculum and professional ideology for most of the twentieth century and is still cherished by the most proper mainstream journalists. Today, we have television news media, especially on cable television, that professional media critics love to hate, new media filled with expressed opinions on the Left and the Right, indifferent, cynical, and pious. The former ABC broadcaster Ted Koppel warns that Fox News and MSNBC "show us the world not as it is, but as partisans (and loyal viewers) at either end of the spectrum would like it to be. This is to journalism what Bernie Madoff was to investment: He told his customers what they wanted to hear, and by the time they learned the truth, their money was gone" (Koppel 2010, B01).

Today, partisan news on cable television is perceived as dangerous in much the same way as the partisan press was of concern to some during the Founding Era. For example, the president's operatives, Democratic or Republican, openly discuss sanctioning opposition television news organizations by denying them access or publicly chiding them (see Menand 2009).[4] In addition to a concern that content will cause offense, another underlying concern is that, especially as it is presented on Fox News Channel and MSNBC, it is overwhelming. It is assailed or celebrated as substantially influencing voters directly or, at a minimum, allowing them to segregate themselves into ends of the political spectrum and grow apart (e.g., Jamieson and Cappella 2008). Among other ills, observers attribute to the contemporary cable news environment a role in making politics angrier, making citizens more cynical and uncivil (Dagnes 2010, 125–26; Mutz and Reeves 2005), and substantially restricting the political agenda to only the most divisive issues of the day (Smerconish 2010).

We are interested in ascertaining how cable news affects public opinion, especially given the fact that today's cable and satellite television providers offer their subscribers, who represent more than 91 percent of American households, unprecedented choice over news and entertainment—over 130 television channels, on average. Before we begin to theoretically and empirically explore media effects, we turn to two final questions in this chapter: Why do we have so many channels? And what are the implications of this choice for media effects and their systematic study?

Technology-Driven Changes in Media Environment

During the last twenty years, we have seen a dramatic proliferation in the number of television channels available to American television viewers, the vast majority of whom subscribe either to cable and satellite television. We show this explosive growth in figure 2.2. In 1964, the average television viewer, more often than not at that time pulling broadcast signals directly off local airwaves, received, on average, five channels, representing the three major broadcast networks of the day and perhaps a public television affiliate. Television service offerings grew exponentially through the last decade of the twentieth century and the first decade of the twenty-first century and continue to expand. As of 2008, the average household received 130 channels. Why?

Cable television was an innovation of the 1940s, originally intended to retransmit the signals of local television stations to consumers who had

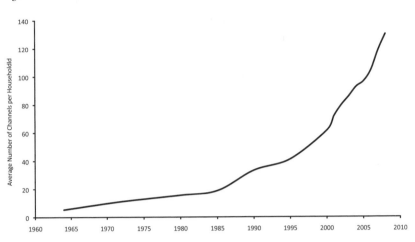

FIGURE 2.2. Increase in average number of television channels in U.S. households.
Sources: Nielsen Media Research Group (1981); Nielsen Media Research Group as reported by PRNewswire (2006) and *Media Daily News* (Mandese 2009).

difficulty receiving them (e.g., people who lived in mountainous places or urban spaces with tall buildings obstructing television signals). The number of channels available to viewers is limited only by the content available for retransmission and the capacity of set-top converter boxes (Ciciora, Farmer, Large, and Adams 2004; Parsons 2008). The distribution of cable television is a relatively simple technology. A cable vendor from a central location distributes television signals via physical cable lines. Inside homes, customers plug the cable either directly into a television, which is able to decode and show individual channel signals, or into a set-top converter box that decodes and presents the individual channel signals on the television.[5]

Improvements in cable distribution technology increased the number of channels available for programming, but it was the response to federal regulations by major players in the entertainment industry that led to the growth of the cable industry. The early 1990s were particularly important in setting the stage for the proliferation of viewing options. Newly developed digital set-top boxes were capable of exploiting more of the capacity of the cable distribution networks in most cities (Parsons 2008, 582). Older analog converter boxes limited cable companies to seventy to eighty channels (Parsons 2008, 435). Many large cable systems nationwide also began to upgrade their distribution network, increasingly relying on hybrid fiber optic and coaxial cable systems that allowed for more efficient transmission (Parsons 2008, 486; see also Ciciora, Farmer, Large, and Adams 2004). Figure 2.3 shows both the expansion of the number of cable providers nationally between 1975 and 2005 and how the capacity of these systems grew dramatically.

Nonetheless, the expansion in capacity would mean little to television viewers without actual channel content and programs to view (or not). The innovation that launched the run-up of cable channels through the last decade of the twentieth century and the first decade of the twenty-first was literally a *creative* deal struck by broadcast television network executives and cable television providers in the wake of the 1992 Cable Television Consumer Protection and Competition Act. From the birth of the cable industry, broadcasters have been at odds with cable companies over whether cable companies are responsible for compensating broadcasters for either the retransmission of their signals or the rebroadcasting of their programming content (Lubinsky 1996). From the earliest efforts to regulate cable television in the mid-1960s, the Federal Communication Commission required cable operators to transmit all the local signals available in their service area.

In the 1992 Cable Act, Congress required cable companies to either negotiate with local stations and compensate them for retransmission rights or carry their signals at no charge. This recognizes that there are

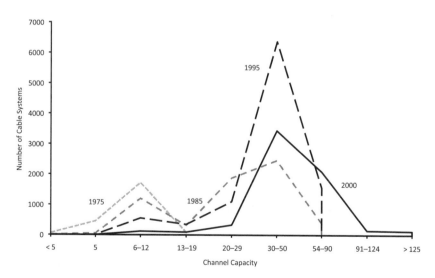

FIGURE 2.3. Channel capacity of U.S. cable systems, 1975–2005.
Source: Parsons (2008).

essentially two types of broadcast station owners. Some have a very lucrative product, such as a major network affiliate for which the owner would want compensation for use by a local cable provider, while other owners are struggling for viewers and would want to essentially force the cable provider to carry their signals. The cable industry fought this compensate-or-carry proposal because potentially it would require cable providers to pay broadcasters large sums of money as part of retransmission agreements. After the legislation passed, several of the major broadcasting companies, led by Fox Broadcasting Corporation, had a better idea. The cable providers had something they wanted more than direct cash payments. The broadcast networks produced and owned the rights to vast quantities of television programming content and possessed expertise in its development. Instead of seeking rent for their retransmitted signals, the networks negotiated with cable companies to allow retransmission in exchange for allowing them to develop *new cable channels* (Kolbert 1993; Lubinski 1996).

As a result of its negotiations with the cable conglomerate Tele-Communications Inc., the parent Fox Broadcasting created the entertainment channel fX. In similar deals, ABC created ESPN2, and NBC created the precursor to both MSNBC and the Fox News Channel, an all-news alternative to CNN called America's Talking (AT). Before joining News Corp. in 1996 to found the Fox News Channel, Roger Ailes was the president of CNBC and AT for NBC. The AT programming lineup of shows included a morning talk show hosted by Steve Doocy and an afternoon show called *Politics with Chris Matthews*, later renamed *Hardball*. This era saw the development of several entertainment cable channels as well, including TV Food Network and Home and Garden Television (Parsons 2008). The 1992 act mandated a reconsideration of the cable-broadcaster retransmission agreements at least every three years. In 1996, this is exactly what happened, facilitating the creation of the Fox News Channel, MSNBC, and others.

Cable News and Partisan Talk Shows Today

Over the last two decades, the twenty-four-hour cable news channels have developed a variety of types of programming. It is worth surveying the contemporary offerings on these channels to clarify the content on which we focus. We are primarily interested in the potential effects of news talk shows that appear on the more partisan cable news outlets, MSNBC and Fox News, and feature a discussion of contemporary issues and the opinions of the hosts and guests on them. In the studies we discuss in chapters 4–8, we use segments from shows on the Left like *Countdown with Keith Olbermann*, which aired on MSNBC from 2003 to 2011, and *The Rachel Maddow Show*, which has aired on MSNBC since 2008. From the Right, we use clips from shows like *The O'Reilly Factor*, which started airing on Fox News as *The O'Reilly Report* in 1996, and *Hannity*, which succeeded *Hannity and Colmes* on Fox News in 2009. These shows feature engaging hosts who provide their own commentary and opinion on news stories of the day in segments like O'Reilly's "Talking Points Memo" or Olbermann's "Special Comment." They also interview generally like-minded guests, feature edited news segments, and occasionally air lighter moments like Maddow's "Best New Thing in the World Today" feature or O'Reilly's "Culture Warriors" panel that may include entertainment stories and more whimsical fare.

Cable talk shows have changed over time in at least one important way. They have become more pure in their ideological or partisan presentation. In the late 1990s and the early years of the twenty-first century, talk shows of this ilk were more likely to feature multiple political perspectives and intense, often uncivil, political conversation. The classic example was CNN's *Crossfire*, which became increasingly acrimonious and internally combative over its twenty-three-year run. But, even on the partisan networks, political competition was de rigueur a decade ago, with Fox News shows like *Hannity and Colmes*, which ran from 1996 to 2009, and *Hardball*, which landed on MSNBC after runs on AT and CNBC. These shows motivated a wave of scholarship on televised incivility (e.g., Mutz and Reeves 2005). But the cable news terrain has shifted; we observe that today these shows offer a preponderance of singularly partisan perspective and far less debate, uncivil or otherwise.

Economics offers a partial explanation for why cable news networks have adopted identifiable ideological orientations while the broadcast networks continue to cultivate an air of impartiality. The presence of other cable news channels creates an incentive for product differentiation (Gentzkow and Shapiro 2006; Hamilton 2005; Peters 2010), and the subscription-based model of cable television allows its news networks to be profitable with smaller audiences. Consequently, cable news networks, unlike the broadcast stations, need not attract advertising aimed at broad audiences. Broadcast networks make their money through advertisement, and a good way to alienate advertisers would be to take sides.[6] Cable news networks, in contrast, make money by attracting small, but devoted, audiences.

How, then, should we categorize partisan talk shows? Patterson (2000, 4) identifies hard news as "coverage of breaking events involving top leaders, major issues, or significant disruptions in the routines of daily life": "Information about these events is presumably important to citizens' ability to understand and respond to the world of public affairs." By this definition, one could categorize partisan news shows as hard news. The shows we focus on feature in-depth discussions of the most pressing issues of the contemporary political era: economic policy, military conflicts in Iraq and Afghanistan, immigration, health care, tax policy. Further, these shows feature knowledgeable political experts, journalists, and political scientists.[7] However, Patterson (2000, 4) describes soft news as "more sensational, more personality-centered, less time-bound, more practical, and more incident-based than other news." Anyone who has watched *Hannity* or *Countdown* will recognize these characteristics as well.

Opinionated news-talk shows can also be usefully distinguished from more pure forms of hard news, like anchored newscasts and softer infotainment. While the latter are not our focus here, MSNBC and Fox News maintain a variety of programming options in both these veins as well. For example, Fox News maintains a straight-ahead evening newscast, *The Fox Report*, hosted by Shepard Smith from 7:00 to 8:00 P.M., as well as a much more whimsical morning chat show, *Fox and Friends*, hosted by Steve Doocy, Gretchen Carlson, and Brian Kilmeade. MSNBC maintains similar hard news (e.g., the midday *MSNBC Live*, hosted by Thomas Roberts) and softer news programs (e.g., *Morning Joe* with Joe Scarborough, Mika Brzezinski, and Willie Geist). In contrast to these anchored newscasts and soft news programs, the partisan talk shows that form the focus of our studies are more boisterous and feature much stronger expressions of opinion.

Coe et al. (2008, 203) offer a useful way to describe news programs broadly defined, proposing two dimensions: a presentation continuum "running from more objective or neutral presentation of the news to more openly opinionated presentation" and a second continuum describing the underlying motive to inform or entertain the audience. The shows we use for our studies vary within this space, from a *relatively* more neutral presentation from a host like MSNBC's Chris Matthews, who is also committed to entertainment values, to the more clearly opinionated presentation of a Hannity or MSNBC's Ed Schultz, both of whom have an interest in entertaining and informing their audiences, albeit from skewed perspectives on the Right and the Left, respectively.

In short, partisan talk shows are not easy to categorize. However, we surmise that, given their content, they will be of greater interest to the types of people who primarily watch harder news than they will be to people who are primarily interested in even softer infotainment (e.g., *Dr. Phil*). Of course, we recognize the plurality of perspectives claiming that soft news can be as informative as hard news (Baum 2003) and, the alternative, that it cannot (Prior 2003). Still others will argue that nothing on Fox News, for one, can be news at all owing to its political orientation (Brock, Rabin-Havt, and Media Matters for America 2012). In this debate, we are lumpers rather than splitters, joining Coe et al. (2008, 203) in considering all these to be *news programs* broadly defined, in part because people certainly turn to Fox News, MSNBC, and these programs in particular as sources of news. Their use by audiences affects our choice to study them.

Implications of the Changing Media Environment for Media Effects Research

Changes in mass media—in the platforms for message dissemination and in the content of programming— influence both the interest of scholars in identifying media effects and the types of media effects identified. For example, Perse (2001, 26) associates a reinvigorated interest in media effects among scholars in the 1970s with the increased penetration of television into American homes, rising dramatically from 64.5 percent of U.S. households in 1955 to 92.6 percent ten years later. This rapid expansion of television availability in homes affected the salience of media effects to scholars and other observers, but it also exposed more people to potential media influence. We have already shown how few channels were available to viewers during much of the twentieth century, in effect forcing people to watch a narrow range of content and heightening its potential influence.

Given the technological and programming changes afoot in the contemporary media environment, the types of effects we observe are likely to change, as are the priorities of researchers. Prior (2007) demonstrates that the limited choices of the broadcast era actually served to facilitate political knowledge. If, prior to the explosion of choice in the 1990s, someone wanted to watch television at a certain time of the day, he or she had little choice but the local and then the national news—creating a large, inadvertent news audience. Today, people have many, many choices at all times of the day. Consumers responded to improvements in cable and satellite services, which include the vast array of programming offered, by selecting these services in greater numbers each year, as shown in figure 2.4.

Cable and satellite television, along with the cornucopia of options these services bring, are now used by nearly all U.S. viewers—a situation similar to the penetration of broadcast television in the 1970s. As figure 2.5 shows, the networks' ratings share has gradually declined as more consumers choose cable and satellite services and those providers expand their offerings. Consequently, people who are not interested in news generally have access to other programming at all times and may select entertainment programming as an alternative to news whenever they so choose, widening the gap in political knowledge between people with high and low interests in politics (Prior 2005, 2007).

Bennett and Iyengar (2008) counsel scholars to consider how recent

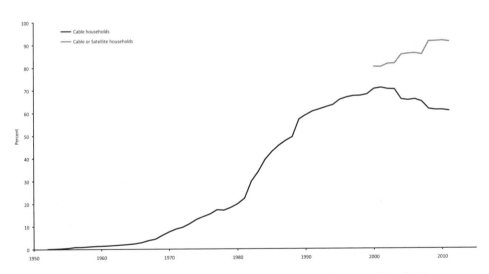

FIGURE 2.4. Percentage of U.S. households subscribing to basic cable or satellite television. *Sources*: 1952–99, Parsons (2008); 2000–2011, TVB (2011).

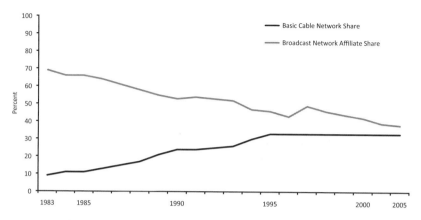

FIGURE 2.5. Rating shares for cable networks and broadcast network affiliates.
Source: Parsons (2008).

"sociotechnical changes" in the media environment may ultimately reduce the reach and impact of news media—especially the prevalence
of more subtle media effects that rely on the presence of a large inadvertent news audience (e.g., agenda setting)—and usher in a new era of
minimal effects. Understandably, in a field devoted in part to cataloging
the effects of the media, Bennett and Iyengar's supposition has not gone
uncontested. In their critique, Holbert, Garrett, and Gleason (2010) argue that the rise of partisan news media forces scholars to reconceptu-
alize news media effects by returning persuasion effects to the center
and treating reinforcement—a central element of the old minimal effects
model—as an end in and of itself. Furthermore, the rise of entertainment
options may only expand the avenues through which the media can influence political attitudes. Entertainment show characters, like the liberal
activist and vegetarian Lisa Simpson, often discuss political topics and
advocate particular viewpoints. Holbert, Garrett, and Gleason conclude:
"A full range of [media] effects is not only plausible, but distinctly prob-
able, even amidst the extraordinary sociotechnical change occurring in
our media system and democracy" (2010, 16).

Although we believe that Holbert, Garrett, and Gleason make an important point about the need to consider the goals of the partisan news
media when theorizing about their possible effects, we contend that they
underestimate how transformative the expansion of choice can be for the
study of media effects. We wholeheartedly agree that scholars should
contemplate the political implications of entertainment programming.

Yet we would be surprised if entertainment shows demonstrate the same capacity to influence political attitudes as the news. After all, entertainment shows tend to touch on political issues in passing, unlike the news, which places politics front and center. We find ourselves concurring with Bennett and Iyengar (2010, 36), who write in response: "Unless Lisa Simpson becomes a mouthpiece for some clever political consultant, the larger utility of understanding communication effects through such entertainment programming seems greatly diminished."

In many ways, media effects research has come full circle. The massive technological changes in the early twentieth century that gave rise to broadcast mass media capable of reaching just about every living room in the country led scholars to fret about the power of the news media to do harm. In particular, this early age of broadcasting made observers worry that the media would stamp out diversity of opinion. Today, it is the reemergence of the partisan news media that concerns many scholars. Not only does it raise the specter of an easily persuaded and polarized mass public, but it also threatens to eat at the common fabric of political life by creating parallel and incommensurable partisan conversations about politics.

Interestingly, many scholars today share the concerns of researchers ninety years ago that technologically induced changes in the news media environment threaten to undermine the foundations of democracy. The contemporary concern is that, by turning away from broadcast news media, people lose their connection with the common conversation about politics—the same mass media–manufactured common conversation that troubled scholars when it was new at the turn of the last century. It is difficult to escape the impression that major technological changes are accompanied by overly simplistic models of what these changes mean. Just as scholars in the mid-twentieth century offered a more nuanced view of news media effects, we believe that current models of massive partisan news effects will give way to models that are primarily focused on identifying boundary conditions rather than potential effects. We seek to offer an entrée into such an approach.

In order to do so, we build on and extend the work of communication scholars actively studying changes in the media environment and its implications. Markus Prior (2005, 2007) identifies one set of sorting behaviors among television viewers—people selecting themselves into audiences for news and entertainment, with profound implications for political knowledge and participation. Others, like Natalie Stroud (2011), focus on another set of sorting behaviors—partisans sorting themselves into congenial news sources. In many ways, our work is synthetic and reflects an attempt to demonstrate that, given the contemporary cable environment, people can engage in complex patterns of sorting into audiences for multiple types of entertainment and news. Other researchers focus on partisan news but more often than not concentrate on the decision people might make among different types of news (e.g., Levendusky 2012), minimizing the fact that many people select themselves out of the audience for news and political information. The people who are left watching news are different from the people who watch news of whatever ideological bent. We contend that these differences affect the influence of partisan news on viewers and hold broader lessons for the study of media effects as well.

CHAPTER THREE

Selective Exposure and Media Effects

What does selective exposure mean for media effects theory and research? Contemporary research tells us that people are increasingly able to sort themselves into more optimally congenial programming, regardless of their specific predispositions. As touched on in the previous chapters, the heightened potential for partisan-motivated selective exposure animates current-day concerns that partisan news media exacerbate ideological rifts in the polity and debase our politics in the process. We offer a different perspective. We primarily expect that opportunities for choosing should blunt the role the media play in changing attitudes and militate against large aggregate effects associated with particular types of television content—including partisan news. Except for the Super Bowl or some universally captivating news story (e.g., the beginning of a military conflict), not enough of the general population pays attention to a single channel or event for there to be large aggregate effects. Instead, we expect that what an individual watches on television increasingly indicates what type of person he or she is—whether that is an angler, a foodie, a sports fan, a dog lover, or a liberal or conservative, assuming an interest in politics in the first place.

In this chapter, we elucidate our thinking about how the expansion of news and entertainment choices on television affects the influence of mass media and establish the foundation for the rest of the book. To motivate both our theoretical model and our empirical approach, we begin with the particularly current and intriguing proposition that the contemporary partisan cable news environment may cause greater ideological polarization in the mass public. As discussed at the conclusion of chapter 2, this proposition brings media research full circle to concerns first raised at the beginning of the twentieth century—that mass media have massive persuasive effects. Moreover, the unabashed ideological nature of partisan media, which makes them potentially polarizing forces, requires us to recontextualize the more subtle effects attributed to the mainstream media, such as attitude reinforcement, agenda setting, and hostile media perceptions.

Our first order of business is to demonstrate that prima facie polarization in political attitudes and differences in political knowledge among cable and broadcast news audiences could just as easily be attributable to individuals sorting into audiences on the basis of interest than to the effects of partisan news shows, consistent with our claim that audiences are active, not passive. Our descriptive analysis sets up a discussion of how an active audience, which seeks out television programming to fill needs and achieve goals, may actually diminish the influence of partisan news shows in a hyperchoice media environment. With the intuitions behind our argument in place, we lay the theoretical foundation of the book by drawing on psychological theories of motivation to develop a more complete model of selective exposure—one that considers the motivation to consume partisan news and the motivation to be entertained by television programming.

The remainder of this chapter is devoted to our empirical approach to testing the expectations generated by the theoretical model. The dominant contemporary approaches to the study of media effects—survey research and traditional laboratory experiments—are limited in their ability to test the effects of media in this new environment. To address these limitations, we develop and describe a novel set of experimental designs, building on and augmenting contemporary political communication experiments, and applying these research designs to investigate a wide range of potential media effects.

The Apparent Effects of Partisan News

How might we go about determining whether partisan news on cable television affects viewers' attitude extremity and political knowledge? A common, but limited, approach would be to identify members of these audiences and ask them their views on political and social issues. The principle weakness of this research design is that, in spite of claims made by many scholars, it does not afford the identification of a causal relationship between media choice and whatever characteristic someone might find of interest. But, at a *minimum*, it should elucidate differences between these audiences. Researchers at the Pew Research Center for the People and the Press regularly conducts exactly this kind of survey research project. They ask a random sample of the American public questions about how they stay informed about politics, covering both the general forms of media they use (e.g., newspapers, television, the Internet) and the specific television networks and programs they watch. Pew generously shares these data with the public, allowing us to analyze the politics of news audiences.

Using Pew's June 2010 media consumption survey (June 8–28), we identify four television audiences: (1) regular viewers of any of the three major broadcast network television newscasts, (2) regular viewers of the Fox News Channel's opinionated talk shows, (3) regular viewers of MSNBC's opinionated talk shows, and (4) those respondents who claim to not regularly pay attention to any source of news, whether newspapers, television, radio, or the Internet.[1] Other than this last group of news-inattentive survey participants, these are not mutually exclusive audiences. At least hypothetically, a survey respondent could be in all three of the viewing audiences if he or she reports regularly watching mainstream television news as well as both Fox News and MSNBC talk shows and newscasts. Obviously, the world is more complicated than this four-group scheme suggests, but we believe it is a useful simplification that allows us to compare regular partisan news watchers to mainstream news viewers and the inattentive public.

The survey included a variety of questions about the respondent's political orientations. We begin with self-reported political ideology. Respondents were asked whether they consider themselves to be very liberal, liberal, moderate, conservative, or very conservative. We coded these identifications running from 1 for very liberal respondents to 5 for very conservative ones, with moderates coded 3. We computed a simple average for each of the four audiences we identified. These averages are graphed in figure 3.1.

The figure conforms to a set of intuitive expectations about these audiences. The inattentive respondents are centrist, on average. The net-

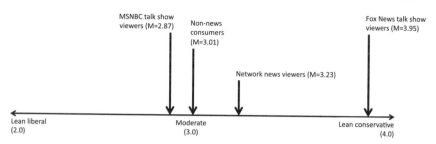

FIGURE 3.1. Ideological self-placement of news audiences.

work news viewers are also in the center of the distribution, on average, but slightly more conservative than the nonnews consumers. Fox News and MSNBC talk show viewers are more conservative and liberal, respectively, creating anchors of a seemingly polarized public. What accounts for this pattern? As we explain in the next section, despite the intuitive appeal, these data do not offer unambiguous evidence that partisan news causes viewer polarization.

Ideological and Demographic Sorting in News Audiences

We go beyond self-reported political ideology in table 3.1, which considers a broader array of political judgments. The table reports the profound differences between broadcast news viewers and viewers of opinionated talk shows in terms of partisanship, evaluations of President Obama, and identification with a variety of social groups. We need not belabor the point but simply highlight two distinctions. In the final two columns, we see that only 12 percent of Fox News talk show viewers but 71 percent of MSNBC talk show viewers approve of the job that President Obama is doing. Broadcast news audiences and the inattentive public fall in the middle, with 54.9 and 44.8 percent approving of the president, respectively. We see the same pattern in social identifications. Respondents were asked if they identify with conservative groups (the Tea Party, Christian conservatives, the National Rifle Association, probusiness interests, and Libertarians) or liberal groups (gay rights supporters, environmentalists, and progressives). In seven of these eight instances, there are substantial differences between the viewers of Fox and the viewers of MSNBC talk shows.

Clearly, these audiences are different from each other politically and discernibly polarized in meaningful ways. But are they politically dif-

TABLE 3.1. **Political Differences among News Audiences**

		Talk Show Viewers		
	Inattentive	Broadcast News Viewers	Fox News	MSNBC
Percentage liberal	23.5	17.0	3.0	32.6
Percentage conservative	28.2	37.8	77.4	25.5
Percentage Democrat	43.8	53.0	12.3	69.8
Percentage Republican	29.6	37.1	81.4	20.6
Approve of Obama	44.8	54.9	11.9	71.4
Disapprove of Obama	27.6	35.0	85.2	26.5
Don't know/refused	27.6	10.1	2.9	2.1
Tea Party	13.8	22.1	68.4	16.4
Christian conservative	37.9	45.7	74.4	32.3
NRA	32.0	38.6	67.0	31.7
Probusiness	35.0	57.3	81.2	59.8
Libertarian	12.8	14.4	22.4	17.5
Gay rights supporter	33.5	36.7	24.0	54.5
Environmentalist	48.8	68.0	48.2	78.8
Progressive	27.1	48.7	22.9	57.4

ferent from each other because people sort by political interest and self-select into different news audiences or because of the differences in news content, reflecting the rhetorical power of the media to persuade people to adopt liberal or conservative views? A third possibility is that both things are happening.

At a minimum, people are sorting themselves into these audiences. In addition to the political differences charted in table 3.1 above, we chart *demographic* differences across these audiences in table 3.2. For example, Fox News and MSNBC talk show viewers express different levels of economic affluence. About 63 percent of Fox News viewers and 54 percent of MSNBC news viewers report incomes higher than the 2010 median U.S. income. Taken together, partisan news show audiences are more affluent than broadcast news audiences (50 percent above median income) and the inattentive public (31 percent above median income). As compelling as Glenn Beck was during his run on the Fox News Channel, we doubt that he was directly generating wealth for his viewers.

We see the same pattern for marriage. A larger proportion of Fox News talk show viewers are married (nearly 68 percent) compared to MSNBC talk show viewers (nearly 52 percent). This pattern holds with

TABLE 3.2. **Demographic Differences among News Audiences**

		Talk Show Viewers		
	Inattentive	Broadcast News Viewers	Fox News	MSNBC
Percentage above median income	31.0	50.0	63.3	54.0
Percentage married	33.5	54.7	67.7	51.9
Average age	40.7	57.6	56.5	54.4
Percentage college educated	15.4	34.6	40.8	39.6
Percentage male	42.9	35.6	48.2	49.7
Percentage white	69.4	76.6	85.7	63.4
Percentage black	10.6	13.9	3.2	17.2
Percentage Latino	12.6	5.4	4.9	10.2

age and ethnic composition as well. As with income, we cannot imagine that anyone would sincerely argue that Keith Olbermann makes people less likely to be married than Bill O'Reilly, that Sean Hannity ages people more than Rachel Maddow, or that Glenn Beck and Chris Matthews change the race or ethnicity of their viewers. In short, these demographic differences suggest that news audiences are socially distinct and polarized but do little to support the argument that the shows' content produces polarization by persuading viewers to adopt more extreme positions.

News Audiences Also Differ in Attention and Knowledge

The Pew survey reveals some other differences among these audiences that we consider to be quite important: differences in the extent to which they pay attention to news, how much they know about politics, and their evaluation of news media. We compare the four audiences across these dimensions in table 3.3. Here, the picture that emerges is qualitatively different than what we saw with political opinions and most of the demographic items. The people who watch talk shows on the Fox News Channel and MSNBC are very engaged with politics and political information. Partisan talk show viewers also see more political bias in news media reports than do network news viewers, and, perhaps as a consequence, they are more likely than the inattentive and broadcast news audiences to prefer news shows that share their point of view. In these regards, partisan news audiences on the Left and the Right are quite *similar.*

TABLE 3.3. **Information Differences among News Audiences**

		Talk Show Viewers		
	Inattentive	Broadcast News Viewers	Fox News	MSNBC
Enjoys keeping up with news "a lot"	4.9	62.2	80.5	79.9
Following condition of the U.S. economy	6.9	47.6	70.6	57.1
Following congressional elections	2.0	23.4	48.0	34.4
Following events in Afghanistan	3.9	38.2	41.7	39.7
Average knowledge items correct	1.0	1.9	2.6	2.4
Percentage registered to vote	66.5	88.2	94.2	91.5
Sees "a lot" of political bias in news	34.5	52.2	81.6	66.1
Trusts a few media more than others	29.1	63.3	81.8	77.8
Prefers news with shared point of view	18.2	23.1	35.4	32.8

Perhaps it should come as no surprise that there are huge gaps in attention, knowledge, and engagement between people who disregard all news sources and people who do pay attention to news (e.g., Zaller 1992). That said, cable talk show viewers are even more interested in the news than are broadcast news viewers, with about 80 percent of talk show viewers reporting that they enjoy keeping up with news "a lot" versus 62 percent of broadcast news watchers. Partisan news viewers at least claim to be paying more attention to the major news stories of the day (Pew asked about the economy, congressional elections, and Afghanistan). They also know more of the news facts that Pew quizzed them about, including identifying the majority political party in the U.S. House of Representatives, the company Steve Jobs headed at the time, Eric Holder's position in government, and the country whose volcanic eruption disrupted international air travel in spring 2010. In each case, broadcast news viewers paid more attention to politics or knew more than inattentive viewers, and the respective cable talk show audiences surpassed the broadcast news audiences.

But Doesn't Fox News Underinform People about Politics?

Evidence that Fox News viewers have levels of political knowledge comparable to or even exceeding those of MSNBC and broadcast news viewers may surprise some readers. Beyond the pervasive perception that partisan talk shows are misleading, in late fall 2011 researchers at Fairleigh Dickinson University earned a great deal of publicity for their study of 612 New Jersey adults and their finding that "some outlets, especially Fox News, lead people to be even less informed than those who say they don't watch any news at all" (Fairleigh Dickinson University 2011). Specifically, they found that survey respondents who said they watch Fox News were far less likely to answer correctly a question about the overthrow of the Egyptian government in February 2011. On the other hand, the researchers characterize news programs like the mainstream media's Sunday morning talk shows as more informative. "Viewers pick up more information from this sort of calm discussion than from other formats," said Daniel Cassino, a scholar at Fairleigh Dickinson (Fairleigh Dickinson University 2011, n.p.). In fact, respondents who said they watch these Sunday morning broadcast shows were much more likely to answer the question correctly.

The researchers want to make a direct causal inference here: Fox News causes ignorance. That may be, but their survey is not designed to provide sufficient evidence. People select into the Fox News audience, which always leaves open the possibility that they are simply different than those who choose to do something else, like watch network news or no news at all. Moreover, reliance on self-reports of viewing behavior further distorts these potential selection problems (Prior 2009). People may say they watch news shows whether they do or not.

The Fairleigh Dickinson researchers are less concerned about the problems of self-selection because they analyzed responses using a statistical technique called *logistic regression*. When estimating the relationship between self-reported viewing of multiple sources of information and correct responses to the question about the removal of former president Mubarak, they accounted for other potential variables that could affect whether survey respondents answered the question correctly, including their party identification. Many people colloquially refer to these as *control variables*; the hope is that they control for the effect of those other factors and allow one to estimate the true causal relationship between the variables of interest: "Because of the controls for partisanship, we know these results are not just driven by Republicans or other groups being more likely to watch Fox News" (Fairleigh Dickinson University 2011).

The major problem with this logic is that statistical controls are insufficient in the face of selection bias. The statistical model employed by the Fairleigh Dickinson researchers makes two assumptions: (1) partisanship and the other controls account for all preexisting differences in knowledge, and the selection into the Fox News audience can therefore be treated as if it were random; and (2) partisanship and the other controls do not causally affect selection into these audiences (i.e., Democrats who watch Fox are no different than Democrats who do not watch Fox). These assumptions strain credulity. It is just as plausible, if not more so, that people choose to watch news *because of* the characteristics measured by the control variables, and, at the very least, it is highly dubious that partisans who watch Fox are no different from partisans who choose not to watch Fox. Treating variables that cause people to select partisan news as if they are exogenous control variables risks *overstating* the effects of cable news shows (see Achen 1986; Arceneaux 2010). In short, selection bias vitiates our ability to disentangle cause and effect from the standard type of methods employed by the Fairleigh Dickinson researchers.

A similar effort by researchers at the University of Maryland in December 2010 came to similar conclusions: Fox News underinforms. This study concluded that Fox News viewers were more likely than others to hold a wide-ranging set of mistaken beliefs. The researchers took essentially the same approach to dealing with the problem of partisan selectivity: "The effect was also not simply a function of partisan bias, as people who voted Democratic and watched Fox News were also more likely to have such misinformation than those who did not watch it" (Ramsay, Kull, Lewis, and Subias 2010, 20). The only difference from the Fairleigh Dickinson study is that the Maryland researchers controlled for partisanship by using a less sophisticated statistical technique to compare partisans to other, similar partisans by news source.

This approach also assumes that the difference between partisans who watch Fox News and those who do not is random. In order to make this problem more concrete, consider the following: if partisans who watch Fox News are, say, more interested in domestic than international politics, we would expect Fox News watchers to be less informed about international politics *irrespective* of Fox's influence; indeed, Fox News could even make these individuals more informed about international events than they would have otherwise been. Neither the Fairleigh Dickinson nor the Maryland research team has access to what statisticians call the *counterfactual*. A counterfactual is the product of a thought experiment:

What would have happened in an alternate reality where Fox News does not exist? Would the same Fox News viewers in the reality we do observe know more or less about politics if they lived in the alternate reality? The fundamental obstacle to causal inference is that we can never simultaneously observe what actually happens and the counterfactual.

All this is not to say that these researchers are necessarily wrong; it very well could be that Fox News is a poor source of information. Our point is that, given the lack of a convincing research design, neither of these attention-grabbing reports should be taken as persuasive. Neither can answer the question of whether Fox News causes viewers to become ignorant about public affairs or whether people who are ignorant about public affairs choose to watch Fox News.

The Implications of Partisan News Choice

At this point, we hope it is clear that partisan news audiences differ from broadcast news audiences along many dimensions. So what? What implications does this have for studying the effects of partisan news? We suspect that the people who choose to watch cable news and cable news talk shows, in particular, have relatively stable opinions about politics. They are certainly more opinionated. For example, table 3.1 above showed that only 3 percent of Fox News talk show viewers and 2 percent of MSNBC talk show viewers were unable to evaluate the job President Obama was doing at the time. Ten percent of regular broadcast network news viewers were unable to do so, and 28 percent of inattentive viewers refused to answer the question or pled ignorance.

Inattentiveness to politics can limit the influence of the news media (Zaller 1992) and underscore our contention that television audiences are active rather than passive. Besides different ideological orientations, demographic characteristics, and political engagement, these audiences also exhibit different patterns of trust in media outlets and use different criteria to select news. Fox News and MSNBC talk show viewers see more political bias in news media reports than do network news viewers. They also extend their trust to news media outlets more narrowly than do network news viewers and the inattentive. Fox and MSNBC viewers are also more likely to indicate a preference for news programming that shares their political point of view. The implication of this audience comparison is that news consumers are *selective* in choosing sources of information, are relatively guarded when considering programming, shop for news and act on their preferences, and sort themselves into audiences for shows on networks they like. What is more, those who change the channel to something other than partisan news are being selective as well. In the next section, we offer a theoretical model of selective exposure and draw from it a set of expectations about how media choice shapes the reach and influence of partisan news shows.

Active Audience Theory

We are certainly not the first to propose that scholars should treat television audiences as active—consisting of individuals who exercise agency over what they consume and what messages they accept. Our theoretical model is heavily indebted to the *uses and gratifications* paradigm that emerged during the minimal effects period of media research. It was conceptualized as a foil to the hypodermic needle model's presumption that individuals are unable to resist media influence. In contrast, researchers applying the uses and gratifications framework argue that people used the media to satisfy their own needs, thus limiting media influence (Cantril 1942). Subsequent research in this mold sought to understand how and why people use the media to attain their needs (e.g., Katz, Blumler, and Gurevitch 1974) but failed to generate a unified theory of media use (Blumler 1979).

Uses and gratifications theory became an eclectic and sometimes contradictory collection of musings. Nonetheless, it is possible to identify common elements that unite disparate articulations of the uses and gratifications framework (Biocca 1988). Active audience members have needs (e.g., desire for information or diversion) that they use media programming to satisfy. Those needs translate into intentional choices about what to consume. Given these choices, individuals actively involve themselves in the media they have chosen (e.g., counterarguing, talking back to the television). Therefore, they do not randomly consume media programming. They select into audiences. Ultimately, uses and gratifications scholars expected the goal-directedness, intentionality, and selectivity of active audience members in the extreme to generate "imperviousness to influence" (Biocca 1988, 54).

Our *active audience theory* shares some but not all elements of the uses and gratifications framework. We, too, presume that individuals are guided by needs and goals when they consume media, leading them to make purposive decisions and, when possible, to select programming that best fits their needs and desires. However, we certainly do not therefore conclude that individuals are impervious to media influence. Just because people select which television shows they want to watch does not mean that they are unaffected by those shows. Instead, our argument is that there is no guarantee that the information presented by the shows people choose to watch will be taken at face value. Selected programming may profoundly affect viewers, but not necessarily in the ways intended by the program's creator; furthermore, the same program could have different effects on different viewers, given their characteristics and interpretations.

We also do not treat the media as a monolithic entity from which all individuals must defend themselves (see Morley 1993). Perhaps this approach made sense, at least as a simplification, during the broadcast television era. The availability of so many news and entertainment outlets on television nowadays (not to mention the radio, the Internet, and social media) compels us to conceptualize the media as a multifaceted, heterogeneous collection of options. Today, more than ever, people can create a media environment that does not challenge their cherished views (Bennett and Iyengar 2008)—if that is what they want.

Finally, at the heart of our active audience theory is a set of midlevel theories recruited from political science and psychology to construct a model of selective exposure that generates empirically falsifiable expectations by specifying how motivations shape reactions to media content. Our approach contrasts with that of many scholars in the uses and gratifications tradition who advance overly abstract functionalist theories of media use that end up explaining everything and, therefore, nothing at all (see Seaman 1992). It is not our goal to explain why people watch what they watch. We take what people watch as a given and proceed to theorize how preferences regarding media programming condition the effects and reach of partisan news media.

A Motivational Model of Selective Exposure

In our effort to understand how selective exposure alters media effects, we start by considering the motivations of television viewers. Psychologists have long considered much of human behavior and reasoning to be rooted in an individual's goals, needs, and desires (Kruglanski 1980;

Kunda 1990). We define *motivation* broadly as any goal-directed preference regarding what to watch on television. These preferences may reflect the desire to defend one's political attitudes (Taber and Lodge 2006), obtain accurate information (Fischer, Schulz-Hardt, and Frey 2008), or be entertained (Prior 2007).[2] Although this is, in many ways, another way of saying that people do the things they want to do, the motivational framework allows for differences in intrinsic individual traits (e.g., personalities) as well as situational constraints and incentives. It offers a valuable starting point for our project because television programming in a free society attracts audiences by catering to people's desires and needs and, when given a choice, people tend to watch the shows that best fit their tastes (Bowman 1975).[3]

In our model of news-viewing behavior, we posit that two fundamental motivations figure into people's viewing decisions: the motivation to receive news from a partisan viewpoint and the motivation to be entertained. The model shown in figure 3.2 makes it clear we assume that both motivations fall on a continuous dimension. Some individuals prefer more partisan news than others, while some individuals

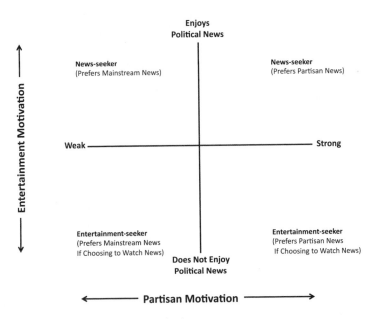

FIGURE 3.2. A motivational model of selective exposure.

are more entertained by the news in general than others. Recently, a great deal of media scholarship has been devoted to partisan motivations in news-watching behavior (e.g., Bennett and Manheim 2006; Garrett 2009a, 2009b; Manjoo 2008; Goldman and Mutz 2011; Iyengar and Hahn 2009; Iyengar, Hahn, Krosnick, and Walker 2008; Mutz and Martin 2001; Stroud 2008, 2011; Sunstein 2009; Valentino, Banks, Hutchings, and Davis 2009). Much of this work focuses on whether the rise of partisan media creates a world in which people consume ideologically congenial news while screening out opposing viewpoints.

Scholars building on a rich literature in psychology on selective exposure to attitude-consistent information (Festinger 1957; Fischer, Jonas, Frey, and Schulz-Hardt 2005; Fischer, Schulz-Hardt, and Frey 2008; Frey 1986; Sears and Freedman 1967) more or less agree that many people gravitate toward attitude-consistent news (e.g., Garrett 2009a, 2009b; Garrett, Carnahan, and Lynch, in press; Iyengar and Hahn 2009; Iyengar, Hahn, Krosnick, and Walker 2008; Mutz and Martin 2001; Stroud 2008, 2011). However, there is some disagreement over the degree to which individuals actively screen out attitude-inconsistent news (see, e.g., Bennett and Iyengar 2008, 2010; Garrett 2009a, 2009b; Holbert, Garrett, and Gleason 2010). It appears that some individual news viewers, albeit a minority, may even seek out contrary viewpoints (Stroud 2011, 169).

Our framework remains agnostic about whether individuals are motivated to screen out oppositional news while consuming only ideologically congenial news. The partisan motivation dimension encapsulates the motivation to watch any partisan news, be it ideologically congenial or otherwise. It is most likely the case that the decision to consume ideologically congenial news at the expense of oppositional news is a function of differences in individual traits and situational factors (for a discussion of the roots of these kinds of motivations, see Kirzinger, Weber, and Johnson [2012]). Some individuals are compelled to view information that comports with their view of the world, while others are equally compelled to hear diverse viewpoints (e.g., Kruglanski, Webster, and Klem 1993). At the same time, particular circumstances motivate people to appear objective and sample from opposing viewpoints (e.g., Fischer, Schulz-Hardt, and Frey 2008). These factors are important but outside the scope of our current study.

Our overarching goal here is to explore the implications of the choice *to screen out news altogether*. In the drive to understand the effects of selective exposure to partisan news, scholars have paid less attention to this related form of selective exposure to political news in general (Bennett and Iyengar 2008). Scholars who have tackled this question conclude that the hyperchoice media environment has made it possible for more and more Americans to wall themselves off from political information (Baum and Kernell 1999; Prior 2005, 2007). In addition to filtering news on the basis of one's partisan predispositions, "selective exposure enables the popular lifestyle choice of political avoidance" (Bennett and Iyengar 2010, 721). We call this *news selectivity* and argue that it is just as important, if not more important, than partisan selectivity.

If we simplify the model presented in figure 3.2, four ideal types emerge. At the top-left corner of the two-dimensional space are individuals who enjoy watching news, but news of a nonpartisan variety, which means that in the current media environment they would likely gravitate toward mainstream news if given a choice. At the top-right corner are individuals who enjoy watching partisan news and, if given a choice, should gravitate toward partisan news programming. In the bottom quadrants are individuals who, if given a choice, would typically not watch political news. All things being equal, these viewers would opt for entertainment programming. If induced to watch the news (e.g., a major event piques their interest), individuals in the bottom-right corner would gravitate toward partisan news, while individuals in the bottom-left corner would opt for mainstream news.

This theoretical model opens a number of avenues for research, but we cannot explore all these questions at once. Because a great deal of research has focused on the effects of partisan selectivity while comparatively less has been devoted to news selectivity, we choose to concentrate on the effects of partisan media given the presence of entertainment choices. Consequently, we hold constant the motivation to watch partisan news and focus on the motivation to watch news as opposed to entertainment, simplifying our typology further to two ideal types: *news seekers* and *entertainment seekers* (see also Prior 2007).

We apply this theoretical framework to investigate how the presence of entertainment choices shapes the influence of partisan news shows. We explore the effects of partisan news on a number of outcomes—attitude polarization, resistance to persuasion, issue salience, hostile media perceptions, and political trust—that have been prominent in previous media effects research. For the purposes of our study, we draw three expectations from our model:

Expectation 1: People view television programming through the lenses of their own partisan motivations. These motivations not only influence what programming individuals choose to watch but also shape how they process the news. People are motivated to defend preexisting attitudes and, therefore, should be more likely to accept messages that are consistent with their predispositions and resist those that are not (e.g., Kunda 1990; Taber and Lodge 2006).[4]

Expectation 2: In the presence of choice, entertainment seekers select out of news audiences and attenuate partisan news effects in the process. The exit of entertainment seekers shrinks the partisan news audience and dilutes its overall effect in the process.

Expectation 3: On average, partisan news shows have smaller effects on news seekers than on entertainment seekers. This expectation is the product of our motivational framework—people's motivations generate chronic viewing habits (e.g., news seekers and entertainment seekers)—combined with scholarship on the effects of chronic exposure to a stimulus (e.g., news). On a general level, research across a wide range of domains, including the biological and the psychological, has found that successive exposure to the same stimulus leads to habituation and diminished responsiveness (see Thompson 2009). In the context of our model, habituation would cause people who regularly watch partisan news to become inured to its effects. On a more specific level, John Zaller's (1992) receive-accept-sample (R-A-S) model of opinion formation predicts that those who chronically avoid the news (i.e., entertainment seekers) are the most susceptible to news media effects but the least likely to experience those effects because they fail to consume information that might affect their views (e.g., partisan news). Meanwhile, those who chronically expose themselves to news (i.e., news seekers) are regularly exposed to messages that could influence their attitudes, but, because they possess very well-formed opinions, they cannot be easily influenced (see also McGuire 1968).

These expectations guide the development of hypotheses that are specific to the media effects under investigation. In the chapters that follow, we elaborate on the rationale for these specific hypotheses, an elaboration informed by these general expectations. Empirically evaluating these hypotheses requires that careful thought be given to the research design, and the remaining sections of the chapter are devoted to explaining and justifying our approach.

The Case for Randomized Experiments

We have already seen that the direct observation of people who watch different news programs does not tell us exactly what we want to know about whether and how partisan cable news talk shows influence public opinion. The shortcoming of the survey research design we discussed at the beginning of this chapter is that it allows us to observe only the correlation between news viewing behavior and political attitudes. This kind of analysis alone cannot conclusively tell us whether watching Fox News causes viewers to become conservative or whether being conservative causes people to watch Fox News. Indeed, given the research on partisan selectivity discussed above, we know that a person's ideology plays a role in deciding what news networks he or she watches (e.g., Stroud 2011) and trusts (Iyengar and Hahn 2009). The analysis of all observational data is complicated by the well-known dictum in statistics that *correlation does not equal causation*. After all, both ice cream consumption and homicides tend to increase in the summer months, but it would be ridiculous to claim on the basis of this correlation that eating ice cream causes people to go on killing sprees. Even though the claim that partisan news causes a shift in political attitudes is far less ridiculous, researchers must still be careful when adducing the effects of partisan media from observational data.

Randomized experiments offer a better strategy for isolating causal effects. The use of randomized experiments to study the effects of political news enjoys a rich tradition in media research, so this is hardly a new approach. The postwar experiments conducted by Carl Hovland and his colleagues contributed significantly to the minimal effects model dominant around the mid-twentieth century (see Klapper 1960). Likewise, the seminal experiments conducted by Shanto Iyengar and Donald Kinder in the 1980s informed our understanding of the impact of network news during the broadcast era. In a randomized experiment, the researcher assigns individuals to different levels of the factor believed to cause something to occur, or *treatments*, in statistics parlance (e.g., watching partisan news or an entertainment program, taking a new drug or a placebo). By making assignment to the different treatments random—imagine the researcher flipping a coin to decide what treatment a person receives—we can be sure that the treatment that people receive is not affected by some other factor that may itself also affect the outcome we are interested in studying, such as the subject's age, political beliefs, and so on.

In essence, random assignment gives researchers a way to create an answer to the counterfactual question underlying all causal inference: What would the same people do if they did *not* watch partisan news shows? Obviously, we cannot directly answer that question. Short of inventing a time machine, we cannot simultaneously observe the state of the world in which the same person does and does not watch partisan news. However, random assignment allows us to create groups of individuals who are highly similar and, therefore, comparable. If we randomly assign some people to watch Fox News and others to watch an entertainment show, we know that the people in the Fox News group will, on average, be similar to the people in the entertainment show group— they come from the same underlying population and differ only in the fact that they are randomly assigned to different treatments. If we simply assigned people at random to different groups and then did not administer the treatment, there should be no differences between the groups with respect to the typical political views these participants express in a survey. As a result, if we do administer the treatment to these groups and find that those who watched Fox News express more conservative attitudes than those who watched the entertainment program, then it is likely that exposure to Fox News caused people to express more conservative attitudes.[5] (We provide a formal proof of this in the appendix.)

Political communication researchers have learned a great deal about the effects of media on opinions using experiments featuring random assignment to fixed treatment conditions. However, the major limitation of these experiments is that they identify the causal effect of political messages provided people are exposed to them—forced to watch. Theoretically, we know that media effects are *conditional* and shaped by audience choices, but this kind of classic experimental design relies on an operational hypodermic needle delivery of stimuli to participants. The only choice participants really have is whether to participate in the experiment at all. More fundamentally, if we ignore the fact that the act of choosing to consume media programming in naturalistic settings is endogenous to the characteristics of the programming, "captive audience" designs can lead to a distorted understanding of media effects (Hovland 1959).

A recent article in the journal *Political Communication* offers an example of this limitation in the context of understanding the effects of partisan news. Lauren Feldman (2011) assigned people at random to view clips of either the conservative commentator Glenn Beck's talk show, the progressive commentator Keith Olbermann's talk show, or the PBS *NewsHour* program. The clips featured discussions of then-president Bush's veto of the State Children's Health Insurance Program bill in October 2007. She found that, independent of partisanship, people who watched Beck were more likely to shift their opinions toward opposition to the bill and that people who watched Olbermann were more likely to shift their opinion toward support of the bill (Feldman 2011, 171, fig. 1). Feldman, for one, sounds what we consider to be an appropriate—if not essential—caution about her findings: "Although the experimental methods permitted causal inferences, by forcing exposure to the stimulus, the influence of selective exposure was obscured" (Feldman 2011, 176).

We do not intend this observation to be a critique of previous experimental studies. For one thing, randomized experiments that assign subjects to forced treatment stimuli are extremely valuable in the scientific study of media effects because they allow researchers to isolate the causal effects of political media far better than do observational studies, such as the ones discussed earlier in this chapter. In addition, the design of initial experiments in an area *should* be parsimonious and aim to capture maximal effects. Establishing the maximal effect of political communication points out the direction in which future research should go. Until recently, scholars could credibly assume that mainstream media coverage would reach most people and that maximal effects were potentially even good barometers of the overall effect of political communication. During the broadcast television era, many people were exposed to political news despite their lack of interest in it (Prior 2007). However, the rise of cable television and the Internet and the fragmented political media market produced in their wake force us to reconsider experimental designs and develop an expanded set of tools to study media effects.

Experimental Design

The design of an experiment is crucial. The inferential power of an experiment comes from its ability to isolate causal effects through the careful manipulation of treatments. The design of those treatments directly affects what can be learned from the experiment. In our project, we rely on three experimental designs to study the effects of partisan news media: a traditional experimental design that assigns participants to one of several specific, forced viewing conditions at random and two novel designs that allow us to assess how the choices that research participants make about viewing options condition the effects of those programs. The broad outlines of these designs are displayed graphically in figure 3.3, and a formal explanation of how these designs jibe with our theoretical model is given in the appendix.

Forced Exposure Design

The traditional experimental design used in political communication research is displayed in figure 3.3*a*. This design proceeds in much the same way as the example discussed above. Study participants are recruited from a population, usually students at a university or nonstudents from the surrounding community, and compensated for their time in some way (e.g., course credit for students or monetary inducements). The study typically takes place in a controlled setting called a *laboratory* where assignment to treatments can be administered and monitored. When subjects arrive at the lab, they are typically asked to answer a set of questions before the study begins. This *pretest questionnaire* measures baseline characteristics (e.g., political ideology, media viewing habits, demographic information) of each of the participants. Next, participants are randomly assigned to treatment conditions. In the simplest design, subjects are randomly assigned to watch some political stimuli, such as a news program, or control stimuli, such as an entertainment program. After watching the experimental stimuli, participants are asked to complete a *posttest questionnaire* that measures the outcomes under investigation, such as political attitudes.

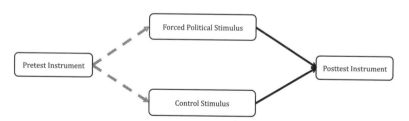

FIGURE 3.3*a*. Experimental design for studying media effects: forced exposure design.
Note: Solid lines indicate nonrandom assignment, and dashed lines indicate random assignment.

The forced exposure design is useful for estimating the maximal effects of political stimuli. Because subjects had little choice in the matter (aside from closing their eyes and ears), any posttreatment differences between the treatment group and the control group likely represent the largest effect of political news possible. In an era of hyperchoice, forced exposure political communication experiments are increasingly plagued by limited external generalizability—a growing disconnect between the ways people use television at home and in a controlled laboratory setting. Experimentalists and other researchers have always been concerned about whether the things that happen in the laboratory meaningfully mirror what happens outside the lab. However, the hyperchoice environment available to cable television subscribers exaggerates these concerns. Thus, if experimental researchers wish to understand the effects of selective exposure, "it is important that [they] use designs that combine manipulation with self-selection of exposure" (Bennett and Iyengar 2008, 724). We do so with the help of two different designs.

Selective Exposure Design

First, we use a novel experimental design, shown in figure 3.3*b*. It builds on the forced exposure design by assigning subjects at random to a forced treatment and a control condition. The added wrinkle is the choice condition, in which participants are given a remote control and allowed to flip among the stimuli showcased in the forced conditions.[6] Participants can spend as much time on each program as they like and can flip back and forth between programs as much as they want, just like they were at home sitting on their own sofas. By comparing posttreatment outcomes in the choice condition to those in the control and forced treatment

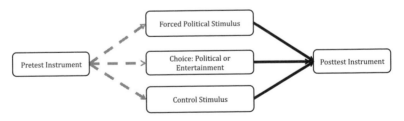

FIGURE 3.3*b*. Experimental design for studying media effects: selective exposure design.
Note: Solid lines indicate nonrandom assignment, and dashed lines indicate random assignment.

conditions, it is possible to gauge the effects of choice and, by extension, selective exposure.

In these studies, participants were recruited to visit our research laboratory at University of California, Riverside, and assigned to one of several conditions, including forced viewing scenarios as well as this novel choice treatment. In the choice treatment, after completing a pretest questionnaire, subjects accessed multiple television channels on their private television monitor. The studies reported here included either three or four channels of programming played for subjects using a four-input audio/video switch unit that emulates a set-top cable box. Research assistants played the programming for each participant using DVD playback devices in a control room adjacent to the viewing rooms in the laboratory, starting all programs at the beginning of the viewing session.

Subjects in the choice condition held a remote control and could change channels among these fixed viewing options as they wished during the viewing sessions. They could watch a given program for the length of time they wished. For example, the subject could linger as long or as short a time as he or she wished on Channel 2, then change the channel to a different option, perhaps Channel 4, and then return to Channel 2 or move to a different channel entirely. Of course, just as in a natural viewing environment, the subject would join each of these options in progress. Consequently, the viewing options were fixed for each choice condition participant and played back in a manner that quite closely simulates the experience of watching television.

Although the selective exposure design simulates conditions present in natural settings, it does not perfectly replicate those conditions. All laboratory experiments trade a degree of generalizability in return for control and, as a consequence, strong internal validity. The selective exposure design is no different. Subjects assigned to the choice condition are not simply sitting on their couch at home. They are sitting in a laboratory, and they know they are being studied. Moreover, they have access to only the number of stimuli present in the experimental design (typically three to four choices) rather than the hundred-plus channels that most Americans have available on their home televisions. As a result, the inference that we can draw from the selective exposure design is *the maximal effect of partisan news when a limited number of choices are available.* On the one hand, if we find little difference between the choice condition and the forced exposure to political stimuli condition, that suggests that limited choice does not mute the effects of partisan media. On the other hand, if we find that the effects of partisan news are muted in the choice condition, that suggests that selective exposure attenuates the effects of partisan media. Ascertaining whether the effects of partisan news are attenuated in the presence of choice—even limited choice—is an important first step because it gives us an indication of what would happen if the choice set were expanded even further.

However, a clear limitation of the selective exposure design is that it does not allow us to investigate conclusively *why* the effects of partisan media are attenuated in the face of choice. Expectation 2 offers one possibility: by allowing entertainment seekers to remove themselves from the audience, choice dilutes the effect of partisan news. Expectation 3 offers the additional possibility that partisan news has a more pronounced effect on entertainment seekers when they cannot look away, as is the case in the forced exposure setting. In technical terms, partisan news may have *differential treatment effects*, typical news seekers being affected differently than typical entertainment seekers. If we force individuals to watch partisan news, the average of these differential treatment effects will not approximate the effect in choice settings. Indeed, in the most extreme case, if news seekers are unaffected by partisan news while entertainment seekers are massively affected by it, then forced exposure designs will greatly exaggerate the effects of partisan news.

So the question is, How do we estimate the existence of differential treatment effects? Again, it may be appealing to use the information obtained in the choice condition to back out the effects of partisan news among those who chose to watch it as opposed to those who chose to watch something else. Unfortunately, this runs afoul of the same problem we encounter in observational studies. Keep in mind that what people choose to watch in the choice condition is endogenous to the characteristics of those shows (e.g., the topic they covered, the likability of the host, etc.). Consequently, we cannot know whether partisan news caused news seekers to think differently than entertainment seekers or whether news seekers simply think differently than entertainment seekers.

Participant Preference Design

In order to investigate possible heterogeneous treatment effects, it is necessary to identify who the news seekers are and who the entertainment seekers are *prior to treatment*.[7] We do so by borrowing an experi-

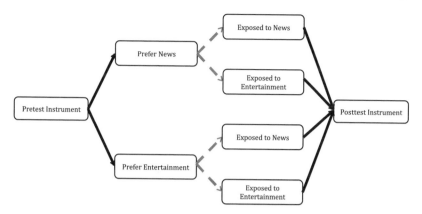

FIGURE 3.3*c*. Experimental design for studying media effects: participant preference design.
Note: Solid lines indicate nonrandom assignment, and dashed lines indicate random assignment.

mental design from the medical trials literature. Medical researchers call this the *patient preference design* (Macias et al. 2009; Torgerson and Sibbald 1998). Given the nature of our research, we refer to it as the *participant preference design*. This protocol asks subjects which treatment they would prefer to receive before randomly assigning them to a treatment. In our studies, we give subjects brief descriptions of the shows they could watch and ask them which one they would choose if it were up to them. After making their preference known, we randomly assign them to one of the shows using the standard forced exposure protocol (for a different approach, see Gaines and Kuklinski [2011]). As shown in figure 3.3*c*, this design allows us to estimate the effects of partisan news separately for those who prefer watching partisan news and those who prefer watching entertainment programs. Because we measure subjects' viewing preferences prior to administering the treatment, we can be sure that some element of the treatment did not simultaneously affect their choice to watch and their resulting political attitude.

Participants

We recruited the nearly seventeen hundred individuals who participated in the studies reported in the chapters that follow using a variety of methods. For some studies, we recruited students at the University of California, Riverside, who received extra credit in their courses in return for participating in research at the Media and Communication Research Lab. For several studies conducted in the lab, we recruited nonstudent adults from the broader Riverside, California, community, working with a temporary employment agency. This agency distributed an initial recruitment notice to its staff of temporary workers, who were hired for a two-hour shift of research participation at a wage rate comparable to their normal earnings, several dollars per hour more than the California minimum wage. One of the attractive aspects of working with this particular agency is the tremendous diversity of its staff, which included unskilled workers, employees from skilled trades, office workers with at least two-year college degrees, and white-collar professionals with four-year college degrees. All participants were informed that they were taking part in a study about "information processing," asked to provide their consent, and welcomed to exit the study at any time.

Finally, in one study, we recruited participants via Amazon.com's Mechanical Turk and administered treatments over the Internet. Subjects in this experiment were adults living in the United States and were compensated with a small monetary credit toward their Amazon.com account ($0.50). The use of Mechanical Turk as a recruitment tool for experiments has been on the rise in psychology and has been shown to produce samples comparable to traditional convenience samples (Buhrmester, Kwang, and Gosling 2011; Paolacci, Chandler, and Ipeirotis 2010). It has been used to successfully replicate canonical experiments (Berinsky, Huber, and Lenz 2012).

Stimuli

We drew stimuli for partisan news and entertainment shows from programs that actually aired on cable television.[8] We collected political stimuli from news talk shows on the major cable networks (i.e., CNN, Fox, and MSNBC). As for entertainment stimuli, we consciously chose programs that draw audiences of equal size to our political stimuli in order to give the political show a fighting chance in the choice condition. If we had offered participants an opportunity to watch a popular entertainment program, it would have been little surprise if most people—even frequent cable news watchers—opted for the popular show over the news program. Of course, there are numerous entertainment programs from which to choose. We narrowed our choices by first drawing up a list of basic cable entertainment programs that aired in the same time slot as the political stimuli and that drew similarly sized audiences. We then randomly selected shows from this list.

We recorded political and entertainment shows using a DVR and edited the shows to fit the time constraints of the experiment (ten to fifteen minutes) as well as to highlight the particular aspects of the show we wished to manipulate (e.g., partisan arguments, hostile interactions, etc.). Before using any clips in an experiment, we first ran a *norming study* in which participants were invited into the lab and asked to rate the shows across a number of dimensions. Armed with these data, we had a better sense that the clips we constructed possessed the characteristics that we wanted them to possess. In general, we selected entertainment shows that norming study subjects did not deem to be overtly political. As for political stimuli, all the liberal news clips were drawn from MSNBC and all the conservative clips from Fox News.

Our stimuli come from political talk shows like Maddow's and O'Reilly's, for several reasons. First and foremost, these shows stand as exemplars of the sort of highly partisan and ideologically motivated discourse that contemporary critics of the partisan media bemoan (e.g., Jamieson and Cappella 2008). We appreciate that some observers are also concerned about the more subtle forms of ideological bias that exist in the more straightforward newscasts that appear on cable news (e.g., Brock, Rabin-Havt, and Media Matters for America 2012), but the crux of most observers' criticism is that cable news programs transmit ideology to their viewers. Opinionated news talk shows exhibit stronger expressions of ideologically motivated reportage and, therefore, are more likely to have the sort of massive direct effects imagined by many media critics. Second, since research on the effects of the partisan news media is relatively new, we consider it necessary to establish measurable media effects. These vivid and highly opinionated shows are designed to provoke more of a reaction than are straight newscasts. By employing these shows as stimuli, we were subjecting one of our main arguments—that choice blunts the overall effects of partisan news show—to a more strenuous test. Finally, we were trying to more realistically capture viewing behavior than others have. These shows were germane because they were selected as sources of information for discernible audiences, as we see in the Pew study discussed above. While many protest, for example, that Fox News is not news but more akin to a political campaign (e.g., Brock, Rabin-Havt, and Media Matters for America 2012), the fact is that it is an information source for a reliable audience of viewers.

TABLE 3.4. **Summary of Experimental Studies**

Study Type and Date	Political Stimuli		Entertainment Stimuli	Participants
	Conservative	Liberal		
Forced exposure: Summer 2008	*The O'Reilly Factor with Bill O'Reilly* (Fox News; composite of three segments aired in July 2008)	*Hardball with Chris Matthews* (MSNBC; composite of three segments aired in July 2008)	N.A.	49 UCR students
Summer 2009	*Hannity and Colmes* (Fox News; composite of two segments aired in April 2006)	*Hardball with Chris Matthews* (MSNBC; August 19, 2009)	N.A.	71 Riverside residents
Fall 2009	1. *The O'Reilly Factor* 2. *The Sean Hannity Show* (both on Fox News; composite of segments aired in late September and early October 2009)	1. *The Rachel Maddow Show* 2. *The Ed Show* 3. *Countdown with Keith Olbermann* (all on MSNBC; composite of segments aired in late September and early October 2009)	N.A.	67 UCR students
Selective exposure: Winter 2009	N.A.	*Hardball with Chris Matthews* (MSNBC; composite of three segments aired in November 2008)	1. *Dirty Jobs* (Discovery Channel) 2. *Log Cabins* (Travel Channel)	167 UCR students
Spring 2009	N.A.	*Hardball with Chris Matthews* (MSNBC; March 17, 2009)	1. *The Dog Whisperer* (National Geographic Channel) 2. *Dhani Tackles the Globe* (Travel Channel)	139 Riverside residents and 43 UCR students ($N = 182$)

Summer 2009	N.A.	*Hardball with Chris Matthews* (MSNBC; August 19, 2009)	1. *The Dog Whisperer* (National Geographic Channel) 2. *Dhani Tackles the Globe* (Travel Channel)	120 Riverside residents
Fall 2009	*The O'Reilly Factor* (Fox News; composite of segments aired in late September and early October 2009)	*The Rachel Maddow Show* (MSNBC; composite of segments aired in late September and early October 2009)	1. *The Dog Whisperer* (National Geographic Channel) 2. *Dhani Tackles the Globe* (Travel Channel)	117 UCR students
Winter 2010	*The O'Reilly Factor* (Fox News; February 2, 2010)	*Countdown with Keith Olbermann* (MSNBC; February 2, 2010)	1. *The Dog Whisperer* (National Geographic Channel) 2. *Dhani Tackles the Globe* (Travel Channel)	132 UCR students
Fall 2011	*The O'Reilly Factor* (Fox News; August 16, 2011)	*The Last Word with Lawrence O'Donnell* (MSNBC; August 15, 2011)	1. *Pet Star* (Animal Planet) 2. *For Rent* (HGTV)	127 Riverside residents
Participant preference: Summer 2010	*The O'Reilly Factor* (Fox News; June 17, 2010)	*Countdown with Keith Olbermann* (MSNBC; June 17, 2010)	1. *The Dog Whisperer* (National Geographic Channel) 2. *Dhani Tackles the Globe* (Travel Channel)	152 UCR students
Fall 2011	*The O'Reilly Factor* (Fox News; August 16, 2011)	*The Last Word with Lawrence O'Donnell* (MSNBC; August 15, 2011)	1. *Pet Star* (Animal Planet) 2. *For Rent* (HGTV)	502 Amazon Mechanical Turk panelists

Note: UCR = University of California, Riverside. N.A. = not applicable.

Studies

Throughout the remaining chapters of the book, we report the results of eleven forced exposure, selective exposure, and participant preference experiments. We conducted these experiments between June 2008 and November 2011. Table 3.4 provides a variety of details about each of the studies, including timing, specific stimuli employed, and number and nature of the participants. We use evidence from these studies to consider a variety of potential effects associated with aspects of the contemporary cable news media environment, including the extent to which cable news talk shows polarize the opinions of viewers about the policies and the job performance of politicians, viewers' openness to policy arguments, differences among viewers in policy priorities driven by attention to different news sources, viewers' perceptions of polarization in the contemporary media environment, and their trust in media and institutions.

Before we present these analyses, we show some preliminary evidence about how people self-select into watching political news programs. Re-

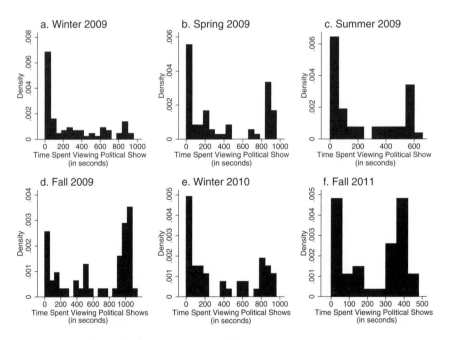

FIGURE 3.4. Distribution of attention to political programs, selective exposure experiments, 2009–11.

call that, in developing our theoretical expectations, we anticipated a fundamental division of attention in the viewing public—some people want to consume political information, while some do not. In figure 3.4, we graph the amount of time people spent viewing the political news or talk show programming we offered them in the choice conditions of each of the six selective exposure studies we conducted. The graphs demonstrate substantial variation in the amount of time devoted to watching the political programs among the research participants. In the appendix, we further break down viewing patterns by ideological group. Moreover, in virtually every study, we see a bimodal distribution of participants. A cluster of participants spends virtually no time viewing political programming, while a sizable group spends substantial time viewing these shows. This is consistent with the deliberate simplification of our theoretical model to essentially two types of people: those who tend to watch cable news talk shows when given the choice (news seekers) and those who tend to watch something else when given the choice (entertainment seekers). It appears that this simplification is empirically justified within the context of our experiments, and, in the remaining chapters, we investigate how news selectivity influences the impact and reach of partisan media.

CHAPTER FOUR

Partisan News and Mass Polarization

Since the mid-1970s, the Democratic and Republican Parties in the U.S. Congress have become steadily more polarized (McCarty, Poole, and Rosenthal 2006). By 2010, the partisan divide in the House of Representatives and the Senate was more acute than it had been since the late nineteenth century in the wake of the American Civil War (Poole 2012). At the same time, it appears that the mass public has become more polarized. Anecdotes of seething partisan divisions abound. One need not look further than the anti–President Obama protest rallies, which included people carrying guns in addition to signs and accusing the president of harboring a socialist agenda, or the raucous town hall meetings where constituents opposed to President Obama's proposed health care legislation often shouted down their members of Congress.

Such displays of partisan animosity are not limited to conservatives. In response to a Republican proposal to curb collective-bargaining rights, public employee unions staged a month-long sit-in at the Wisconsin state legislature. Beyond Wisconsin, for months, thousands of people across the country occupied public parks and college campuses, among other places, to protest income inequality and government-backed "crony capitalism," ultimately leading to violence as police officers moved to evict them. Contemporary politics seems to offer little of the reasoned discourse that constitutes the idealized democratic polity of many democratic theorists.[1]

Some scholars and public intellectuals blame the rise of the partisan media for this predicament. In their study of conservative news media, Kathleen Hall Jamieson and Joseph Cappella (2008, 214) argue: "The increasingly partisan nature of news media coupled with the human tendency to seek out ideologically comfortable information could have the effect of increasing polarization and distortion." The Harvard Law professor Cass Sunstein reaches the same conclusion in his work on the rise of the partisan media. The fragmentation of the television news media has allowed a diverse set of opinions to flourish (Webster 2005), but, "at the same time, the growth of a wide variety of issues-oriented programming—expressing strong, often extreme views and appealing to dramatically different groups of listeners and viewers—is likely to create group polarization" (Sunstein 2007, 73). Farhad Manjoo, a journalist and media critic, pushes the argument even further: "No longer are we merely holding opinions different from one another; we're also holding different facts" (Manjoo 2008, 2).

Any time at all spent watching partisan cable television news and opinion shows makes it clear how they could be construed as a polarizing force. These broadcasts are often visceral, intensely partisan, and apparently designed to tear the other side down while building up their own. Two examples are particularly telling. In October 2009, on his Fox News talk show, the conservative commentator Sean Hannity and a guest, the former presidential counselor Karl Rove, raised a horrifying allegation: President Obama and his assistant deputy secretary of education had ties to the North American Man/Boy Love Association (NAMBLA), an organization well-known for promoting "consensual" relationships between men and boys. Shocking. Disgusting. Until, of course, one inspects the details of this purported association and discovers how very weak it is.[2] Fox News is not the only purveyor of provocative invective. In December 2011, a news anchor on the progressive MSNBC news channel reported the shocking revelation that the Republican presidential candidate Mitt Romney was tied to the Ku Klux Klan through his supporters' use of the slogan "Keep America American" (Whitlock 2011). The MSNBC host Chris Matthews delivered the network's on-air apology for the report, saying that it represented an "appalling lack of judgment." If we focus on the content itself, as early propaganda researchers like Harold Lasswell might have, it is difficult to escape the suspicion that the programs drive wedges in the electorate and push us further apart.

One thing is clear. Partisan cable news shows are designed to persuade and bolster the opinions of like-minded viewers. In the process of purveying ideologically slanted news, have the partisan cable news networks deepened ideological polarization within the broader public? In this chapter, we investigate this question. In doing so, we sidestep the debate about whether mass-level polarization exists to the same degree elite-level polarization does (e.g., Abramowitz and Saunders 2008; Fiorina, Abrams, and Pope 2006; Levendusky 2009). We assume an ideological divide in the American public and ask whether the partisan media are to blame.

Partisan Media and Mass Polarization

One can build a strong case for partisan news shows serving as a polarizing force, a case rooted in the psychology of information processing. In Abelson's (1986) apt analogy, beliefs are like possessions. People value their beliefs in the same way they value their homes or their family possessions, and they do not part easily with beliefs that are particularly valuable to them. High-value beliefs motivate individuals to assess information in ways that allow them to maintain these beliefs (Kunda 1990). One way to accomplish this goal is for people to latch on to *proattitudinal information*, which psychologists use as shorthand for information that is consistent with preexisting attitudes.

For some individuals, political beliefs are tied to their social identities and are endowed with a great deal of value. The belief that one political party is better than the others is an especially relevant example. The attachment to a political party is for many individuals a central aspect of their personal identity (Green, Palmquist, and Schickler 2002), and these partisan identities can color how individuals evaluate information (Arceneaux and Vander Wielen, in press). As the leaders of the nation's two major political parties have sorted more cleanly along ideological lines, ideological identities have become inexplicably tied with partisan identities (Levendusky 2009; but see Baldassarri and Gelman 2008). Consequently, politics is very much an example of intergroup competition, with liberals and Democrats on one team and conservatives and Republicans on the other.

In a political environment where the major political parties are clearly divided along ideological lines, it is easy to see why proattitudinal partisan news reinforces and perhaps even strengthens preexisting attitudes.

First, people are motivated to incorporate the attitudinally consistent spin espoused by ideologically congenial news outlets. Second, even in the absence of such a motivation, encountering a stream of proattitudinal information, as would be the case with watching proattitudinal news, bolsters the confidence that one's initial position is accurate and supported by the facts (Baron et al. 1996). Third, because the partisan news media tap into the us-versus-them mentality of intergroup competition, partisans are more likely to see the attitudes and beliefs espoused by personalities on cable talk shows, with whom they share a partisan identity, as an element of the group's identity. Possessing and defending such views is not just a means to maintaining preexisting attitudes; it becomes an element of group solidarity and endows it with greater value (Spears, Lee, and Lee 1990).

Building on a mountain of evidence from psychology research that proattitudinal information reinforces and strengthens preexisting attitudes, Sunstein (2009) makes a compelling case that partisan selectivity should polarize political attitudes in the United States as each side retreats to its own corner and attends only to ideologically congenial news. The concern is that, if left unchecked, partisan selectivity will cause the nation to splinter into opposing groups each of which possesses its own conception of reality (Manjoo 2008), and Sunstein warns that at some point we will be only a step away from the sort of fanatical extremism that led to the rise of fascism in Germany after World War I. He proposes a voluntary dose of news from the other side as a solution. If people expose themselves to *counterattitudinal* information, the thinking goes, it will serve as a moderating force and help partisans converge on a common answer (Sunstein 2009, 158). President Obama articulated this notion quite well in his commencement speech at the University of Michigan in 2010: "If we choose to actively seek out information that challenges our assumptions and our beliefs, perhaps we can begin to understand where the people who disagree with us are coming from" (Obama 2010). In sum, this line of reasoning holds that partisan news shows are not so much polarizing as they are persuasive (Feldman 2011). Just as long as viewers mix up their viewing options, we need not worry about the polarizing effects of partisan news.

As currently articulated, the partisan news polarization thesis depends, in part, on the existence of partisan selectivity, itself a topic of debate (Garrett 2009a; Holbert, Garrett, and Gleason 2010). If people do not actively avoid counterattitudinal information, or if they encounter it inadvertently on a regular basis, then perhaps we already live in the world President Obama envisions. Unfortunately, the same literature in psychology from which Sunstein builds his case for the polarizing force of partisan news undermines his proposed solution. Exposure to counterattitudinal news can be just as polarizing as exposure to proattitudinal news.

In one study, Lord, Ross, and Lepper (1979) exposed strong opponents and proponents of capital punishment to a mixture of evidence in support of and against the death penalty. Importantly, this approach is the same as the proposed solution to proattitudinally fueled polarization: provide people with a balanced set of arguments on both sides of a controversy and facts to back them. If exposure to a mixture of proattitudinal and counterattitudinal information is a moderating influence, the death penalty attitudes of their participants should have converged at the end of the study. Instead, the opposite happened. People left the study with more extreme attitudes on the issue, with proponents more in favor of capital punishment and opponents more strongly opposed to it than they were when they entered the study.[3]

Subsequent research on polarization suggests that the findings that Lord, Ross, and Lepper report might also be explained by cognitive engagement with the topic—that is, simply thinking about it (Kuhn and Lao 1996). However, this still suggests that, contrary to the hopeful expectations of many of our colleagues, people do not necessarily assimilate information in an unbiased fashion. Indeed, political controversies may be the sort of topics that do not lend themselves to unbiased processing. Numerous studies in political science also find evidence of resistance to counterattitudinal information (e.g., Fischle 2000; Gaines, Kuklinski, Quirk, Peyton, and Verkuilen 2007; Rudolph 2006; Taber and Lodge 2006).

That said, it is possible that with a sufficient amount of counterattitudinal information people may begin to moderate their attitudes.[4] As Kunda (1990, 482) puts it: "People do not seem to be at liberty to conclude whatever they want to conclude merely because they want to." Perhaps, then, we need only refine Sunstein's solution: if people avoided like-minded news altogether and exposed themselves only to counterattitudinal news, they would be forced to contend with inconvenient facts, and the problem of polarization would be solved. The implicit assumption here is that, by getting out "the facts," news media—even partisan news media—can challenge people's preexisting beliefs. When it comes to partisan news, we have strong reason to doubt that even this would reliably be the case. Many political beliefs and attitudes are *distal* in the sense that they are "only remotely experienced or not sensibly verifiable" (see Abelson 1986, 229). Did the economic stimulus bill of 2009 save three million jobs? Did the Community Reinvestment Act of 1977 lead to the financial crisis of 2008? These are the assertions of political argument, and they are also not directly verifiable by experience.

We suspect that distal beliefs are much easier to defend from counterattitudinal arguments. It is easy for people to dismiss evidence trotted out for distal claims by counterattitudinal sources as suspect or motivated by bias. Consequently, political actors often attempt to rhetorically attach distal beliefs (e.g., that President Obama's economic policies hurt the economy) to *testable* ones based on direct personal experience (Abelson 1986), such as an increase in the price of gasoline. Even here, however, people may reinterpret testable beliefs in ways that decouple them from the distal belief in question (Gaines, Kuklinski, Quirk, Peyton, and Verkuilen 2007). For instance, one might accept that gas prices are indeed higher but assert that the increase in global demand for oil, not President Obama's policies, is responsible. One can even place different valence interpretations on testable beliefs. Perhaps the price of gasoline is not all that high if we consider it in relationship to its price in other countries, or perhaps higher gas prices are good because that will depress demand for gas and reduce the release of greenhouse gases. It is these sorts of reinterpretations and counterarguments that can insulate individuals from counterattitudinal news.

Finally, it is important to bear in mind that information on partisan news is relayed in a passionate manner. Personalities on cable news talk shows do not present the news in a calm, even-keeled voice. They raise their voice in outraged frustration, badger hostile guests, and hurl insults at the other side. These shows are designed to elicit a reaction from the audience. The apparent goal is to steel and energize the in-partisans while taunting the out-partisans. In other words, it is the perfect recipe for enraging rather than mollifying the opposition, and we know from psychological research that anger suppresses openness to persuasion (Lerner and Keltner 2000; Petersen 2010; Valentino, Brader, Groenendyk, Gregorowicz, and Hutchings 2011) and that name-calling and insults polarize the attitudes of those on the opposite side (Abelson and Miller 1967). Consequently, psychological research presents us with a demoralizing picture. Partisan news should, by its very nature, polarize viewers—whether it be preaching to the choir or throwing stones at the other side.

However, the discussion up until this point has considered only one type of selective exposure—the motivation to consume partisan news. Making the leap from partisan selectivity to mass polarization requires the implicit assumption of hypodermic media effects. If we relax this assumption and allow for the motivation to consume entertainment options in lieu of the news, we may find that, while partisan news has the *potential* to polarize viewers, its polarizing effects are muted in a media environment with choices. It is this heretofore untested possibility that we turn to in the next section.

The Effects of Partisan News and Choice

Studies

We investigate the effects of partisan news—both in potential and in a limited-choice environment—with the help of three selective exposure experiments (SEEs) conducted in spring 2009, fall 2009, and winter 2010. Participants in these studies were randomly assigned to four conditions: (1) a control condition where participants watched a nonpolitical entertainment option, (2) a forced exposure to proattitudinal news condition (e.g., a liberal watching a liberal show), (3) a forced exposure to counterattitudinal news condition (e.g., a conservative watching a liberal show), or (4) a choice condition that includes the partisan news and entertainment stimuli used in the other experimental conditions. These studies are summarized in table 3.4 above, and each offers different advantages.

The spring 2009 SEE focuses on a one-sided information environment with the political show mostly discussing the state of the economy. Subjects were assigned to watch a liberal talk show (*Hardball with Chris Matthews* from MSNBC), entertainment programming, or a choice condition that consisted of entertainment programming or the liberal option. The advantage of this design is that it holds the ideological content of the political stimulus constant and creates an uncomplicated choice environment. The disadvantage is that the design confounds the proattitudinal news condition with being liberal and the counterattitudinal news condition with being conservative. We address this disadvantage in the remaining studies, which feature both a liberal and a conservative partisan news stimulus.

In the fall 2009 SEE, we focus on a particular controversy alive during this time period: the debate over Barack Obama's health care reform bill. We combined multiple segments from both a liberal show (*The Rachel Maddow Show* from MSNBC) and a conservative show (*The O'Reilly Factor* from Fox News Channel) that were devoted to the health care debate. The winter 2010 SEE takes a different tack, presenting participants in the forced exposure condition with a fifteen-minute portion of a liberal (MSNBC's *Countdown with Keith Olbermann*) or a conservative (*The O'Reilly Factor*) show taken from the same day. The winter 2010 SEE allows us to consider the effects of partisan news in a more naturalistic form since these shows do not always address the same issues. It also allows us to hold the gender of the host constant.

All the partisan media clips were chosen with the help of norming studies that allowed us to be confident that the shows were perceived to have a liberal or conservative bias. The fifteen-minute *Hardball* clip in the spring 2009 SEE featured the guest host, Mika Brzezinski, discussing the economy and the war in Iraq with Ron Christie, a former aide to former vice president Richard B. Cheney, and the Democratic strategist Karen Finney. The discussion centered on the extent to which former president Bush or President Obama bore responsibility for U.S. economic conditions at the time. Since the clip aired only two months into the Obama administration, the answer naturally gravitated toward placing the blame on Bush.

Both the liberal and the conservative shows for the fall 2009 SEE are composites compiled from several original broadcasts. Using composites allows us to focus both stimuli on the politics of health care reform in the United States, holding the issue constant across the programs. The segments of conservative and liberal shows we used originally aired in late September and early October 2009. The conservative show featured O'Reilly discussing health care and the Obama administration with the former adviser to President Clinton Dick Morris, the author Ann Coulter, the Fox News anchor and business editor Neil Cavuto, and the Fox News senior political correspondent Carl Cameron. These segments tended to focus on the costs and complexity of the proposed health care legislation as well as on the influence of liberals in Congress and in the Obama administration. The liberal show discusses and criticizes former New York lieutenant governor Betsy McCaughey's efforts to oppose health care reform, interviews the *Cleveland Plain Dealer* columnist Connie Schultz, and interviews the *Newsweek* senior Washington correspondent and columnist Howard Fineman. Maddow focuses on the need for health care reform, potential procedures for passing the legislation, and the tactics of the legislation's opponents.

For the winter 2010 SEE, we selected segments from MSNBC's *Countdown with Keith Olbermann* (the liberal show for this study) and *The O'Reilly Factor* from a day at random—February 2, 2010—so as not to constrain the show agendas to a single issue. Olbermann featured the *Newsweek* national affairs columnist Jonathan Alter discussing the inefficacy of torturing U.S. detainees for information, referencing the alleged successful interrogation of Christmas 2009 bombing suspect Umar Abdulmutallab. A segment on U.S. policy regulating the service of homosexuals in the military follows, with exchanges between U.S. Senator John McCain and military and civilian leaders in Senate testimony as well as an interview between Olbermann and Lawrence Korb, the assistant defense secretary for President Reagan. Olbermann's third segment is a "Comment" on health care and allegations by U.S. Representative Michelle Bachman that, under congressional legislation, political dissenters would be denied access to medical care. The last segment focuses on financial regulation reform and conflicts of interest in the political consultant Frank Luntz's work with Republicans and large banking firms.

The O'Reilly Factor segment featured a somewhat different agenda and framing space. This stimulus begins with O'Reilly's "Talking Points Commentary" on federal spending under the Obama administration, which he characterizes as "President Obama's biggest gamble." The second segment of this show focuses on the legal treatment of captured suspected foreign terrorists and the appropriateness of civilian and military trials. O'Reilly then interviews the Fox News military analyst Colonel David Hunt and Lieutenant Colonel Anthony Shaffer from the Center for Advanced Defense Studies about the U.S. military's "kill-capture" program aimed at reducing the terrorist threat on the Afghanistan-Pakistan border. Finally, O'Reilly hosts a segment with the commentators Monica Crowley and Alan Colmes debating President Obama's performance confronting the House Republican Retreat at the end of January, which addresses health care, among other issues. On the same day, these news commentary shows discussed substantially different topics, and, where there was some overlap, for example, in discussing terrorism, military policy, and health care, the two shows focused on entirely different aspects of these issues.

Results

Because President Obama's handling of the economy was the main focus of the *Hardball* segment in the fall 2009 SEE, we asked participants to rate the president's job performance across five areas—the economy, the Iraq War, health care, terrorism, and immigration—and then to give an overall assessment of his job performance as president. Participants gave their answers in terms of a four-point scale: 1 = strongly disapprove, 2 = somewhat disapprove, 3 = somewhat approve, and 4 = strongly approve. For the analyses, we measured attitude polarization on Obama's job performance by coding these variables such that larger values go in the direction of the subject's predispositions. Larger values for liberals indicate stronger approval, whereas larger values for conservatives indicate stronger disapproval. (For all the empirical analyses in this chapter and those that follow, a complete description of question wording, coding decisions, and full model results for all statistical tests can be found in the appendix.)

Self-described moderates represent something of a challenge for us. Since they did not reveal their predispositions to us, we have to decide how to treat them in the analysis. We could remove them entirely, treat them as if they expressed liberal or conservative orientations, or assign them at random to one of these orientations. In our study samples, we have generally found that our self-described moderates tend to express views more similar to our conservative study participants than to our liberal participants.[5] Consequently, we coded them as conservatives for the sake of parsimony. However, we obtain similar results if we code them as liberals or remove them from the analysis altogether.

Figure 4.1 displays the difference in means between each of the treatment groups and the control group. Consistent with concerns that exposure to proattitudinal news is a polarizing force, we find that liberals who watched *Hardball* were more likely to rate President Obama's handling of the economy more positively.[6] In contrast to concerns that counterattitudinal news can be just as polarizing, we do not find evidence that conservatives rated Obama more negatively after viewing *Hardball*. In fact, it appears that conservatives rated Obama's handling of the economy slightly more positively, though we cannot rule out the possibility that watching *Hardball* had no effect on conservatives.[7] It is of note that the effects of the *Hardball* segment are localized to Obama's handling of the economy. Evaluations of his performance in other policy areas,

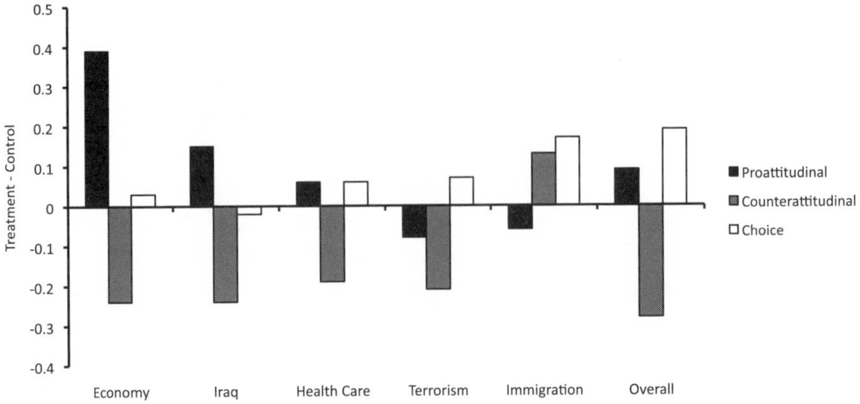

FIGURE 4.1. The effects of partisan news on presidential approval, spring 2009 SEE.
Note: Bars represent difference in means between the treatment group and the control group. For the full statistical model results, see table A4.1.

which received less discussion, if any at all, were unaffected by the show. We also do not find effects with respect to the president's overall rating. Taken together, the *Hardball* segment did not have diffuse effects, leading viewers to focus on the particular topic of the broadcast, Obama's handling of the economy.

However, if we introduce a minimal amount of choice into the information environment (i.e., two entertainment options), the polarizing effects of the partisan news show are attenuated. Participants assigned to the choice condition rated Obama no differently than did subjects in the control group.[8] It does not appear to be the case that the lack of a treatment effect in the choice condition is due to the show pushing conservatives away from their predispositions and liberals toward their predispositions, canceling one another out in the process. Not only are there no differences in effects between liberals and conservatives in the choice condition,[9] but we also obtain the same results if we code the Obama evaluation in the same direction for everyone. Moreover, it is not the case that subjects in the choice condition chose not to watch the *Hardball* segment at all. The median viewing time for *Hardball* was 3.41 minutes, meaning that half the group watched the show for three minutes or more.

As we mentioned above, this study is not without limitations. We did not manipulate the ideological bias of the news program and, thus, confounded the attitudinal direction of the stimulus with the self-identified ideological orientation of the participant. The study also fails to capture the naturalistic setting in which individuals can choose to watch programming that is congenial to their ideological predisposition, mimicking instead a one-sided information environment. We also conducted the study at the very beginning of Obama's term, when the argument that he cannot be blamed for the economy may have been naturally stronger than the obverse. All things considered, then, our experimental design may underestimate the effects of polarization.

We address these limitations in the remaining studies. Recall that the fall 2009 SEE included both a liberal and a conservative news option and focused on a highly partisan debate in Congress over health care reform. We included questions on the posttest survey that probed the participants' opinions on various aspects of the proposed law. These include questions about which party will do the best job on health care, how much the issue affects participants personally, support for a public option, a requirement for individuals to maintain health insurance, and increased taxes on wealthy Americans to pay for reforms. Subjects gave their answers in terms of six- or seven-point Likert scales. We coded answers such that higher values corresponded with proattitudinal positions. So, for example, higher values on the public opinion question indicate support among liberals and opposition among conservatives. Figure 4.2 displays the treatment effects for the fall 2009 SEE.

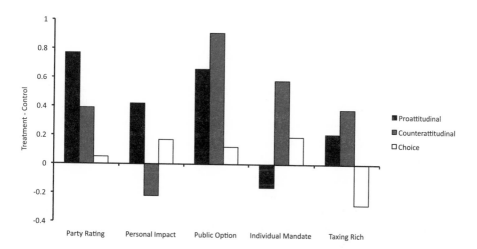

FIGURE 4.2. The effect of partisan news shows on issue attitudes, fall 2009 SEE.
Note: Bars represent difference in means between the treatment group and the control group. For the full statistical model results, see table A4.2.

Consistent with the previous study, the results displayed in figure 4.2 demonstrate that forced exposure to ideologically congenial news shows led participants to adopt more extreme attitudes. Proattitudinal messages caused individuals to trust the party aligned with their ideological faction to do a better job with the issue of health care, to view health care as having an impact on them personally, and to adopt more extreme positions on the question of whether a public option should be included in health care reform legislation.[10] We also now find evidence that exposure to counterattitudinal news can have a polarizing effect. Participants who were exposed to the other side were more likely to take attitude-consistent positions on the public option and individual mandate.[11]

Across all these issues, however, the effects of ideologically biased programs dissipate when people are placed in an information environment with choice. Subjects assigned to the choice condition do not express attitudes that are different from the control group with respect to which party they trust to handle health care reform, the perceived personal impact of the legislation, opinion about the public option, view of the individual mandate, or preferences regarding taxing the rich.[12]

Interestingly, subjects in the choice condition devoted roughly the same amount of time to watching proattitudinal and counterattitudinal shows. Among self-identified liberals and conservatives, subjects spent 62.1 percent of the time watching one of the political shows on average: 30.6 percent of the time watching the proattitudinal show and 30.4 percent of the time watching the counterattitudinal show. Because subjects in the choice condition were placed in a limited-choice environment in which half the shows to choose from featured political content, it should not be surprising that we find weak evidence of ideological sorting (Fischer, Schulz-Hardt, and Frey 2008). Nevertheless, we can rule out lack of attentiveness to the political shows as an explanation for the attenuation of polarization effects.

In the two previous studies, we presented subjects with partisan news that focused on a particular issue. In the winter 2010 SEE, we presented subjects with a liberal show and a conservative show that featured divergent issue content, which is a common occurrence on partisan talk shows. The only common element relates to assessing the job performance of Barack Obama, but that assessment is made across a variety of issues. Consequently, rather than focusing on assessments of his job performance on a single issue, we investigate an aggregate assessment of the president's performance, constructing an index of six posttest measures: evaluations of Obama's handling of the economy, the Iraq War, health care, terror-

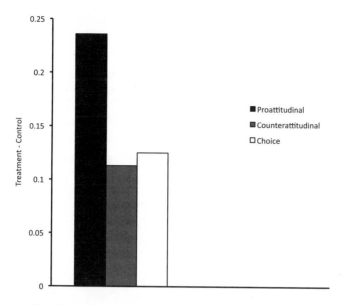

FIGURE 4.3. The effect of partisan news shows on evaluations of presidential job performance, winter 2010 SEE.
Note: Bars represent difference in means between the treatment group and the control group. For the full statistical model results, see table A4.3.

ism, and immigration and his overall job performance. Subjects gave their answers in terms of a four-point scale: 1 = strongly disapprove, 2 = somewhat disapprove, 3 = somewhat approve, and 4 = strongly approve. We recoded each of these variables such that larger values go in the direction of the subject's predispositions. Larger values for liberals indicate stronger approval, whereas larger values for conservatives indicate stronger disapproval.[13] To capture a latent evaluation of President Obama, we create a single index from the six items by averaging the responses.[14] The results shown in figure 4.3 reveal a familiar pattern. Exposure to proattitudinal news polarizes, while neither exposure to counterattitudinal news nor the introduction of choice has statistically significant effects.[15]

Why Does News Selectivity Attenuate the Effects of Partisan News?

We find consistent evidence that giving participants the option to watch entertainment programming considerably dampens the overall influence of cable news programming. In this section, we ask the simple question, Why? As we outlined in chapter 3, *dilution* offers one explanation for the attenuation of media effects in an information environment that contains choices. Cable news cannot directly affect those who do not watch it. As people opt for entertainment programming in lieu of news programming, the overall effects of cable news shrink. Cable news may have an equally polarizing effect on news seekers and entertainment seekers, but we observe it only among those who actually tune in.

It is undoubtedly the case that dilution accounts for some of the attenuation of partisan media effects. But we also consider the possibility that partisan news shows have less of an effect on news seekers than they do on entertainment seekers. As we sketched out in chapter 3, it may be the case that typical entertainment seekers are heavily influenced by something with which they are relatively unfamiliar. Because they normally do not watch partisan news, they may be unfamiliar with the structure of these programs, the types of arguments, and the style of argumentation. Consequently, when they have no other choice but to watch partisan news, the shows may have a sort of novelty effect that leaves more of an impression. In contrast, news seekers know what they are in for and may be less affected by these shows. After all, they may already have heard the arguments being made on previous shows and either incorporated them into their beliefs or developed counterarguments.

Furthermore, the receive-accept-sample (R-A-S) model developed by John Zaller (1992) proposes that individuals who regularly watch the news are less likely to be influenced by persuasive messages than are those who rarely watch the news. News seekers have a stable store of political considerations from which to draw, and these considerations are unlikely to be displaced or considerably augmented by new information. As a result, their attitudes tend to be more stable, given their exposure to persuasive communication. In contrast, entertainment seekers tend to have fewer accessible considerations about political issues, and their attitudes are heavily influenced by exposure to new information. The R-A-S model generates two important implications. First, it suggests that the sizable polarizing effects of partisan news observed in the forced exposure conditions are explained, in part, by the response of entertainment seekers, who would have avoided exposure if given the choice. Second, it suggests that, in an environment that includes entertainment choices, the attenuation of cable news effects is caused by more than just dilution.

As entertainment seekers select out of the cable news audience, the partisan media have a more modest effect on those who remain.

We should also consider whether differential effects vary by exposure to proattitudinal and counterattitudinal news shows. The R-A-S model predicts that, when exposed to the news, entertainment seekers should be more accepting of counterattitudinal information than news seekers. Without available "contextual information" (Zaller 1992, 121), entertainment seekers are less likely to realize that new information conflicts with their predispositions, and they are, therefore, likely to unwittingly incorporate such inconsistent considerations in their on-the-spot attitudes. News seekers already possess enough information about politics to resist and even argue against inconsistent considerations. It is worth noting that the R-A-S model was developed during the broadcast news era, when television news reporting strived for journalistic objectivity and balance.

Partisan news is a different animal. Show hosts clearly communicate their partisan and ideological agendas, and cable news outlets possess ideological reputations (Baum and Gussin 2008). These shows often feature discourse that disparages the opposing side while extolling their own side. In short, partisan news shows provide viewers with contextual information and easily interpretable cues about the applicability of the considerations they raise. Consequently, we expect that even entertainment seekers will be able to recognize that the considerations raised by counterattitudinal shows are at variance with their predispositions and reject them (see also Arceneaux and Kolodny 2009).

We investigate the presence and nature of differential effects using the fall 2011 participant preference experiment (PPE). This study followed the participant preference design protocol discussed in chapter 3. It used a forced exposure design where subjects are randomly assigned to view a proattitudinal news clip, a counterattitudinal news clip, or an entertainment show (the control group). The key difference from the standard forced exposure design is that, before watching the assigned clip, subjects are asked which show they would choose to watch if given a choice. Because we measure their preference before exposing them to the clip, we are able to identify individuals who prefer to watch partisan news rather than entertainment programs and those who prefer to watch entertainment programs rather than partisan news. Accordingly, we are able to assess whether proattitudinal news and counterattitudinal news affect news seekers and entertainment seekers differently.

The political shows were drawn from *The O'Reilly Factor*, a conservative talk show appearing on Fox News, and the *Last Word with Lawrence O'Donnell*, a liberal talk show appearing on MSNBC. These shows focused on the same topic: the billionaire Warren Buffet's August 2011 *New York Times* op-ed arguing for higher tax rates on the wealthiest Americans. The liberal show extolled Buffet's column, while the conservative show excoriated it. Helpfully, both shows addressed similar arguments for and against raising taxes on the rich, with the liberal show blaming tax cuts for the steady increase in income inequality over the past thirty years and the conservative show arguing that low taxes are necessary for economic growth. Not surprisingly, both shows came to diametrically opposed conclusions about the fairness of the current tax system with respect to how much (or how little) it taxes the wealthy. Consistent with the protocol in our selective exposure experiments, subjects assigned to the control group watched a clip from one of two basic cable shows, *Pet Stars* or *For Rent*.

After viewing the clip, participants were asked several questions about tax policy: which party they trusted most to deal with tax policy, whether households that earn more than $250,000 a year should see an increase in taxes, whether lowering taxes on corporations would spur economic growth, and whether the "American tax system is unfair because the rich do not pay their fair share of taxes." Participants gave their answers in terms of six- or seven-point scales, and we coded those answers such that higher values correspond with the attitude-consistent response. For example, a higher value would be given to a liberal who wants to tax the rich, while a higher value would be given to a conservative who disagrees with the statement that the rich should pay more in taxes.[16]

The effects of ideological news shows are displayed in figure 4.4. The bars represent the difference between the treatment group and the control group in the mean response to the items. Similar to the analysis in previous studies, a positive difference offers evidence of polarization: liberals and conservatives who watched the partisan news clip staked out more extreme positions than did liberals and conservatives who watched the entertainment show. Among participants who preferred to watch entertainment shows, we find consistent evidence that exposure to ideological news shows polarizes attitudes about tax policy, and both pro- and counterattitudinal shows have similar polarizing effects.[17] These findings are consistent with our expectations. Entertainment seekers exposed to partisan news are more likely to adjust their attitudes and stake out more

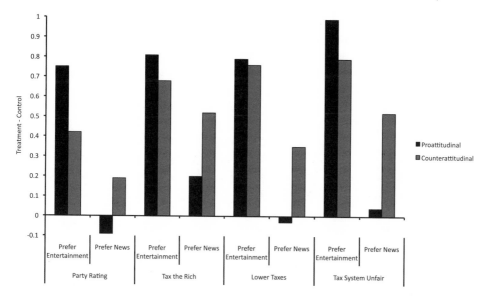

FIGURE 4.4. The effects of partisan news on tax policy attitudes, among news seekers and entertainment seekers, fall 2011 PPE.
Note: Bars represent difference in means between the treatment group and the control group. For the full statistical model results, see table A4.4.

extreme, ideologically consistent positions in the process. What is more, partisan news causes entertainment seekers to reject counterattitudinal messages, suggesting that they either glean enough information from the program itself to realize it espouses counterattitudinal views or rely on source cues to reach the same conclusion.

The data also demonstrate that partisan news shows have different effects on those who prefer to watch them. Consistent with the R-A-S model, ideological news has less of an influence on news seekers than it does on entertainment seekers. Both pro- and counterattitudinal news appear to have less of a polarizing effect on news seekers. However, we can say this confidently only with respect to the effect of proattitudinal news. Across all four of these items, news seekers are much less likely than are entertainment seekers to be influenced by proattitudinal news.[18] Indeed, the effects of proattitudinal news are close to nil. In contrast, counterattitudinal news has a sizable polarizing effect on each of these issue attitudes, and, while the polarizing effects are smaller than the ones we observe for entertainment seekers, we cannot rule out chance as explaining these relatively small differences.[19]

In sum, these data suggest that the substantial polarizing effect of proattitudinal news is concentrated among entertainment seekers. Ideologically congenial shows appear to have relatively small effects among those who choose to watch them. This finding fits with the notion that individuals who wish to watch proattitudinal news shows already have an ideologically consistent opinion on many issues, and, as a result, these shows end up preaching to the choir. It is also possible that news seekers have already been treated by previous exposure to proattitudinal news and that there is no additional effect to be had. The fact that counterattitudinal shows appear to have substantial effects among individuals who enjoy watching cable news shows suggests that these shows strike a nerve and that, in the process of defending their attitudes, individuals end up adopting more extreme views than those they held before watching the show (e.g., Lord, Ross, and Lepper 1979).

Summary

It is undeniable that discourse in American politics has become more polarized and shrill, and plenty of anecdotes suggest that Americans have become more ideologically polarized as well. Whether Americans are becoming more polarized is a topic of debate beyond the scope of this project. What we *can* say is that, *if* Americans are becoming more polarized, the rise of the partisan media on cable television is not the likely culprit. The evidence presented in this chapter shows that, while partisan news *can* polarize those who watch, the ample presence of entertainment programming likely mutes the overall effect of partisan media on mass attitudes.

In terms of potential effects, forced exposure to proattitudinal news shows consistently leads to attitude polarization across our experiments. These findings are consistent with the contention that given exposure to ideological congenial sources, such as partisan media, "like-minded people tend to move to a more extreme version of what they thought before" (Sunstein 2009, 4). There is some merit to the concerns voiced by public intellectuals that partisan selectivity might lead to mass polarization. More troubling, however, is the fact that we find little evidence that exposure to counterattitudinal news is a moderating force. If anything, it can be just as polarizing as exposure to proattitudinal news. These results are consistent with motivated reasoning accounts of attitude formation in which the motivation to protect preexisting attitudes leads people to become more extreme in the process of rejecting attitude-inconsistent arguments. Because counterattitudinal arguments—unlike proattitudinal ones—do challenge people to defend their preexisting attitudes, we suspect that the effects of counterattitudinal news are more complicated than the effects of proattitudinal news. In the next chapter, for instance, we consider the role played by the ability and willingness to develop counterarguments to attitude-inconsistent information.

Suffice it to say, these findings leave us unconvinced that a balanced mix of exposure to pro- and counterattitudinal news would reliably lessen mass-level polarization. Indeed, it may sometimes heighten it. Those concerned by the polarizing effects of partisan news are unlikely to find a simple solution in getting people to voluntarily expose themselves to crosscutting information. If both proattitudinal news and counterattitudinal news have the potential to polarize, then the structure of the partisan media would likely need to be targeted for reform—not just the viewing habits of citizens.

All that said, we believe that the most important takeaway from our experiments is the fact that introducing even a modicum of agency in the choice to watch partisan news as opposed to entertainment significantly attenuates the polarizing effects of partisan news. The entertainment options were not stellar fare, either. Participants in our experiment could choose among basic cable shows that attract audiences similar in size to the partisan news shows on display. In all our studies, a sizable portion of participants assigned to the choice group chose to watch partisan news at least some of the time (and some watched it the entire time). Just imagine what would happen to the overall effects of partisan news if subjects were given the option to choose from hundreds of channels, including popular entertainment and sports programs?

Moreover, because the forced exposure treatments demonstrate that exposure to counterattitudinal programs can cause attitude polarization, we discount the possibility that exposure to pro- and counterattitudinal frames in the choice condition simply canceled out both sides' effects. Our findings are consistent with previous research on motivated reasoning that demonstrates that, when individuals are confronted with both pro- and counterattitudinal information, they tend to reject counterattitudinal arguments and accept proattitudinal ones, increasing attitude polarization in the process (e.g., Lord, Ross, and Lepper 1979; Taber and Lodge 2006). Furthermore, Druckman, Fein, and Leeper (2012) find that when individuals are given the opportunity to choose what information they receive—as our studies allow—exposure to competing arguments does not cancel out the effect of the initially received argument.

So, all told, it is unlikely that partisan news has the sort of massive direct effects that often animate hand-wringing about the partisan media. Part of the reason for this is simple dilution. The partisan media cannot polarize those who do not tune in—at least not directly. But we also find evidence that the partisan media may have smaller effects on those who choose to watch than those who would typically choose not to watch. What do we make of these differential effects? First, they suggest that the massive effects we uncovered in the forced exposure treatments are driven, in part, by the reactions of entertainment seekers who are forced to watch something they would normally avoid. Consequently, we would mostly expect massive effects, on the order that we uncovered in the forced exposure treatments, *when people cannot turn away.* In the current hyperchoice media landscape, people rarely are in a position in which they cannot turn away. Second, these differential effects suggest that the effects of partisan media may decrease as people become inured to partisan news shows. News seekers know what to expect from these programs. What is more, as we showed in chapter 3, people who choose to watch these shows do so *because* they have strong opinions in the first place.

CHAPTER FIVE

Hearing the Other Side and Standing Firm

We have presented preliminary evidence that choice can substantially blunt the effects of the contemporary news environment on viewers. When entertainment seekers remove themselves from the audience for partisan news, these shows are less effective at pushing partisans in the direction of their ideological biases. This is a useful first step, but, given the multifaceted ways in which partisan news might polarize partisan viewers, we recognize it as just that, a first step. Here, we consider a somewhat different proposed effect of partisan cable news: the role it could play in hardening the attitudes of viewers against opposing arguments.

Cable news talk shows appear to be designed both to bolster pre-existing attitudes and to help hone viewer defenses to arguments from the other side. Hosts of cable news talk shows work to undermine other hosts, as we have emphasized elsewhere (Arceneaux, Johnson, and Murphy 2012). Take, for example, *Countdown with Keith Olbermann*, formerly on MSNBC. Olbermann, the host, often derided his counterparts on Fox News during his melodramatically titled "Worst Persons in the World" segment. Reflecting on the role that Fox News played in the ouster of Shirley Sherrod from the Department of Agriculture over comments of hers taken out of context, he blustered in a July 2010 "Special Comment": "What you see on Fox News, what you read on right-wing websites, is the utter and complete perversion of journalism, and it can have no place in a civilized society. It is words crashed together, never to inform, only to inflame. It is a political guillotine" (Olbermann 2010b). Strikingly similar segments castigating MSNBC or the mainstream news often air on *The O'Reilly Factor* and *Hannity*.

These show hosts also trade accusations of collusion with or service to parties and candidates. For example, in an interview with Slate.com, MSNBC's Maddow said: "Fox is operating with a political objective to elect Republican candidates and particularly to elect Republican candidates who [Fox News Channel president] Roger Ailes likes" (Slate.com 2011). While on his show in April 2009 Fox's O'Reilly insinuated that MSNBC was providing favorable coverage of President Obama and airing critical coverage of Tea Party organizations in exchange for government contracts provided to MSNBC's parent company, General Electric. "That kind of corruption would make Watergate look small. We hope it is not true," O'Reilly opined (O'Reilly 2009).

It seems that, to these hosts, it is not nearly enough for their shows to promote their own views—they must also tear down others with whom they disagree. As these examples suggest, they criticize the quality of the other side's journalism, its motives, the illegitimacy of its views, and the venality of its behavior. These kinds of communication seem designed to wall off like-minded viewers from "hearing the other side" (Mutz 2006a). In fact, this is one of the many specific concerns of critics of contemporary partisan news that we have previously elaborated (e.g., Jamieson and Cappella 2008).

These critics offer a hypothetical counterfactual to current conditions in political communication. Instead of the polarized news and divided electorate that we now have, in this alternative reality we would have more unified news programming and more moderate voters, fused by their consideration of views from more than one political perspective. This vision draws on two major assumptions. The first is what we have been dealing with—exposure to politically congenial news reinforces predispositions and thus divides. The second assumption is that hearing countervailing messages moderates the opinions of a partisan. In lieu of a counterfactual news media, observers, including President Obama, actively encourage people to expose themselves to both sides of the national ideological debate or, at a minimum, lament that people seem to not be doing this (Mutz 2006a). By sampling from the other side as well, they envision that people will grow to understand the perspective of those with whom they disagree and will develop more reasonable opinions.

In this chapter, we test both whether exposure to counterattitudinal media helps reduce resistance to opposing views and how media choice affects reactions to arguments from political opponents. We identify an alternative to the second assumption here. Despite the intuitive appeal, hearing the other side does not necessarily moderate the views of partisans. People may be motivated to reject counterattitudinal information (e.g., Kunda 1990) or argue against it. So, while it may be true that people have a tendency to selectively watch ideologically congenial news shows (Bennett and Manheim 2006; Iyengar and Hahn 2009; Iyengar, Hahn, Krosnick, and Walker 2008; Stroud 2008), it is not clear that watching counterattitudinal shows would make people more open to the views of their political opponents. In fact, exposure to countervailing views might also harden partisans against those arguments. We address the role that choice plays and, again, expect that the ability to select into and out of political programming blunts the effects of these shows on how viewers evaluate political arguments.

The Potential Effects of Opinionated News on Openness to Opposing Views

A multitude of psychological studies show that people express more extreme positions and are less open to opposing arguments after exposure to proattitudinal views (cf. Sunstein 2009). A number of psychological processes are at work here. As we discussed in chapter 3, exposure to proattitudinal information makes people confident that the facts are on their side and bolsters the perception that their initial opinion is the correct one (Baron et al. 1996), and exposure to proattitudinal information primes intergroup competition (e.g., liberals vs. conservatives). When an in-group member articulates the group's shared beliefs (e.g., "this is what liberals believe"), it signals that those viewpoints are an element of group identity that should be defended against opposing views expressed by out-group members (Spears, Lee, and Lee 1990).

Extrapolating from these studies, many scholars are concerned that the current state of the partisan media imperils civil society (e.g., Stroud 2010; Sunstein 2009). But these studies offer no support for the notion that exposure to counterattitudinal news will obviate the polarizing effects of partisan news. Indeed, recall from our previous discussion that many studies show the opposite: exposure to counterattitudinal informa-

tion backfires and ultimately reinforces preexisting opinions and polarizing attitudes (e.g., Lord, Ross, and Leeper 1979; Pomerantz, Chaiken,
and Tordesillas 1995; Taber and Lodge 2006).

Intergroup psychology partially explains why exposure to counterattitudinal information fails to moderate people's attitudes. Counterattitudinal information can be viewed as an out-group threat, increasing
the salience of in-group identity, and motivating people to defend their
group's positions (Moskalenko, McCauley, and Rozin 2006). Simply
forewarning an individual that he or she is about to encounter a counterattitudinal argument is sufficient to activate defensive processing by
developing counterarguments that allow the maintenance of the preexisting attitude (McGuire and Papageorgis 1962). We see these considerations as especially relevant to partisan news media because people tend
to know the ideological orientations of partisan news outlets (Baum and
Gussin 2008) and because these shows often purvey "outrage discourse"
designed to be provocative and threatening to those who are on the other
side (Sobieraj and Berry 2011). Consequently, we continue to be less san-
guine about the promise of exposure to counterattitudinal news to promote active consideration of those countervailing views. It would not be
surprising to find that exposure to partisan news shows on the other side
does more to divide than to unite people.

Individual Differences in Processing Political Arguments

Psychological research suggests that individual differences in the motivation to critically evaluate arguments affect receptivity to persuasive
appeals. With this research in mind, we refine our underlying model of
opinion change to incorporate how audience members might vary in
their receptivity to pro- and counterattitudinal arguments. In particular, we incorporate elements of the elaboration likelihood model (ELM)
of receptivity to persuasive communication (Petty and Cacioppo 1986b)
into our model. The ELM anticipates that some individuals have a strong
need to intellectually process, or elaborate, arguments while others are
less inclined to do so. Thinking through something thoroughly is cognitively taxing and requires mental effort. Not everyone is motivated to
expend this effort, and those who do typically do so because they enjoy
it. Petty and Cacioppo anticipate that people vary on this quality, which
they call *need for cognition* (1986a, 8). Individuals who possess a high

need for cognition are much more adept than others at dissecting arguments as well as at generating their own counterarguments.

Although the ELM posits that people are generally motivated to reach an accurate opinion, it does not assume that they necessarily process arguments in an unbiased fashion. Those who have strong beliefs about the accurate answer may process arguments in a biased fashion (Petty and Cacioppo 1986a, 1986b; Pomerantz, Chaiken, and Tordesillas 1995). In situations where individuals possess weak preexisting attitudes, counterattitudinal information causes high need for cognition message recipients to moderate their opinions (Rudolph and Popp 2007). In contrast, when individuals possess strong preexisting attitudes and are exposed to counterattitudinal information, high levels of need for cognition lead to counterarguing (Petty and Briñol 2002), which may cause the message recipient to build up a larger store of proattitudinal considerations than he or she possessed before being exposed to the counterattitudinal message (Petty and Wegener 1998, 351; see also Druckman and Nelson 2003). As a result, the need for cognition can lead to attitude strengthening and polarization when people possess strong partisan goals. Furthermore, people with a high need for cognition are more likely to rehearse counterarguments, strengthening their attitudes in the process, especially when they distrust the counterattitudinal source (Priester and Petty 2003).

Accordingly, we anticipate that exposure to counterattitudinal news media is likely to induce resistance to persuasion, especially among people who are motivated to cognitively process arguments. Once again, however, this discussion has proceeded with only partisan selectivity in mind. The choices that viewers make matter as well, especially the decision to avoid news altogether. If people select out of watching partisan news altogether, this will dilute its influence on resistance to opposing arguments. In the remaining sections, we empirically test these expectations.

Open-Mindedness, Need for Cognition, and Selective Exposure

Studies

We recruit the fall 2009 and fall 2011 selective exposure experiments (SEEs) to investigate the effects of partisan news. We discussed the fall 2009 SEE at length in chapter 4, but recall that this study featured Rachel Maddow (a liberal) and Bill O'Reilly (a conservative) discussing the health care reform controversy on their shows. The fall 2011 SEE is similar to the fall 2009 SEE in that we assigned participants to watch a proattitudinal show, a counterattitudinal show, an entertainment show, or their choice of shows (the latter being a choice condition in which they could flip among stimuli using a remote control). We also restricted the subject matter to a single topic—tax policy—so that we could manipulate pro- and counterattitudinal messages on the same issue. Restricting the political stimuli to a single issue is an important feature of these designs since we are interested in understanding the effects of partisan news on viewers' openness to persuasion. The key difference between the two studies is that the fall 2011 SEE drew on a broader population—the surrounding community in Riverside, California—rather than only university students. In this sense, the fall 2011 SEE allows us to gauge whether we can replicate the findings in the fall 2009 SEE using a broader sample.

The political stimuli in the fall 2011 SEE included *The Last Word with Lawrence O'Donnell*, which is a liberal talk show appearing on MSNBC, and *The O'Reilly Factor* on Fox News. The segments from both shows aired a day apart in August 2011 and focused on Warren Buffet's op-ed piece criticizing the tax system for not taxing millionaires enough. Remarkably, both segments covered similar arguments for and against raising taxes on the wealthy. Chris Hayes, who is an editor-at-large for *The Nation*, filled in for Lawrence O'Donnell and provided evidence supporting Buffett's claim that the wealthy are able to duck payroll taxes by obtaining their earnings through capital gains, which are taxed at a lower rate. He went on to critique conservative arguments that the tax base should be broadened since nearly 50 percent of Americans do not owe *federal* income taxes after deductions and tax credits. The conservative radio talk show host Laura Ingraham, filling in for Bill O'Reilly, made a case for low capital gains tax rates, opined that raising taxes on the wealthy would just add to the size of the federal government, and noted that Warren Buffet could choose to pay payroll taxes if he wanted.

For both experiments, we measured openness to persuasion by asking participants to watch the stimuli and then rate the persuasiveness of counterattitudinal arguments on a nine-point scale that ranged from "very strong argument" to "very weak argument." These arguments are shown in table 5.1. Participants in the fall 2009 SEE rated the persuasiveness of four arguments (two liberal and two conservative), and

TABLE 5.1. **Political Arguments**

Fall 2009 SEE: Health Care Reform Debate

Conservative arguments:

Antireform Argument 1. The current health care legislation in Congress will increase big government and continue America's slide toward socialism. The nanny state is not our solution to better health. Our government already provides Medicare (for senior citizens) and Medicaid (for low-income citizens). The costly programs already substantially contribute to our skyrocketing deficits. Rather than create a government medical bureaucracy, Congress and the president should reform, improve, and enhance these programs. Washington, DC, should produce a truly bipartisan plan that won't raise taxes (for anyone), regulate personal medical choices, or ration health care.

Antireform Argument 2. The current health care legislation in Congress is being rushed. This sweeping health care reform plan is being enacted in a world-record time. Just like the stimulus packages and bogus bailout, this legislation is being shoved down America's throat without explanation and propelled like a ramrod through Congress without examination. The president and congressional Democrats promised a more open and transparent government but are making backroom deals that could increase taxes on American families, cut Medicare for seniors, cripple state budgets, and allow a government takeover of health care.

Liberal arguments:

Proreform Argument 1. The current health care legislation in Congress is popular with voters. In the latest opinion polls, a majority of Americans favor giving everyone the option to join a government-sponsored health care plan like Medicare. Even a majority of doctors support the public option. Of course, the health insurance companies don't support a public option because they make billions of dollars under the current system. President Obama should not listen to the insurance companies. He should listen to the doctors and to the American people, who overwhelmingly want a public option.

Proreform Argument 2. The current health care legislation in Congress would save money across the medical system and ease the financial burden on families who cannot afford insurance today. It would give much-needed competition to the private insurance industry. It would provide a huge relief to millions of Americans without health insurance and millions more who are underinsured. Every day, we hear unfortunate stories of families denied coverage because of health problems the insurance companies call *preexisting conditions*. The human costs of failing to reform the system are too great to be ignored.

Fall 2011 SEE: Tax Policy Debate

Conservative arguments:

Tax Increase Opposition Argument 1. Raising taxes on job creators, like small business owners, investors, and corporations, will only hurt the economy. If we really want to spur economic growth and create jobs, we should lower the tax burden on those who fuel our economy.

Tax Increase Opposition Argument 2. The United States has an unsustainable debt of $14 trillion. This is a spending problem, not a revenue problem. Taxes are high enough. If the federal government would live within its means, like the rest of American families, and balance its budget, we wouldn't have a problem with national debt.

Tax Increase Opposition Argument 3. Income should be taxed only once and at a low rate. Currently, we ask people who invest money in the stock market—money that is taxed as income—to pay a second round of taxes on capital gains and dividends. This kind of double taxation is unfair and should be abolished.

(*continued*)

TABLE 5.1. *(continued)*

Liberal arguments:

Progressive Tax Argument 1. The poorest Americans pay a much larger percentage of their income in taxes than the wealthiest Americans, who pay a lower percentage of their income in taxes. This regressive tax system redistributes wealth upward from the poor to the rich, and it should be reversed. Superrich people should pay a higher tax rate.

Progressive Tax Argument 2. In 2009, one of the largest corporations in the world, General Electric, made $10.3 billion in profit and paid no taxes. Before we talk about cutting Medicare and Social Security to balance the budget, we should first ask megacorporations to pay their fair share in taxes.

Progressive Tax Argument 3. The American tax code has many loopholes and deductions that allow the superrich and corporations to dodge taxes while the middle and working classes do not have the same opportunity to take advantage of loopholes. A fairer tax system would end tax loopholes so the country doesn't have different tax rates for those who can afford accountants and those who can't.

participants in the fall 2011 SEE rated six arguments (three liberal and three conservative).[1] These arguments were drawn from the broader debate on health care reform (the fall 2009 SEE) and tax policy (the fall 2011 SEE) and were related to the arguments encountered on the shows that individuals watched.

Both studies also allow us to test predictions drawn from the ELM about the influence of the need for cognition on openness to persuasion. We included on the pretest instrument the need for cognition battery, which was developed by the psychologists who proposed the ELM, John Cacioppo and Richard Petty (Cacioppo and Petty 1982). The need for cognition battery measures the extent to which people enjoy effortful processing of information and arguments. Participants are asked to read a series of statements and evaluate how much each one describes them, using a five-point scale that ranges from "extremely uncharacteristic" to "extremely characteristic." It includes statements like, "I find satisfaction in deliberating hard and for long hours," and, "Thinking is not my idea of fun." We employ the short-form, eighteen-item battery (Cacioppo, Petty, and Kao 1984).[2]

Results

We measure openness to persuasion by coding how resistant individuals are to counterattitudinal arguments. If conservatives (liberals) evaluate liberal (conservative) arguments as weak after watching cable news talk shows, it suggests that these shows have the power to harden people's

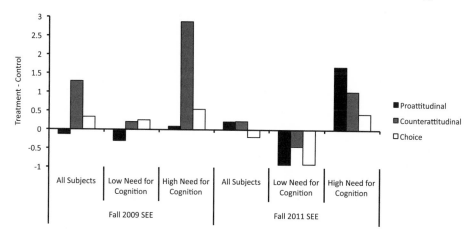

FIGURE 5.1. The effects of partisan news on resistance to opposing arguments, fall 2009 and fall 2011 SEEs.

Note: Bars represent difference in means between the treatment group and the control group. For the full statistical model results, see table A5.1.

opinions and make them less open to opposing viewpoints.[3] The bars in figure 5.1 represent the difference of means on the resistance to opposing arguments scale between each of the treatment groups and the control group. Positive values indicate that subjects in the treatment group were more resistant to opposing arguments than were subjects in the control group, while negative values indicate that subjects in the treatment group were less resistant to opposing arguments than were subjects in the control group.

If we focus our attention on the treatment effects for the full samples in the fall 2009 and fall 2011 SEEs, we find no evidence that watching proattitudinal talk shows hardens people against opposing arguments. Subjects who watched the proattitudinal show did not evaluate counterattitudinal arguments as any less persuasive than did subjects assigned to the control group. In statistical parlance, the difference in persuasiveness ratings between the two groups is statistically indistinguishable from zero (i.e., there is no difference).[4] We also find no evidence that watching counterattitudinal shows increases openness to opposing views. If anything, as we discovered in chapter 4, watching counterattitudinal shows may *increase* resistance to opposing arguments. In the fall 2009 SEE, subjects who watched the counterattitudinal show were significantly more likely to rate opposing arguments as weak compared to subjects assigned to the control group.[5] We uncover a similar pattern in the fall 2011 SEE, but the difference in persuasiveness rating between the counterattitudinal group and the control group is quite small and not statistically different from zero.[6]

Above, we argue that, if partisan news shows increase resistance to opposing arguments, it is likely through providing viewers with counterarguments and that, according to the ELM, individuals who are high in need for cognition are more likely to absorb counterarguments from proattitudinal shows as well as to generate their own counterarguments when they are exposed to counterattitudinal shows. We evaluate this argument in figure 5.1 as well. Subjects who scored above the median on the need for cognition scale included on the pretest were coded as "high" in need for cognition, and those who fell below the median were coded as "low."

The treatment effects were estimated separately for both subsamples. The results are consistent with the predictions that we drew from the ELM. Subjects who do not enjoy processing arguments were more or less unfazed by the cable news talk shows. In both studies, low need for cognition subjects in pro- and counterattitudinal groups did not evaluate arguments differently than low need for cognition subjects in the control group—the treatment effects for low need for cognition subjects were not statistically different from zero in either study.[7] In contrast, the political stimuli caused high need for cognition participants to be more resistant to opposing arguments. In both studies, subjects who scored high on the need for cognition scale evaluated opposing arguments as much weaker after watching the counterattitudinal shows compared to subjects in the control group who also scored high on the need for cognition scale.[8] In the fall 2011 SEE, we uncovered additional evidence that watching the proattitudinal talk shows can increase resistance to opposing arguments among individuals who are high in need for cognition.[9]

Once again, we find that introducing a modicum of choice in the viewing environment attenuates the deleterious effects of cable talk shows. As figure 5.1 demonstrates, subjects in the choice condition do not evaluate opposing arguments all that differently, on average, than subjects assigned to the control group.[10] What is more, the effects observed in the choice condition are much smaller than the effects uncovered in those instances where the forced exposure conditions increased resistance to opposing viewpoints. These results suggest that allowing people to sort into news or entertainment blunts the effects of cable news. We explore explanations for this attenuation effect in the next section.

Are News Seekers Affected Differently Than Entertainment Seekers?

As we discussed in chapter 4, news selectivity may attenuate attitude re-inforcement through *dilution* (entertainment seekers selecting out of the cable news audience) and *differential effects* (partisan news shows having a more modest effect on news seekers relative to entertainment seekers). We suspect that the same mechanisms account for the attenuation of reinforcement effects in the selective exposure studies reported in this chapter. Partisan news shows cannot directly affect those who tune them out, and those who tune in probably need less help defending against counterattitudinal arguments. People who watch partisan news shows tend to have strong opinions and are motivated to maintain those opinions (see chapter 3). So news seekers should be capable of recognizing and resisting counterattitudinal arguments *even in the absence of exposure to partisan news shows*.

Entertainment seekers, on the other hand, may benefit from exposure to proattitudinal news. Because they typically choose to avoid the news, especially partisan news, they may have fewer defenses against counterattitudinal arguments (Zaller 1992). Exposure to proattitudinal news provides them with ready-made counterarguments, inoculates them against attempts at persuasion, and reinforces predisposition-consistent attitudes. Of course, whether proattitudinal news performs this service depends on the degree to which individuals are willing to cognitively engage arguments. People who do not enjoy cognitive tasks may not be as motivated to connect the arguments discussed on a proattitudinal show with the arguments they face after being exposed to the show. Consequently, we expect that the reinforcing effects of proattitudinal news shows will be most evident among individuals who possess a high need for cognition.

We test these expectations using the fall 2011 participant preference experiment (PPE), which employed shorter versions of the same stimuli used in the fall 2011 SEE (for details, see chapter 4). Before being randomly assigned to a proattitudinal clip, a counterattitudinal clip, or an entertainment clip, subjects were asked which of the four possible television shows they would prefer to watch if given the choice, allowing us to identify news seekers and entertainment seekers. We also measured need for cognition on the pretest instrument using a shorter version of the standard battery used in the selective exposure studies.[11] After viewing the clip, subjects were asked to rate the persuasiveness of the same arguments as were used in the fall 2011 SEE (shown in table 5.1 above). Averaging across these responses, we measured how resistant participants were to opposing arguments, with positive values indicating that participants viewed opposing arguments as weak.

Figure 5.2 shows the differences in resistance to opposing arguments between treatment and control groups, broken down by viewing preferences and need for cognition. Consistent with our expectations, we find that partisan news shows have a larger effect on individuals who would not, if given the choice, prefer to watch these news programs.[12] Exposing entertainment seekers to proattitudinal news substantially increases their resistance to opposing arguments, suggesting that proattitudinal news aids entertainment seekers in recognizing and resisting counterattitudinal arguments.[13] We also find some evidence that exposure to counterattitudinal news boosts resistance to opposing arguments among entertainment seekers.[14] We did not have strong theoretical expectations regarding the effects of counterattitudinal news on entertainment seekers, but this finding is consistent with the notion that even individuals who do not regularly watch partisan news are capable of recognizing which shows espouse an opposing perspective and, therefore, which political arguments should be viewed with suspicion. In contrast, neither pro- nor counterattitudinal news shows did much to reinforce the attitudes of news seekers.[15] We do find, however, that news seekers in the control group were more likely than entertainment seekers in the control group to resist opposing arguments.[16] Since control group subjects did not watch the partisan news clip, this finding offers evidence for our a priori expectation that news seekers already possess the ability to resist opposing arguments and that, in many situations, partisan news shows may only marginally improve on this ability.

In addition, we also explore whether need for cognition facilitates attitude reinforcement among entertainment seekers exposed to proattitudinal shows. These results are also displayed in figure 5.2. Interestingly, we find that exposure to proattitudinal news causes entertainment seekers who are low in need for cognition to resist opposing arguments.[17] But, as expected, entertainment seekers who possess a high need for cognition are substantially more likely to resist opposing arguments after exposure to proattitudinal news.[18] In contrast, partisan news has little impact on news seekers, irrespective of their need for cognition.[19] These

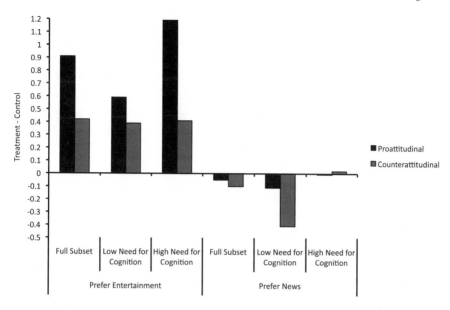

FIGURE 5.2. The effects of partisan news on resistance to opposing arguments among news seekers and entertainment seekers and by need for cognition, fall 2011 PPE.
Note: Bars represent difference in means between the treatment group and the control group. For the full statistical model results, see table A5.2.

results support the thesis that differential effects also attenuate the effects of partisan news in a choice environment. In the absence of choice, exposure to partisan news substantially reinforces the attitudes of those who would generally tune out cable news shows. Once these individuals are given the opportunity to watch something else, the remaining audience is already resistant to opposing political arguments. Partisan news, at least in our study, does little to harden their attitudes further.

Summary

Across three separate studies, we find evidence that exposure to proattitudinal news can reinforce preexisting attitudes and cause people to be more resistant to opposing arguments. It appears, however, that proattitudinal news shows do not uniformly protect viewers from opposing arguments. Viewers who enjoy thinking—those who are high in need for cognition—are more resistant to opposing viewpoints after exposure to proattitudinal news programming than are those who enjoy thinking less. Exposure to proattitudinal news causes these individuals to see opposing arguments as weaker than they would have deemed them to be if they had watched an entertainment show.

Moreover, in spite of the hopeful notion that exposure to alternative views will ameliorate political division in the United States, we find little evidence that exposure to counterattitudinal news causes viewers to be more open-minded. If anything, exposure to counterattitudinal news programs *also* reinforces preexisting attitudes and makes people more resistant to counterarguments. Once again, we find this to be the case mostly among individuals who enjoy thinking. The simple and appealing idea that we can mechanically balance people's views hypodermically has little empirical support here. People are more committed to their predispositions than that. They stand firm.

Our findings lend support to the ELM and models of motivated reasoning. When people have partisan (i.e., directional) goals, they tend to reject counterattitudinal information so that they can maintain their preexisting attitude. However, doing so requires them to develop plausible arguments against counterattitudinal information. As Kunda (1990, 482) explains, motivated reasoners try "to construct a justification for their desired conclusion." Individuals who are high in need for cognition are in the best position to construct justifications because, through actively engaging the attitude-discrepant information they encounter, they are capable of developing counterarguments.

Importantly, we also discover that allowing entertainment seekers to select out of partisan news audiences attenuates the overall effects of partisan news shows on closed-mindedness. Building on the evidence presented in chapter 4, we demonstrate that the attenuation of partisan news effects is caused by more than the simple dilution of the message given media choice. Partisan news—both pro- and counterattitudinal shows—has the largest effects among entertainment seekers when they are forced to watch news programming they would prefer to avoid. These individuals appear to be substantially different from news seekers in their susceptibility to media effects. Differences across members of the potential audience suggest that partisan news has the *potential* to have massive effects, but these are likely unrealized because the most susceptible tune out opinionated cable news programs.

Taking stock, then, it seems that the effects of media choice may be neutral. It does not appear to make things worse and merely preserves extant divisions. When entertainment seekers are allowed to choose, they select diverting programming less likely to make them entrenched ideologues, opposing the other side. Bully for them! The dark side of this is that, in our experiments, these entertainment seekers are alienated by the partisan news shows that could inform them about politics and implicitly relegated to viewing shows that do very little to inform them.

In the next chapter, we explore another dimension of political division that partisan media are alleged to exacerbate. Many observers suggest that different sources of partisan news offer their viewers different priorities, informed by their competing perspectives on political events and issues (e.g., Koppel 2010). Presumably, this would then affect the salience of issues, the concerns people identify as the most important problem, and responses to issue frames. We explore these next and find, consistent with the findings of the previous two chapters, that self-selection into entertainment and types of partisan news substantially blunts the effects of these partisan programs.

The Salience and Framing of Issues

In his study of the relationship between the press and the public's views on foreign policy, Bernard Cohen (1963, 13) argued: "[The mass media] may not be successful much of the time in telling people what to think, but it is stunningly successful in telling its readers what to think about." When he wrote these words, conventional wisdom held that news media had little impact. Two recent Ph.D.'s in journalism at the University of North Carolina saw Cohen's observation as an opening for a new kind of media effects research as it focused attention away from persuasion—for which scholars failed to find much evidence—and toward the media's ability to set the public agenda. In their path-breaking work, McCombs and Shaw (1972) coined the term *agenda setting* and argued that, by reporting on some issues at the expense of others, news media influence what issues the mass public sees as most important and, therefore, in need of the most attention from politicians.

McCombs and Shaw's study took place in Chapel Hill, North Carolina, amid the 1968 U.S. presidential election. They conducted a content analysis of the campaign coverage in the news outlets available to Chapel Hill residents, including print and broadcast television, and found a striking amount of convergence in the issues covered. Of all the possible issue areas that these outlets could report on in the 1968 campaign, five dominated: foreign policy, law and order, economics, public welfare, and civil rights. McCombs and Shaw also conducted a survey of undecided voters living in Chapel Hill and asked them to rank issues by their importance. They found an almost perfect correspondence between what issues the news covered and what issues voters perceived to be the most important. Hundreds of studies have replicated this finding across a diverse set of situations and conditions (see McCombs 2004, chap. 1).

News media do not directly persuade citizens to adopt particular positions, but they do shape how much importance people attach to issues, which turns out to be politically consequential. In their seminal use of randomized experiments to study news media effects, Iyengar and Kinder (1987) demonstrate that, by transferring *salience* to issues, news media can influence what considerations figure into people's political evaluations. The news *primes* people to rely on some issues rather than others when constructing political attitudes. News media are also capable of constructing shared perceptions about the collective experience, which can have more of an influence on people's political judgments than their own personal experiences (Mutz 1998). News media have the ability to shape, not only the salience that viewers attach to issues, but also the characteristics ascribed to them (McCombs 2004). How a problem is defined, or *framed*, affects what people think are its causes and the appropriate solutions as well as which political arguments are viewed as the most compelling (e.g., Entman 1993; Gamson 1992; Iyengar 1991; McCombs 2004).

Of course, this discussion of agenda setting focuses on the power of the mainstream broadcast media during the mid-twentieth-century broadcast era. Does the rise of partisan media alter agenda setting? One possibility is that partisan media may focus on different issues—issues that serve partisan goals. Liberal outlets may focus on issues over which Democrats have a built-in advantage, while conservative outlets focus on Republican-advantaged issues. If this were the case, it would undermine the common conversation about national politics historically constructed by the mainstream broadcast media (cf. Mutz and Martin 2001).

Echoing McCombs and Shaw's seminal study, Stroud (2011) conducted a content analysis of partisan media coverage of the 2004 U.S. presidential election and found some evidence of partisan agendas: CNN and newspapers that endorsed the Democratic nominee, John Kerry, tended to devote proportionally more coverage to the Iraq War (a Democratic-advantaged issue) than did Fox News and newspapers that endorsed the Republican nominee, President George W. Bush. Nevertheless, the differences in agendas were not stark. All of these news outlets, including

Fox News and Bush-endorsing newspapers, focused more attention on the Iraq War than on terrorism, suggesting that, although partisan media may attempt to craft different agendas, they face some constraints in creating radically different agendas and perhaps preserve some semblance of a common conversation.

However, Stroud did find more significant differences with respect to how partisan outlets framed these issues. Even though all news outlets devoted more coverage to the Iraq War than to terrorism, conservative news outlets framed the war differently—and on more favorable terms for President Bush—than liberal outlets did. More generally, Morris and Francia (2010) find that Fox News framed the presidential campaign in a way that was much more negative toward and critical of John Kerry and that CNN's approach was more evenhanded.

So, with respect to agenda setting, we expect that partisan media have the *potential* to create multiple agendas such that the audience of one news outlet will have a different conversation from that of the audiences of other news outlets. Just as the identification of the agenda-setting power of mainstream news in the 1970s caused researchers to expect influences other than persuasion, pro- and counterattitudinal news programs may have similar effects on issue priorities beyond changing people's political positions. If a counterattitudinal show focuses on a particular issue, it necessarily induces the viewer to contemplate that issue—even if the viewer engages in the kinds of motivated reasoning we have uncovered in chapters 4 and 5.

However, once the agenda is set, we expect to see evidence of agency in viewers' acceptance or rejection of the way in which an issue is framed. Partisan news shows may be capable of getting viewers—whether like-minded or not—to think about the same issue, but they will not necessarily get those viewers to accept their definition of the problem. As we have seen in previous chapters, we expect that prior attitudes and sources will influence whether individuals accept or reject the frames offered (cf. Brewer 2001; and Druckman 2001), with individuals tending to reject the frames of counterattitudinal shows and to accept the frames of proattitudinal shows.

Yet, as should be familiar to readers by now, these hypotheses assume exposure to partisan news. Those who remove themselves from the news audience obviously cannot be affected by its attempt to set the agenda—at least not directly. We expect that allowing even a modicum of choice will attenuate the agenda-setting power of partisan news programs. Furthermore, we expect that, as we saw in chapters 4 and 5, audience dilution explains part of the attenuation effect, but we are left to speculate about the existence and nature of differential treatment effects among news seekers and entertainment seekers. Some scholars contend, consistent with the expectations outlined in chapter 3, that individuals who have little interest in the news are more likely to be "victims of agenda setting" (e.g., Iyengar and Kinder 1987, 59). Conversely, others suggest that news seekers who view the news purveyor as a trusted source view the news as signaling which issues are the most important and, therefore, are most likely to be susceptible to agenda setting (Miller and Krosnick 2000). We sort out these expectations empirically in the remainder of this chapter.

Agenda Setting, Partisan News, and Selective Exposure

Issue Salience

The fall 2009 and winter 2010 selective exposure experiments (SEEs) offer a useful place to start. As we discussed in chapter 4, the liberal and conservative shows in the fall 2009 SEE were exclusively devoted to President Obama's health care reform bill in Congress. In contrast, the winter 2010 SEE presented participants with a liberal or a conservative show drawn from the same day. Both shows spent some time discussing President Obama's health care bill, but both also devoted a considerable portion of their airtime to different topics. The liberal show (*Countdown with Keith Olbermann*) spent much of its time discussing the inappropriateness of torture, while the conservative show (*The O'Reilly Factor*) spent much of its time on the budget deficit and its drag on the economy. Consequently, both studies allow us to test whether partisan news shows can affect the salience participants attach to an issue (health care) and whether the divergent issues covered by the shows in the winter 2010 SEE also have the ability to detract from the common conversation.

To investigate the effects of partisan news shows on common perceptions, both studies included a question on the posttest that asked participants to rank how much they "personally care" about the "health care legislation currently being discussed" on a four-point scale that ranged from "very little" to "a great deal." The bars in the graph shown in figure 6.1 represent the difference in means between the treatment groups and the control group on this item. The results are consistent with the

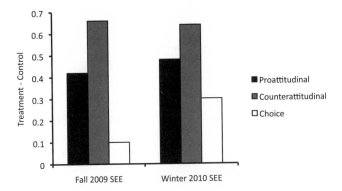

FIGURE 6.1. The effect of partisan news on the salience of health care issue, fall 2009 and winter 2010 SEEs.
Note: Bars represent difference in means between the treatment group and the control group. For the full statistical model results, see table A6.1.

expectation that exposure to both pro- and counterattitudinal news shows can boost the salience of an issue. The effects of partisan news shows on the perceived personal salience of the health care reform bill were considerable, and they were strikingly similar in both studies.[1]

We find that both pro- and counterattitudinal shows can shape perceptions of issue salience. It is worth noting, however, that health care reform was a controversial and prominent issue during the time that both the fall 2009 and the winter 2010 SEEs were conducted. Would we find such equivalent effects for a new issue? Using actual news broadcasts poses a key obstacle to investigating this question. Simply put, we do not control what issues the partisan news outlets cover, making it difficult to find a novel issue that both liberal and conservative shows address. In August 2011, such an opportunity presented itself. Political talk shows appearing on Fox News and MSNBC spent time addressing Warren Buffet's *New York Times* op-ed in which he blasted the superrich for not paying their fair share of taxes and charged that lowering tax rates for the rich over the past twenty years had caused income inequality to worsen. We were lucky to complete the fall 2011 SEE, which used these clips, before the Occupy Wall Street protest caused the mainstream media to devote time to income inequality. Indeed, only two participants in the control group volunteered on an open-ended question that income inequality is "the most important problem facing the country."

In order to study the effects of pro- and counterattitudinal news shows on perceptions of issue salience, we coded the responses to the open-ended most-important-problem question into two categories: as having to do with income inequality or tax policy (the central topics of the partisan new shows) or as having to do with something else. Figure 6.2 shows the effects of the treatment conditions on the probability that a participant named income inequality or taxes as the most important problem. Participants exposed to the proattitudinal show were more likely to view income inequality or taxes as the most important problem, while those exposed to the counterattitudinal show were no more likely than subjects in the control group to view these issues as the most important problem.[2] Given that this dependent variable differs from the one employed in the fall 2009 and winter 2010 SEEs, it is not surprising that the pattern among participants exposed to the counterattitudinal program is somewhat different.

Much like broadcast media, partisan news shows have the ability to affect the importance that viewers attach to issues simply by discussing certain issues and not others. But this occurs when those shows spend time talking about the same issues (even if briefly). What happens when they discuss different issues? The winter 2010 SEE provides a useful guide here. In this study, we also asked subjects to volunteer which issue they saw as the "most important problem" using an open-ended question. We coded the verbatim answers they provided into a single, overarching category that best summarized the answer. The breakdown of these categories is shown in figure 6.3. The economy was considered by participants to be by far the most important problem facing the coun-

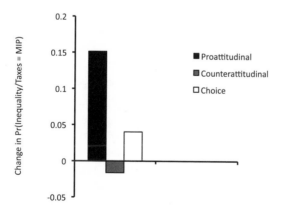

FIGURE 6.2. The effects of partisan news on the salience of income inequality or tax policy, fall 2011 SEE.
Note: Bars represent difference in probabilities between the treatment group and the control group. MIP = most important problem. For the full statistical model results, see table A6.2.

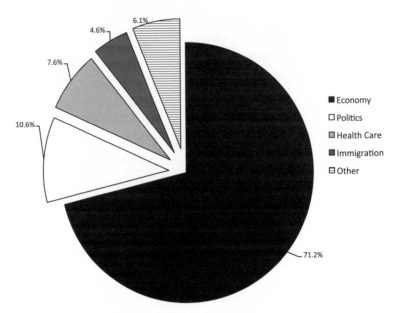

FIGURE 6.3. Answers to most important problem open-ended question, winter 2010 SEE.

try. Given the dire state of the economy in early 2010, this should hardly be surprising. Not only was the economy a common staple in news coverage at the time; its importance was also likely reinforced by participants' personal experiences (for a discussion of how personal experiences shape perceptions of issue salience, see Mutz [1998]).

We investigate whether cable news shows can influence perceptions of salience by modeling the effects of watching either the liberal show (*Olbermann*) or the conservative show (*O'Reilly*) on the probability that subjects named the economy as the most important problem. Because O'Reilly's show devoted a good bit of the time to the economy—or at least the federal budget deficit's effect on the economy—while Olbermann did not discuss the economy at all, we expect that participants assigned to watch Olbermann's show should be less likely to name the economy as the most important problem. The results, displayed in figure 6.4, are consistent with our expectations. Olbermann viewers were nearly 14 percentage points less likely than were O'Reilly viewers to mention the economy as the most important problem.[3] By focusing on issues other than the economy, Olbermann was able to shift the focus of many viewers away from a pressing issue of the day.

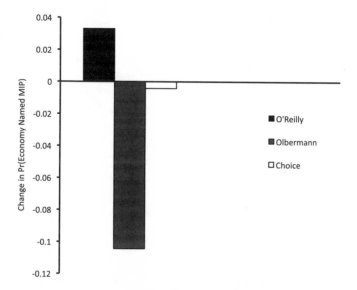

FIGURE 6.4. The effects of different agendas on perceptions of the most important problem, winter 2010 SEE.

Note: Bars represent difference in probabilities between the treatment group and the control group. MIP = most important problem. For the full statistical model results, see table A6.3.

Turning our attention to the effects of news selectivity, we once again find evidence that allowing even a modicum of choice between partisan news and entertainment shows attenuates the agenda-setting effects of cable news shows. In the fall 2009 and winter 2010 SEEs, participants in the choice condition did not view health care as more salient than participants in the control group did (see fig. 6.1 above).[4] Channel changers in the fall 2011 SEE were no different from those in the control group in their propensity to name taxes or inequality as the most important problem facing the country (see fig. 6.2 above).[5] And participants allowed to change the channel in the winter 2010 SEE were neither more nor less likely than control group participants to rate the economy as the most important problem (see fig. 6.4).[6]

Issue Priming

In their study of agenda setting, Iyengar and Kinder note that the influence of the news media extends beyond imbuing issues with salience to a more subtle form of attitude change, which they call *issue priming*.

As they explain: "By calling attention to some matters while ignoring others, television news influences the standards by which governments, presidents, policies and candidates for public office are judged" (1987, 63). Their theory of issue priming derives from psychological research on priming, which demonstrates that when forming an opinion—such as an evaluation of the president—people often use the information at the top of their heads. In the process of focusing on a particular event or problem, news media make some considerations more accessible than others in the minds of viewers. Iyengar and Kinder demonstrate the existence of priming by showing that news coverage influences the correlation between people's evaluation of the president on particular issues (e.g., energy, defense, and inflation) and their overall evaluation of him. When the news focuses on energy issues, for example, people's evaluations of the president's performance on energy correlates more strongly with their overall rating of him.

We are able to investigate the priming effects of partisan news using the winter 2010 SEE. Recall that both the liberal and the conservative news shows spent some time discussing President Obama's health care reform bill. On the posttest, subjects were asked to give an overall evaluation of the president using the standard question, "How do you feel about the job that Barack Obama is doing as president? Do you strongly approve, somewhat approve, somewhat disapprove, or strongly disapprove?" Participants were also asked to evaluate the president (using the same scale) on specific issue areas, including health care.

These measures allow us to employ the same approach that Iyengar and Kinder used to assess the presence of priming and to investigate whether the specific evaluation of Obama's handling of health care has a stronger correlation in the forced exposure groups. However, we must make one adjustment to accommodate for an important difference between the broadcast newscasts that form the basis of the *News That Matters* experiments and the partisan talk shows that form the basis of our experiments. Because the broadcast news media's coverage of policies tends to be similar across networks, Iyengar and Kinder were simply interested in the correlation between the raw evaluations.

In our case, we face the fact that the liberal and conservative shows both presented diametrically opposed presentations of Obama's health care reform plans. Unlike the mainstream media, the partisan news media have overtly partisan goals: liberal shows generally want to burnish evaluations of Democratic politicians, while conservative shows gener-

ally want to diminish evaluations of Democrats. The aim of a proattitudinal show is to reinforce partisan evaluations of the president, while
that of a counterattitudinal show is to weaken partisan evaluations of the
president. We investigate this possibility using the same directional measures used in chapter 4 and 5 and coding evaluations of the president in
the direction of one's ideological predispositions. Larger values indicate
approval of the president on the part of liberals and disapproval on the
part of conservatives.

The results are shown in table 6.1. The numbers in the first column
represent the linear relationship between the specific evaluation of
Obama's handling of health care and the evaluation of his overall performance as president, broken down by treatment groups with standard
errors in parentheses. The numbers in the second column represent the
proportion of the variance in the overall evaluation that is explained by
the variance in specific evaluations—or, in statistical parlance, the r^2.
There is virtually no relationship between health care and overall performance evaluations in the control group. The slope of the line that represents the relationship between these two evaluations is essentially flat,
and specific evaluations explain almost none of the variance in overall job evaluations. Simply put, in the absence of partisan news coverage, subjects did not really connect how they evaluated Obama's performance on health care with their overall opinion of him.

The story is quite different in the partisan news treatment groups,
particularly the counterattitudinal group. Participants assigned to this
group were more likely to bring their health care–specific and overall

TABLE 6.1. **Priming Health Care Evaluations, Winter 2010 Selective Exposure Experiment**

Treatment	Relationship between Health Care Rating and Overall Rating	r^2
Proattitudinal	.30	.06
	(.24)	
Counterattitudinal	.70	.31
	(.25)	
Choice	.11	.01
	(.20)	
Control	−.05	.001
	(.21)	

Note: Numbers in first column represent the OLS regression slope coefficient summarizing the correlation between President Obama's performance rating on health care and his overall performance rating, with the numbers in parentheses representing the standard error. Numbers in the second column represent the proportion of
the variance in Obama's overall performance rating that is explained by his performance rating on health care
within each treatment condition. For full statistical model results, see table A6.4.

performance evaluations of Obama in line with each other, with the specific evaluation explaining 31 percent of the variance in the overall evaluation.[7] What's more, the performance evaluations became more partisan in this group—with liberals rating both Obama's performance on health care and his overall performance positively and conservatives rating his performance on both dimensions negatively. We see a similar, but weaker, pattern in the proattitudinal group, so we cannot rule out the possibility that the participants in the proattitudinal group behaved no differently than did those in the control group.[8]

Partisan news shows, especially counterattitudinal shows, appear to have the capacity to prime the issues relevant to their evaluations of the president. However, as we have seen in previous chapters, counterattitu-dinal shows appear to have the unintended effect of magnifying the par-tisan flavor of issue-specific presidential evaluations by bringing them in line with their partisan evaluations of the president's overall job per-formance. Nonetheless, consistent with our expectations, introducing choice into the mix attenuates the magnitude of issue priming. As we have seen with other media effects, the priming effect observed in the choice group is small and statistically indistinguishable from the effect observed in the control group.[9]

News Selectivity and Agenda Setting

We now turn our attention to the question of how news selectivity condi-tions the effects of partisan media. The degree to which news seekers and entertainment seekers respond differently to agenda setting has implica-tions for why we observe the attenuation of agenda-setting effects in the choice condition. For instance, it is possible that, as Iyengar and Kinder (1987) found with respect to broadcast newscasts thirty years ago, par-tisan news shows have a stronger influence on which issues infrequent news viewers deem important than it does on the issues that frequent news viewers see as important. Entertainment seekers may literally be unaware of the issues discussed by the news, whereas news seekers may already have strong impressions about what issues are important—and these impressions are difficult to dislodge with exposure to a ten-minute news clip. If this were the case, it implies that the agenda-setting effects observed in the forced exposure conditions are driven by the inability of entertainment seekers to turn away and that attenuation of the agenda-setting effect observed in the choice group is caused by a combination of dilution (i.e., entertainment seekers tuning out) and the smaller effect that partisan news has on the perceptions of salience among those who do tune in.

Other scholars pose the opposite possibility. Because entertainment seekers avoid the news, they may lack the political sophistication to put the pieces together and appreciate how the issues discussed in the news media fit in the broader scheme of the nation's major issues. In contrast, individuals who tune in to the news do so because they trust it to tell them what is important (Miller and Krosnick 2000). If this were the case, it would suggest that the agenda-setting effects observed in the forced exposure conditions are driven by news seekers and that the attenuation of these effects in the choice condition is driven mostly by dilution. It would suggest that partisan news media have the capacity to powerfully shape the perceptions of salience among their regular viewers.

We investigate these alternative accounts with the help of two participant preference experiments (PPEs). The partisan news clips in the summer 2010 PPE focused on the Deepwater Horizon incident, in which a deep water oil well uncontrollably spewed oil into the Gulf of Mexico. The second study comes from the fall 2011 PPE, in which we used shorter versions of the partisan news shows featured in the fall 2011 SEE. These clips focused on income inequality and the federal tax system (for a more complete discussion, see chapter 4). We asked participants to name the most important problem facing the nation on the posttest questionnaire. Consistent with our measurement protocol for the selective exposure studies, these open-ended responses were coded into dichotomous categories where 1 = mentioned the issue discussed in the show (i.e., the environment in the summer 2010 PPE and inequality or taxes in the fall 2011 PPE) and 0 = did not mention the issue discussed in the show.

Figure 6.5 shows the agenda-setting effects in the summer 2010 PPE for participants who would have chosen to watch one of the partisan news shows if given the option and for participants who would have chosen to watch one of the entertainment shows instead. The pattern of results is most consistent with Iyengar and Kinder's account of agenda setting as well as with our general expectations. Agenda setting is most likely to happen among entertainment seekers but only among entertainment seekers assigned to watch the proattitudinal news show.[10] The counterattitudinal show had basically no agenda-setting effect among entertainment seekers.[11] In contrast, we do not observe any evidence of agenda

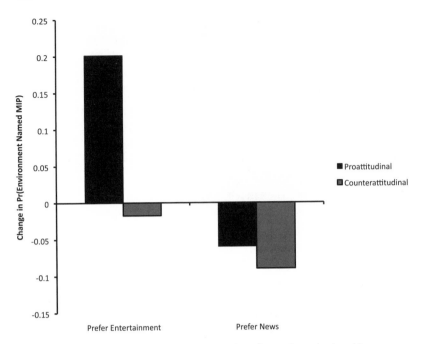

FIGURE 6.5. Effects of partisan news on perception of most important problem among news seekers and entertainment seekers, summer 2010 PPE.
Note: Bars represent difference in probabilities between the treatment group and the control group. MIP = most important problem. For the full statistical model results, see table A6.5.

setting among news seekers. Unlike entertainment seekers, the proattitudinal show had no discernible effect on news seekers.[12] News seekers assigned to the counterattitudinal condition appear to resist agenda setting, as they are nearly 10 percentage points less likely to mention the environment as the most important problem. However, we cannot rule out chance as a possible explanation for this finding.[13]

A different picture emerges from the fall 2011 PPE (fig. 6.6). The data from this experiment show that exposure to partisan news caused both news seekers and entertainment seekers to be more likely to view either income inequality or taxes as the most important problem. Exposure to proattitudinal news shows increased the salience of the issues covered in the program by 11.5 and 6.8 percentage points, respectively, and, while it appears that the most-important-problem responses of news seekers were somewhat less influenced by proattitudinal shows than were the responses of entertainment seekers, the difference is not statistically significant.[14] Exposure to counterattitudinal news shows

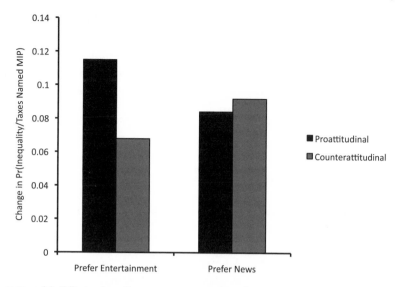

FIGURE 6.6. Effects of partisan news on perception of most important problem among news seekers and entertainment seekers, fall 2011 PPE.
Note: Bars represent difference in probabilities between the treatment group and the control group. MIP = most important problem. For the full statistical model results, see table A6.6.

also appears to increase the salience of inequality and taxation among both news seekers and entertainment seekers (by 9.2 and 6.8 percentage points, respectively).[15]

These disparate findings suggest that partisan news has a reliable agenda-setting effect among entertainment seekers but a less consistent agenda-setting effect among news seekers. One possibility is that the issue covered in the summer 2010 PPE—the seemingly uncontrollable gushing of a deep water oil well in the gulf—had been in the news daily for approximately two months before the study, whereas the issue covered in the fall 2011 PPE—income inequality—was relatively new on the scene, at least in mass media news coverage. This supports the intuition that, among regular news seekers, the partisan news media have the power to set the agenda, but only on novel issues.

Issue Framing

The foregoing analysis suggests that partisan news can alter *what* issues viewers think about, but can it also alter *how* viewers think about issues?

Certainly, partisan media are not just interested in setting the agenda. Partisan talk shows also wish to affect how viewers define issues within the agenda space. Proattitudinal shows encourage viewers to select problem definitions that are consistent with their predispositions, while counterattitudinal shows intend viewers to adopt problem definitions that are at variance with their predispositions. The extent to which counterattitudinal shows are successful in this gambit likely depends on the characteristics of the viewer. As discussed in previous chapters, individuals who prefer to watch partisan news should be more likely to reject attempts to define problems in a counterattitudinal fashion. Entertainment seekers, on the other hand, may be less capable of resisting such subtle attempts.

We use the fall 2011 PPE to sort out the effects of issue framing. Participants were presented with six problem definitions of federal tax policy and asked to rank how important each was from "most important" to "least important." These definitions were gleaned from the partisan news clips, with three coming from the liberal show and three coming from the conservative show. The liberal definitions were as follows:

- Rich people not paying their fair share.
- Big corporations not paying enough taxes.
- Too many deductions.

The conservative definitions were as follows:

- High tax rates on the wealthy.
- Not enough people paying federal taxes.
- Out-of-control government spending.

The survey interface allowed participants to physically drag each definition to the spot where they believed it belonged.

We use rank-ordered logit to analyze whether exposure to partisan news shows caused participants to define the tax policy issue in an attitude-consistent fashion (e.g., conservatives ranking conservative definitions higher and liberals ranking liberal definitions higher). The results are displayed in figure 6.7. Participants who enjoy watching partisan news were highly likely to choose attitude-consistent problem definitions without the aid of partisan news (nearly 70 percent chance), and their problem definitions were unaffected by both pro- and counterattitudinal shows.[16] In contrast, partisan talk shows had some impact on

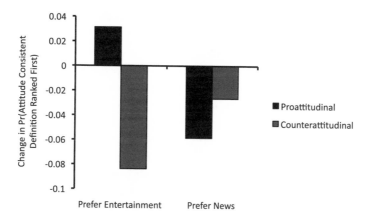

FIGURE 6.7. Effects of Partisan news on problem definition among news seekers and entertainment seekers, fall 2011 PPE.

Note: Bars represent difference in probabilities between the treatment group and the control group. For the full statistical model results, see table A6.7.

how entertainment seekers defined the tax policy issue.[17] Proattitudinal shows appeared to facilitate an attitude-consistent problem definition among those who would rather not watch partisan news shows, although the small increase is not statistically different from zero.[18] Counterattitudinal shows lowered the probability that entertainment seekers chose an attitude-consistent definition as their first choice by 8.4 percentage points (relative to the control group).[19] Entertainment seekers exposed to the counterattitudinal show had only a 56 percent chance of ranking an attitude-consistent definition first, which, given the fact that three of the six choices were attitude consistent, is only somewhat better than chance. All told, these results illustrate that, at least in this particular study, partisan news is not guaranteed to have substantial influence over a problem definition but that counterattitudinal shows may be successful in altering problem definitions among those who prefer to not watch partisan news.

Summary

In tune with more than forty years of media research, we find that, just like the mainstream media, partisan news can increase the salience of political issues simply by discussing them. Even in a fragmented media environment, partisan news has the power to set the agenda. Across our studies, we consistently find that exposure to proattitudinal news programs causes viewers to see the issues discussed as more important and salient to them. In contrast, we find less consistent agenda-setting effects for counterattitudinal news programs. In some studies exposure to counterattitudinal programs boosted issue salience, whereas in others it did not. We could speculate about the reasons for the differences across these studies, but determining the conditions under which counterattitudinal programming can prime the importance of an issue will require additional research, which we discuss further in chapter 8.

We do find that both proattitudinal news and counterattitudinal news have the ability to prime which issue considerations viewers draw on when evaluating the president, and it is possible that counterattitudinal news shows have a stronger priming effect. The added wrinkle here is that it appears that, unlike the passive priming effects induced by exposure to mainstream media coverage, exposure to counterattitudinal news leads to a defensive response owing to the *partisan* character of the priming. Liberals exposed to conservative news coverage see the denigration of liberal policies as more reason to support the Democratic president. Conservatives exposed to liberal news coverage see the burnishing of liberal policies as more reason to oppose the president. Perhaps this is as it should be. Cable news talk shows are overtly partisan, and, consequently, in the process of highlighting the salience of an issue, they prime partisan considerations. While these findings are based on only one study, we suspect that, because counterattitudinal shows attack people's core predispositions and partisan identities, a defensive priming effect may be more robust than simple agenda-setting effects are.

To the extent that liberal and conservative news shows talk about different issues, partisan news media also have the power to construct different agendas. Of course, this power appears to be constrained by viewers' own experiences. In the one study where we are able to investigate this question, we found that most viewers continued to list the economy as the most important problem, even after being exposed to a partisan news show that did not discuss the economy. Nonetheless, we did find that those exposed to this show were less likely to list the economy as salient. Unfortunately, the size of this study did not allow us to investigate whether pro- and counterattitudinal shows have differential success rates in constructing different agendas. If our findings in other studies shed light on this question, they suggest that proattitudinal shows may be able to more reliably change the topic, so to speak.

More important, as we have discovered in previous chapters, including entertainment choices in the mix substantially reduces the agenda-setting effects of partisan news media. Much of this reduction appears to be caused by dilution, and while one of our pretest preference studies found evidence of differential treatment effects—with entertainment seekers more susceptible than news seekers—the other did not. One possibility, we speculate, is that the novelty of the issues varied between these two studies. Perhaps, when an issue is regularly in the news, the partisan news media can set the agenda on that issue only among those who do not regularly tune in to the news. But, when an issue has just come to the fore, the partisan news media can set the agenda among news seekers as well. While additional research would be necessary to confirm if our hunch is correct, we expect that the agenda-setting power of the partisan media is at its height when an issue is new.

Finally, we find limited evidence of media framing effects. In some sense, framing the issues is the ultimate goal of the partisan media. They do not just want viewers to think the issues they cover are important; they also want them to think about issues through a particular ideological lens. Income inequality exists, but is it a good thing or a bad thing? If it is a good thing, who deserves the credit? If it is a bad thing, who is to blame? The partisan media have answers to these questions, and, more important, they want viewers to accept their answers as the correct ones. On this score, we find differences between news seekers and entertainment seekers. News seekers do not need help from proattitudinal shows defining problems in ideologically consistent ways, and counterattitudinal shows do not successfully get them to define issues in ideologically inconsistent ways. Entertainment seekers, in contrast, may benefit somewhat from exposure to proattitudinal news, but not from watching counterattitudinal news. In fact, exposure to counterattitudinal news reduces the probability of defining an issue in an attitude-consistent manner to a coin flip. While this effect is short of the goal of counterattitudinal news shows, which is to get viewers to see it *their* way, it does suggest that, if entertainment seekers are inadvertently exposed to counterattitudinal news, they may walk away with a less ideologically coherent handle on the issues.

Thus far, we have explored how audience choice affects the influence of partisan media over issue positions, candidate evaluations, issue salience, and the receptivity of viewers to arguments and frames. In the next chapter, we investigate the extent to which partisan media affect other judgments about politicians, the political system, and the mass media. Some scholars have expressed concerns that the partisan media affect these judgments in a manner detrimental to the polity (e.g., Mutz 2006b). We examine these concerns experimentally, applying our designs with the aim of identifying the choice behavior and preferences of audience members.

CHAPTER SEVEN

Bias and Incivility in Partisan Media

Jon Stewart, the comedian and host of *The Daily Show* on Comedy Central, appeared on Chris Wallace's public affairs show, *Fox News Sunday*, in June 2011. Fox News hosts often accuse Stewart and *The Daily Show* of having a liberal bias. From the beginning, the discussion between Stewart and Wallace was heated, with each taking the position that the other's show was ideologically biased. At some point in the interview, Stewart asked Wallace if he believed that Fox News is "exactly the ideological equivalent of NBC News." Wallace responded: "I think we're the counterweight. I think they [NBC News] have a liberal agenda and we tell the other side of the story" (Benen 2011). Stewart mocked this line of reasoning on his own show the following day, affecting the personality of the stereotypical stoner: "Hollywood, comedians, every single news organization, the Internet, facts, history, science, it's all just left-wing bullshit, man" (Stewart 2011).

The charge that the mainstream news media have an ideological bias is not new. Despite a professed commitment to report the news in an objective fashion, they have often been accused by observers on both the Left and the Right of being biased against *their* point of view (e.g., Alterman 2003; Goldberg 2002). Moreover, political elites consistently use claims of media bias as a way in which to undermine trust in the media among their followers (Ladd 2010, 2012). Perhaps all this is understandable because people tend to see the world from their point of view and it is only natural to see bias in accounts that give equal weight to sides that are not perceived to deserve equal weight (Vallone, Ross, and Lepper 1985).

The partisan news media, as Chris Wallace articulates, offer a chance for partisans to receive the news in a way that is consistent with their view of the world. In the process, those media also create a news environment in which there are real distinctions in news accounts across networks. For example, take the coverage surrounding the killing of Osama bin Laden. The day after the announcement, Sean Hannity on Fox News reacted with qualified praise of President Obama's decision to send in an elite Navy SEAL team to carry out the risky job. At many points in his show, he asserted that Osama bin Laden's whereabouts were likely learned through enhanced intelligence techniques, which have been at the center of the debate over the use of torture to obtain intelligence: "And by the way, and I give President Obama a lot of credit here. Because I thought it was a gutsy choice. A gutsy choice, not to drop a 2,000-pound bomb but to send these guys in, so we can confirm that it's him [bin Laden]. . . . But as I look at this, would President Obama not now realize that without [enhanced intelligence], he wouldn't have had the ability to make this decision, I would hope that it might change his mind" (Hannity 2011). Meanwhile, on MSNBC, amid the mocking of the president's critics, Ed Schultz, who hosts a liberal talk show, was offering a full-throated congratulations. At one point in the show, he played a video of Sarah Palin, the former Republican governor of Alaska and John McCain's running mate in 2008, criticizing the president's commitment to the war on terror in which she charged: "And to win that war we need a commander-in-chief, not a professor of law standing at the lectern." Schultz (2011) repeated this line before asking in taunting tone: "So, Sarah Palin, how is this commander-in-chief doing now? Palin has just been a small part of the smear job on President Obama's national security credentials."

Conservatives watching Hannity's show and liberals watching Schultz's show may come away with the view that the news media are on their side. At the same time, it is also possible that, if conservatives become aware of the taunting on Schultz's show, and liberals become aware of what they would perceive as a whitewash on Hannity's show, their overall disdain for news media will only deepen. Indeed, in today's partisan news environment, the hosts of cable news shows regularly inform their viewers what outlandish things the other side is saying. So, while it is possible that avoiding opposing viewpoints may improve people's view of news media, it is also possible that the presence of unabashedly oppositional news coverage (as opposed to the purportedly balanced news coverage in the mainstream media) may erode their trust in the media even more.

More generally, cable news talk shows feature a great deal of vitriol and negativity, which has the potential to erode viewers' trust in political institutions (Mutz and Reeves 2005). These shows draw audiences, in part, by featuring brash, "in-your-face" discourse (Mutz 2007, 621), but, in the process of ramping up incivility to increase ratings, they may also create an unflattering caricature of the American political system. If partisan news talk shows reduce politics to puerile bickering and grandstanding, then how can we blame viewers who ask themselves, What's the point? and become more cynical about politics in general.

In this chapter, we investigate the potential for the news media to influence viewers' evaluations of politicians, institutions of government, and the news media themselves. Whether and how media influence trust in institutions constitute the underlying questions for a great deal of research (e.g., Cappella and Jamieson 1996; Ladd 2012; Mutz and Reeves 2005). In these investigations, we make no assumptions about how much faith or doubt viewers *should* have in social institutions. Philosophically, of course, some amount of trust in institutions is required for people to perceive their legitimacy, but this trust must be tempered as a check on power. A somewhat common view is that the "healthy skepticism" people have had toward government and the media has been replaced by a "corrosive cynicism," borrowing the terms Mann and Ornstein (1994, 1) apply to assessments of Congress.[1] We recognize that the polity is well served by a limited trust in social institutions and ask how political communication affects relative judgments about the trustworthiness of the government and the media. We investigate hostility toward both the news media themselves and politicians and the government within the new partisan media environment.

The Hostile Media Phenomenon

In mid-September 1982, all the broadcast news channels inundated their viewers with coverage of the massacre of civilians in the Sabra and Shatila refugee camps during the Israeli occupation of Beirut, Lebanon.

The previous June, Israel sent troops into southern Lebanon to stop missile attacks on northern Israeli cities. According to ABC's coverage of the Sabra and Shatila massacre, on Wednesday, September 15, Israel sent military forces "deep" into Beirut, partially in response to the bombing assassination of Lebanon's president-elect, Bashir Gemayel, a Maronite Christian whom Israel supported (Reynolds 1982). Over the next several days, Beirut became "the first Arab capital ever to be completely under Israeli control" with Defense Minister Ariel Sharon threatening to continue the occupation "until 2,000 Palestinian guerillas . . . either leave the city or are eliminated" (Jennings 1982a). On the night of Friday, September 17, an estimated "300 Palestinian civilians were murdered in the Sabra and Shatila camps . . . most of them by straight execution" (McCourt 1982). The killings were directly attributed to the right-wing Kataib militia led by Amin Gemayel, the brother of the slain president-elect. Some observers also blamed Israel, whose military had allowed the Christian militia into the camps (Jennings 1982b). U.S. Senator Howard Baker, speaking of Israel, contended: "It's clear that [Israeli armed forces] were there and in the vicinity at least to those camps and did not prevent it. And to the extent that they went back in and created a military climate, the Israelis did, then they must assume some heavy share of the responsibility for what flowed from that" (Donaldson 1982). Israeli prime minister Menachem Begin rejected the notion that his country had any responsibility for the attacks.

This tragic turn of events served as the setting for an important and seminal study conducted by Robert Vallone, Lee Ross, and Mark Lepper (1985). In the six weeks following the massacre, they recruited pro-Arab and pro-Israeli students at Stanford to participate in a study of media perceptions. These participants were asked to watch six news segments reporting on the massacre, segments that aired between September 15 and September 24, 1982, and were drawn from the three major broadcast networks' nightly news programs. After watching the segments, participants rated the programs and the editors.

Even though they had watched the same segments, pro-Arab and pro-Israel participants perceived the programs and the editors as biased, but in diametrically opposed directions. Pro-Arab participants thought that the segments were too friendly toward Israel's arguments and version of events, while pro-Israeli participants reached the exact opposite conclusion. Not only did these two groups perceive that the news programs were biased against their side; they also remembered the segments differently, recalling more negative than positive references to their particular side. Remarkably, both groups perceived hostility toward their side in news reports that were designed with twentieth-century standards of journalistic balance in mind, and perceptions of hostility were most pronounced among those with the highest knowledge of the Israeli-Palestinian conflict. Vallone, Ross, and Lepper interpret what they call the *hostile media phenomenon* as evidence that individuals have a tendency not only to see the world from their own point of view but also to assimilate information about it in a biased fashion. Partisans see the truth as either "black" or "white" and "complain about the fairness and objectivity of mediated accounts that suggest that the truth might be at some particular hue of gray." Consequently, when confronted with a balanced account of the issue: "One side reports it to be largely white (instead of the blackish hue that the other side thinks it should be), the other side reports it to be largely black (instead of the whitish hue that the first side thinks it should be), and both sides believe the discrepancy between the mediated account and the unmediated truth to be the intended result of hostile bias on the part of those responsible" (Vallone, Ross, and Lepper 1985, 584).

The hostile media phenomenon has been verified across a variety of situations since Vallone, Ross, and Lepper's original study. A second study, conducted after the fever pitch of the incident subsided, uncovered similar hostile media perceptions among pro-Arab and pro-Israeli groups who were asked to view old coverage of the massacre (Perloff 1989). Beyond international disputes, which may tap into nationalistic pride, other scholars have uncovered the hostile media phenomenon in media coverage of college football teams (Arpan and Raney 2003), animal rights (Gunther, Christen, Liebhart, and Chia 2001), elections (Dalton, Beck, and Huckfeldt 1998), and politics in general (Lee 2005).

If partisans tend to view the mainstream media as hostile to their side, how should they view the partisan media? After all, by mainstream journalistic standards, partisan news programming *is* biased. In a modern update of the original hostile media study, Coe et al. (2008) presented study participants with segments from CNN, Comedy Central's *The Daily Show*, and Fox News. Although participants recognized that these shows possessed an ideological point of view, self-identified liberals and conservatives reached different conclusions about their level. Liberals rated Fox News as more biased than conservatives did, while conservatives rated *The Daily Show* as more biased than liberals did.

Consequently, the partisan news media may create two opposing forces. On the one hand, partisans who watch proattitudinal news come to see it as friendly to their views and interests (Goldman and Mutz 2011). Indeed, perceptions of hostility on the part of mainstream news may drive some partisans to seek out information from friendly sources that present the world in the hue they believe it to be. As the anecdote with which we began the chapter suggests, Fox News views itself as fair and balanced—not in the sense of mainstream journalistic standards, but in the sense that it offers the side not covered by hostile mainstream news. On the other hand, the existence of ideologically oppositional news outlets creates, not just a perceived, but a real difference in the slant of news coverage within the partisan media. As such, partisans may come to view counterattitudinal news outlets with deep suspicion and hostility (see Baum and Gussin 2008), and this *oppositional media hostility* may spill over into general perceptions of media bias.

But, as should be familiar from previous chapters, we believe that the availability of entertainment options may moderate oppositional media hostility. We continue to posit two possible mechanisms. First, as entertainment seekers tune out partisan news, the overall level of oppositional media hostility is diluted. Second, because news seekers are familiar with partisan media, they may be more inured to the hyperbolic rhetoric on these shows. Consequently, while news seekers may perceive oppositional media hostility, it may seem to them less stark than the hostility perceived by entertainment seekers who cannot turn away. As a result, forced exposure studies, like Coe et al. (2008) conducted, likely overestimate the existence of oppositional media hostility.

Establishing the Existence of Oppositional Media Hostility

We employ the summer 2008, summer 2009, and fall 2009 forced exposure experiments (FEEs) to first establish the existence of oppositional media hostility. These studies, summarized in table 3.5 above, were conducted with the help of both student and community participants. We drew stimuli from Fox News and MSNBC and selected segments that featured partisan commentary. For example, in the fall 2009 FEE, we featured clips from *The O'Reilly Factor, Hannity, The Rachel Maddow Show, The Ed Show* with Ed Schultz, and *Countdown with Keith Ol-*

bermann. Each of these was a composite of multiple broadcasts featuring commentary on the health care legislation advanced by the White House in 2009. We chose health care reform as a topic because it has been a heavily contested and partisan issue in the United States.

The *Hannity* stimulus drew on shows from September 22, September 30, and October 7, 2009. We had to use so many segments because Fox News hosts were less likely to spend time discussing the issue relative to MSNBC talk show hosts. Nonetheless, these shows provide lively and intensely partisan discussions of the issue. Take the following as a representative example. In the October 7 segment, Hannity discusses the campaign for health care reform with a guest commentator, the conservative Michelle Malkin. Specifically, they complain to each other about a recent White House event that brought President Obama together with doctors and other supporters, organized in part by the group Doctors for America:

> HANNITY: Isn't this the definition of propaganda? I mean, think about this, it's intended to manipulate the American people. It's intended—"We're going to put white coats on everybody and we're going to make the American people think all the doctors want this," you know, which contradicts every poll, every doctor that I know, but this was basically a propaganda event you'd expect in another country. . . .
>
> MALKIN: Who's behind it? Who's behind Doctors for America and this Organizing for America propaganda event? Well, I traced it to the Center for American Progress. They're the ones . . .
>
> HANNITY: (talking over) Ah, Podesta.
>
> MALKIN: . . . that launched this Doctors for America campaign. Yes, the Soros-funded left-wing outfit that has been, that has acted basically as hit men for Obamacare since the beginning of the year. (Hannity 2009)

Throughout their discussion, the on-screen slate described the segment as presenting "THE TRUTH BEHIND PRES OBAMA'S MONDAY MEETING W/ 150 DOCTORS." The other stimuli offered similarly contentious discussions of the health care bill.

Participants were randomly assigned to view a proattitudinal show or a counterattitudinal show. After watching the show, they completed a questionnaire for which they used a semantic differential test to rate the level of bias and hostility on the shows they had seen. The semantic differential test places a positive trait and its antonym (e.g., *fair* vs. *unfair*) on opposite sides of a continuum and asks the rater to mark on the continuum which word best describes the stimuli. Raters who believe the show was completely fair would place the mark close to fair. Those who believe the show was fair in some ways and unfair in others would place the mark in the middle of the continuum. On the summer 2008 and summer 2009 FEEs, participants could rate the show they viewed using four semantic differential items (*fair/unfair; friendly/hostile; good/bad; quarrelsome/cooperative*), and, on the fall 2009 FEE, these items were augmented with three more (*balanced/skewed; one-sided/even-handed; American/un-American*). For each of these items, participants rated each video clip stimulus using the pair of words on a scale ranging from 1 to 9.

The mean responses to the semantic differential items for each treatment group are displayed in figure 7.1. Across all three experiments, participants consistently rated the counterattitudinal show as more unfair, hostile, bad, and less cooperative than the proattitudinal show. This pattern extends to the expanded set of items in the fall 2009 FEE, where participants viewed the counterattitudinal show as more skewed, less evenhanded, and more un-American than the proattitudinal show.[2]

In addition to rating the relative level of bias and hostility, participants in all three studies rated how illuminating and intellectually stimulating they found the shows, with two items that asked if the show they watched was "informative" and "gave food for thought." The mean responses for these items for each treatment group are shown in figure 7.2. Echoing the results reported above, participants across all three studies tended to view the counterattitudinal show as less informative and intellectually stimulating than the proattitudinal show.[3]

In the fall 2009 FEE, we went beyond the content of the shows and asked participants to rate how much they liked the host. They were also asked to answer a battery of questions that measured how trustworthy they perceived both the news media generally and the television news media in particular to be.[4] The mean rating of the show host by treatment group is displayed in figure 7.3. On average, participants rated the host of the counterattitudinal show nearly 30 points lower than they did the host of the proattitudinal show on a 101-point scale. Proattitudinal show hosts were viewed as warm ($M = 78.8$), while counterattitudinal hosts were viewed as cold ($M = 44.7$).[5] Figure 7.4 displays the mean of the media trust scales by treatment group. Participants who viewed the

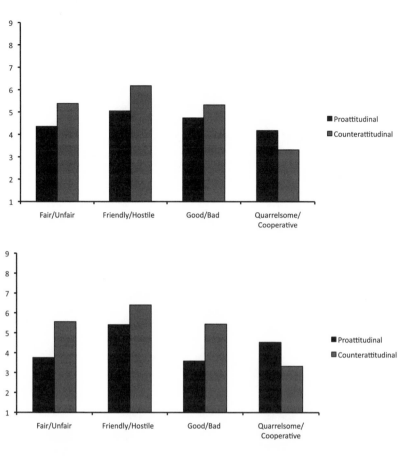

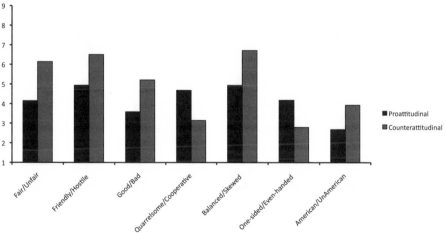

FIGURE 7.1. Perceptions of hostility in proattitudinal and counterattitudinal news shows. *a*, Summer 2008 FEE. *b*, Summer 2009 FEE. *c*, Fall 2009 FEE.
Note: Bars represent mean rating for each treatment group. For the full statistical model results, see table A7.1.

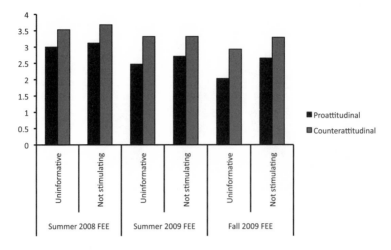

FIGURE 7.2. Ratings of informativeness and intellectual stimulation of proattitudinal and counterattitudinal news shows.
Note: Bars represent mean response for each treatment group. For the full statistical model results, see table A7.1.

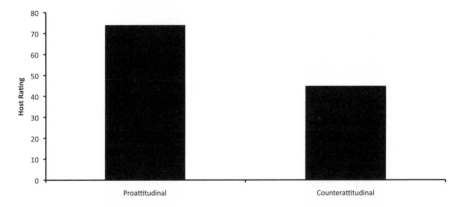

FIGURE 7.3. Rating of host on proattitudinal and counterattitudinal news shows, fall 2009 FEE.
Note: Participants rated the show host using a thermometer score that ranges from 0 (not warm) to 100 (very warm). Bars represent the mean response for each treatment group. For the full statistical model results, see table A7.1.

counterattitudinal show were more likely to say that they did not trust the news media generally and that they did not trust the television news media in particular.[6]

Taken together, these findings are consistent with Coe et al.'s (2008) study of hostile media perceptions and cable news shows. People find

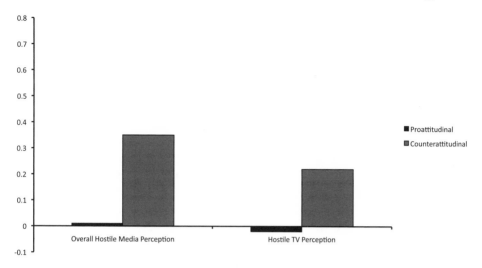

FIGURE 7.4. Hostile media perceptions after exposure to proattitudinal and counterattitudinal news shows, fall 2009 FEE.
Note: Bars represent mean of factor score for media hostility scales, where positive numbers indicate distrust and negative numbers indicate trust. For the full statistical model results, see table A7.1.

counterattitudinal shows to be more biased and less interesting than proattitudinal shows. Negative appraisal of the counterattitudinal show's content also extends to the host and spills over to general perceptions of the news media. Exposure to counterattitudinal shows causes viewers to perceive the media in general and television news in particular as hostile. In sum, partisan news talk shows have the potential to affect people's perception of media hostility. A steady diet of counterattitudinal shows would lead to oppositional media hostility, while partisan selectivity would potentially engender friendly media perceptions. Next, we turn to a consideration of the effects of choice on hostile media perceptions.

Selective Exposure and Oppositional Media Hostility

Does choice attenuate the presence of oppositional media hostility? We investigate this question using the now-familiar selective exposure design with the help of the fall 2009 and winter 2009 selective exposure experiments (SEEs). Recall from chapter 4 that the winter 2009 SEE simplifies matters by restricting the information environment to a one-sided flow of information. Participants assigned to the forced news condition were asked to watch a segment of *Hardball with Chris Matthews*, which has a liberal slant. The show aired just following the election of Barack Obama as president of the United States in November 2008 and featured a tendentious discussion of outgoing president Bush's handling of the economy. The entertainment options in the choice condition and the control group were drawn from the Discovery Channel (*Dirty Jobs*) and the Travel Channel (*Log Cabins*). While this study allows us to hold the ideology of the political show constant, it does so at the expense of confounding assignment to pro- or the counterattitudinal treatment with participants' ideology. We address this drawback in the fall 2009 SEE by including a conservative show in the mix. Recall that both political shows covered the debate over Obama's proposed health care reform bill in the fall of 2009. *The Rachel Maddow Show* served as the liberal news program and *The O'Reilly Factor with Bill O'Reilly* served as the conservative news program. The entertainment shows in the choice condition and the control group were drawn from the National Geographic Channel (*The Dog Whisperer*) and the Travel Channel (*Dhani Tackles the Globe*).

After watching television, participants were asked to complete a questionnaire that included the four-item battery of news media trust used in the fall 2009 SEE. The differences in means between each of the treatment groups and the control group are displayed in figure 7.5. The winter 2009 SEE shows what should be a familiar pattern by now. Forced exposure to partisan news shows affects hostile media perceptions. Consistent with the evidence from the forced exposure studies, exposure to the counterattitudinal show leads to hostile media perceptions, and the addition of the control group allows us to say that exposure to proattitudinal shows may actually decrease hostile media perceptions.[7] Nonetheless, affording participants a minimal amount of choice causes these effects to be diminished in the choice condition. We find that the level of media hostility in the choice condition is not statistically different from the level of media hostility in the control group.[8]

The results from the fall 2009 SEE, which featured a two-sided flow of information, echo the findings from the winter 2009 SEE, but the attenuation in the choice condition is much less pronounced.[9] Indeed, it appears that limited choice in a two-sided information environment reduces, but does not eliminate, hostile media perceptions. These findings raise additional questions ripe for study. The simplest explanation is that participants in the choice condition watched a sufficient amount of the

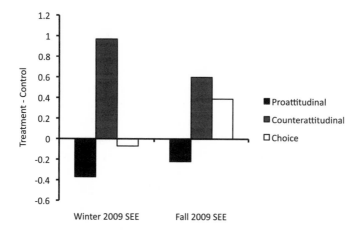

FIGURE 7.5. The effects of partisan news shows and selective exposure on hostile media perceptions in one-sided and two-sided information environments, winter 2009 and fall 2009 SEEs, respectively.

Note: Bars represent the difference in mean between the treatment groups and the control group. For the full statistical model results, see table A7.2.

counterattitudinal show to generate hostile media perceptions. After all, half the choices in this condition were political news, and participants spent, on average, 62 percent of their time watching these shows. With a greater degree of choice, as is the case in the modern cable television environment, we would expect the oppositional media hostility effects to be attenuated further. That said, as we discuss in the next section, the presence of counterattitudinal shows may engender some degree of oppositional media hostility—at least among partisan news viewers.

Why Does News Selectivity Attenuate Oppositional Media Hostility?

Why do we observe less oppositional media hostility in choice environments? We have thoroughly explained our twofold answer to this question in previous chapters, and our story remains the same. First, as entertainment seekers select out of the news audience, they dilute the overall effect of news programs. Second, partisan news shows have a smaller effect on the remaining audience of news seekers. People who typically do not watch partisan news shows may be particularly dismayed by the tendentious arguments made on counterattitudinal programs, whereas those who typically tune in to these shows might view the hyperbolic rhetoric as par for the course. Liberal news seekers know what Fox News is all about, while conservative news seekers know what MSNBC is all about.

We investigate the possibility of heterogeneous treatment effects using the summer 2010 participant preference experiment (PPE). The experiment was conducted with the help of students attending the University of California, Riverside. In all, 152 participants were recruited for this study. Following the participant preference protocol, participants were given four possible viewing options from which to choose and then randomly assigned to one of them. Two of the options were cable news shows. The liberal show was a segment from *Countdown with Keith Olbermann*, and the conservative show was a segment from *The O'Reilly Factor*. The other two options were the same entertainment shows used in the fall 2009 SEE, discussed above.

The political news segments were taken from shows that aired on June 17, 2010, and focused on the Deepwater Horizon British Petroleum (BP) oil spill. At the time, oil had been uncontrollably spewing from a deep water oil well off the coast of Louisiana since April 22, 2010, when an explosion sank the Deepwater Horizon drilling rig that had tapped the exploratory well. Both these show segments discussed the appearance of BP's then-CEO Tony Hayward at the House Committee on Energy and Commerce the day after the corporation had negotiated with the Obama administration to establish a $20 billion fund to support recovery efforts and compensate victims of the spill. During the committee hearing, U.S. Representative Joe Barton (D-TX) apologized to BP for its treatment by the White House. "I do not want to live in a country where any time a citizen or a corporation does something that is legitimately wrong is subject to some sort of political pressure that, again, in my words amounts to a shakedown," Barton said in a sound bite that aired on both programs.

While both Olbermann and O'Reilly offered criticism of BP, Hayward, and Barton, there were profound differences in the treatment of the incident on their shows. Olbermann castigated BP, Barton, and the Republican Party, saying that the apology was "revealing the pained contortions of the GOP, now the G-O-B-P is going through as the defender of big oil" (Olbermann 2010a). O'Reilly was more nuanced—critical of Barton and BP but also critical of the federal government under

Obama and, to a certain extent, the fund, saying: "BP has been coerced by the president to put up at least $20 billion in a fund to benefit those hurt by BP's dereliction." O'Reilly's guest, Laura Ingraham, went further in criticizing the president, arguing: "Joe Barton, before he apologized, had a legitimate point. First of all, this administration has taken a very aggressive and, I would say, strong-arm approach to private industry across the board whether it is health insurance companies or banks or hospital groups, and now with BP" (O'Reilly 2010). Ultimately, these were both contentious segments featuring partisan criticism.

We measured perceptions of hostility on the posttest questionnaire with the help of the thought-listing task, which is a well-worn psychometric tool to gauge gut-level assessments and information processing (Cacioppo and Petty 1981). The measure is more finely tuned than the blunter indicators employed in our previous studies. The thought-listing task was administered right after participants finished watching the show. In order to ensure that we captured top-of-the-head reactions, participants were asked to write down as many thoughts as they could in two and a half minutes (for the logic behind the time constraint, see Cacioppo and Petty [1981, 316]). After the study, two research assistants independently coded the valence of the thoughts. Positive thoughts indicated that the participant enjoyed the show (e.g., "I really loved watching this show"), while negative thoughts indicated hostility (e.g., "I can't believe they allow shows like this on TV"). The overall valence of participants' reactions is measured by taking the difference between the total number of positive thoughts and the total number of negative thoughts. A zero indicates balance in positive and negative thoughts, positive numbers indicate that thoughts were mostly positive, and negative numbers indicate that thoughts were mostly negative.

The results are shown in figure 7.6. Entertainment seekers reacted negatively to *both* the proattitudinal show and the counterattitudinal show.[10] There is also a glimmer of evidence for oppositional media hostility—the reaction to the counterattitudinal show was more negative—but this difference is not statistically significant, and it should be noted that entertainment seekers reacted quite negatively to the proattitudinal show as well. In contrast, we observe small negative reactions to the partisan talk shows among news seekers, and we cannot rule out the possibility that these shows had no effect on the hostility perceptions of news seekers.[11] These results are consistent with the explanation that both dilution

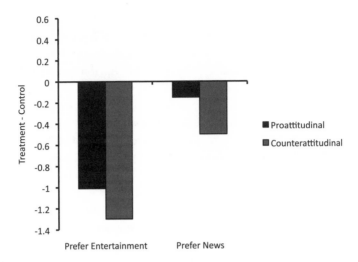

FIGURE 7.6. The effects of partisan news shows on affective reactions, by viewing preferences, summer 2010 PPE.
Note: Bars represent the difference in mean between the treatment groups and the control group. For the full statistical model results, see table A7.3.

(entertainment seekers removing themselves from the audience) and habituation (news seekers reacting less strongly to cable news content) lead to the attenuation of oppositional hostility in choice environments.[12]

Partisan News and the New Videomalaise

Noting the simultaneous rise in the American public's dependence on television news and cynicism toward and distrust of the political system during the late 1960s and early 1970s, Michael Robinson proposed the *videomalaise* hypothesis. He described videomalaise as a diffuse phenomenon in which negative portrayals of politics on television news cause people to develop a sense of detachment from the political system and political leaders. Robinson argued: "Our doubts about ourselves and hostility toward our institutions would be far less severe were it not for the images we receive from the electronic media, more specifically, from network journalism" (1975, 98). A number of researchers have shown that the content of television news—particularly its focus on strategy and political process—alienates voters and promotes distrust in and negative evaluations of institutions (Cappella and Jamieson 1997; Hibbing and Theiss-Morse 1995; Moy and Pfau 2000; but see Norris 2000).

If this is the effect of exposure to broadcast news, just imagine how terrible exposure to the partisan news media must be. Partisan news talk shows, in particular, feature a daily diet of negativity. Hosts routinely mock and berate public officials who earn their ire and excoriate guests who espouse different viewpoints. Keith Olbermann, for example, featured a segment at the end of his show titled "The Worst Persons in the World" in which he strongly criticized individuals, usually politicians or other media pundits, who have behaved in ways he finds repugnant. Bill O'Reilly has a similar recurring segment on his show called "Pinheads and Patriots" in which he denounces people he considers to be pinheads and praises those he views as patriots.

The rise of incivility in political discourse on cable news has reinvigorated interest in the videomalaise hypothesis. Mutz and Reeves (2005) focus on how televised incivility affects distrust of politicians and political institutions. They contend that the intensity of incivility on cable news shows violates norms of conflict avoidance and causes viewers to develop negative reactions toward politics and government. Through a series of carefully crafted experiments, they demonstrate that exposure to uncivil political debate lowers trust in politicians and the political system and that uncivil debate has particularly deleterious effects on individuals who possess a high aversion to conflict. They conclude that the ubiquity of uncivil discourse on television debate shows may ultimately "threaten the stability of political institutions" and that, because the negatively of these shows is the reason for their success, it illustrates that in the current environment "market forces do not best serve the interests of democracy" (13). Their findings are consistent with a number of complementary studies. Conflict-oriented coverage of the State of the Union address affected evaluation of institutions and lowered government trust (Forgette and Morris 2006). Similarly, the content of coverage of the 9/11 Commission hearings affected trust in government and evaluations of public officials (Cooper and Nownes 2005).

Yet all the experiments that inform these studies rely on captive audiences and assume hypodermic effects. When Robinson developed the videomalaise hypothesis, broadcast news was at its zenith. As we know, however, partisan news shows have relatively small audiences, and more Americans are tuning out the news—any news—altogether. It is possible that, because of shrinking news audiences, the videomalaise phenomenon could be on the decline even as cable news ramps up its incivility. What is more, we should also consider whether televised incivility plays into people's decisions to tune in to cable news shows in the first place. Mutz and Reeves find that conflict-averse individuals display the most negative reactions to these shows; we have demonstrated that conflict aversion makes it less likely that people will tune in to cable news talk shows (Arceneaux and Johnson 2007; Johnson and Arceneaux 2010). If those who are most susceptible to videomalaise are less likely to tune in, partisan news talk show audiences are most likely filled with those who relish conflict and are either unaffected or less affected by uncivil political debate.

Selective Exposure and Videomalaise

We investigate the effects of choice on videomalaise with the summer 2009 and fall 2009 SEEs. The summer 2009 SEE was designed to test specifically the effects of incivility. Participants were assigned to a treatment in which they watched a particularly uncivil exchange on a political talk show, a control group in which people watched one of two entertainment shows, or a choice group in which participants could flip among all three shows. The political clip was drawn from a pugnacious segment of *Hardball with Chris Matthews* that aired August 19, 2009. In this clip, the host, Chris Matthews, discusses whether people attending presidential appearances should be allowed to carry firearms with John Velleco, a spokesman for Gun Owners of America, and Brian Levin from the Center for the Study of Hate and Extremism. The interaction among Matthews and his guests ranges from lively to badgering and curt, with a great deal of interruption, raised voices, and participants talking over each other as they tried to make points. The show ends with more discussion of the town hall meetings in summer 2009 with the commentators Joan Walsh (Salon.com), Ken Vogel (*The Politico* news organization), and Matthews discussing U.S. Representative Barney Frank's (D-MA) contentious interaction with a belligerent constituent. The fall 2009 SEE, in which participants could watch either a liberal or a conservative show discussing the health care reform debate, added a partisan dimension by introducing a pro- and counterattitudinal political shows.

After watching television, participants in both studies completed a posttest questionnaire that measured political trust using the same twelve-item battery that Mutz and Reeves (2005) employed. The results are shown in figure 7.7. Beginning with the summer 2009 SEE, we find evidence, consistent with previous scholarship, that subjects forced to watch uncivil political debate scored lower on the political trust scale (fig. 7.7a).[13] However, when given a choice, the negative effects dissipate. There is no difference in political trust between those in the choice condition and those who were forced to watch one of the entertainment shows.[14]

When we allow for both pro- and counterattitudinal shows, an intriguing pattern emerges (fig. 7.7b). Participants exposed only to the proatti-

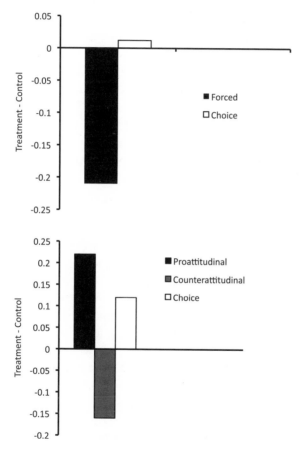

FIGURE 7.7. The effects of partisan news and selective exposure on political trust. a, One-sided information environment (summer 2009 SEE). b, Two-sided information environment (fall 2009 SEE.

Note: Bars represent the difference of means on the political trust scale between the treatment group and the control group. For the full statistical model results, see tables A7.4 (col. 1) and A7.5.

tudinal show expressed significantly higher levels of political trust compared to those exposed only to the counterattitudinal show.[15] Watching proattitudinal news coverage has an effect similar to the one Mutz and Reeves documented for watching civil debate. Subjects in the proattitudinal condition were more trusting of politicians and government than subjects in the counterattitudinal condition. Once again, the effect of partisan news is attenuated when participants are given a choice. Relative to the control group, the effect size is cut nearly in half when compared to the that of the forced exposure treatments.[16] Intriguingly, if any effect does exist, it is a positive one—there is no statistically significant difference between the level of political trust in the choice condition and that in the proattitudinal condition, while there is a difference between the choice condition and the counterattitudinal condition.[17] This suggests that having access to a proattitudinal current affairs talk show in the media environment may overcome the negative effects of counterattitudinal shows.

Conflict Aversion, Choice, and Videomalaise

Are those who are most susceptible to videomalaise more likely to select themselves out of cable news audiences? In our previous work, we show that conflict aversion is negatively correlated with viewing cable news shows (Johnson and Arceneaux 2010). We also know from Mutz and Reeves's (2005) research that those individuals who are conflict averse respond the most negatively to televised incivility. We investigate the interaction between conflict aversion and exposure to cable news shows with the help of the summer 2009 SEE, which included on the pretest questionnaire the same five-item measure of conflict aversion that Mutz and Reeves used in their study.

Figure 7.8 shows the mean level of political trust for each treatment group separately for those low and high in conflict aversion. Among participants with a below-average aversion to conflict, exposure to uncivil debate has no effect on their level of political trust.[18] In contrast, those with above-average aversion to conflict are less likely to trust politicians when forced to watch uncivil political debate relative to the choice condition, where they are free to change the channel.[19] These results suggest that, once subjects who are averse to conflict have an opportunity

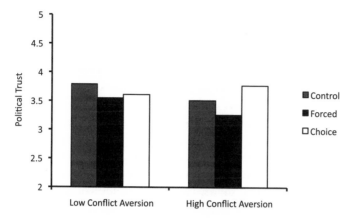

FIGURE 7.8. The effects of uncivil debate on political trust by level of conflict aversion, summer 2009 SEE.
Note: Bars represent mean levels of political trust by experimental condition. For the full statistical model results, see table A7.4 (col. 2).

to select themselves out of watching uncivil debate, the negative effects associated with it diminish, making their level of trust in government no different from that of those who are less averse to conflict.

Summary

In this chapter, we asked whether partisan news shows on cable television engender hostility toward the media and the political system. Both the hostile media and the videomalaise literature provide strong theoretical rationales for concern. Yet we find that the broadening of choices on television that has made the partisan media both possible and profitable also undercuts its ability alter people's perceptions of the media and government. As we have demonstrated in previous chapters, having the option to change the channel diminishes the power of partisan news talk shows to influence public perceptions.

With respect to media hostility, we demonstrate that viewing oppositional news has the potential to make people less trusting of the news media in general. When we introduced a limited amount of choice over news and entertainment options in the mix, we find that hostile media perceptions are less pronounced. We offer evidence that the attenuation of oppositional hostility is partially explained by entertainment seekers selecting out of partisan news audiences and the diminished impact of partisan news on those who do tune in.

We do find some evidence that hostile media perceptions can be obtained in choice environments where news seekers are consuming counterattitudinal news. Of course, this may be an artifact of the limited amount of choice offered in our selective exposure experiments, as there may be a higher degree of partisan selectivity in hyperchoice settings (see Stroud 2011). Nonetheless, there is also reason to believe that cable news viewers *are* exposed to counterattitudinal shows, even if they tune in only to proattitudinal shows. How so? The hosts of these cable news talks shows routinely talk about each other, across network and ideological lines, in order to criticize each other. For example, in October 2009, Rachel Maddow invested a segment in an extensive critique of Fox News, rhetorically asking, "Is Fox a news station?" She argued that it is not because of the political activities of several of its hosts, including Glenn Beck, who worked for the network at the time, and John Stossel: "Opinion has always been a kissing cousin to news, and one man's ideology is another man's objective passion. The difference between Fox and news, the way in which one of these things is not like the other, is that only one of these organizations is organizing antigovernment street protests. There's nothing wrong with that. It's perfectly legal, as far as I know. It just makes Fox an opposition political outlet to the Democratic Party and the Obama White House, rather than a normal news channel." Importantly, in the segment, Maddow (2009) aired clips of Fox News personalities and promotional messages, essentially airing the other side on her program, although with intense criticism. Similar examples can be found on Fox News, but with criticism of MSNBC news clips.

We similarly find that videomalaise can at times affect viewers in a choice environment. Cable news channel programming that features incivility can dampen trust in the political system, but only in the situation in which people do not have the option to look away, and primarily among people who would most want to change the channel if given the opportunity. Introducing choice into the mix, once again, attenuates the negative effects of incivility and negativity in partisan news. Moreover, when effects are observed, they are mostly among those who are averse to conflict and, when given a choice, typically choose to watch something other than cable news talk shows.

CHAPTER EIGHT

Media Effects in the Age of Choice

Communication technology has changed in dramatic ways over the last four decades. We focus on television[1] and the proliferation of viewing options that are the result of entertainment industry reactions to the 1992 Cable Act (e.g., Lubinsky 1996). As a result of this expansion of choice, viewers can tailor the time they spend watching television to their most particular, if not peculiar, tastes. Many of our colleagues focus on the political dimensions of this choice and the increased availability of news and commentary clearly branded as coming from the Left and the Right of the political spectrum, exemplified by MSNBC and Fox News Channel (e.g., Stroud 2011; Levendusky 2012). We consider these political choices to be of critical importance as well. However, they do not occur in a vacuum. Viewers choose between types of news, to be sure, but first they have to choose news. The diversion of entertainment programs, from the edifying to the banal, is constantly available alongside partisan news.

This book demonstrates that partisan news programs are not as influential as many observers expected. Their influence is meaningfully limited by the choices viewers make, especially the availability of entertainment options. The members of the Sloan Commission (1971, 122) are as right today as they were forty years ago: "No one can be forced to twist the dial to the channel carrying political information or political news." The influence of Bill O'Reilly, Rachel Maddow, and their colleagues is limited by the fact that the audience is fragmented, diluting the reach of these shows. The evidence we accumulate here suggests that, when people are allowed to choose what they view, the direct effects of partisan news talk shows are limited to the people who actually tune in to them.

However, the diminished influence of partisan news is only partially explained by its limited reach in a hyperchoice information environment. Just as important is the tendency of partisan news shows to have a smaller effect on those who regularly watch them. *News seekers* want to watch political shows because of their interest in politics and knowledge of politics, while *entertainment seekers* avoid political content and have interests that lie elsewhere among the 130 or more channels the typical person receives today. News seekers are less susceptible to opinion change than are entertainment seekers because they have far more political knowledge anchoring their opinions (Zaller 1992). If the entertainment seekers were somehow forced to watch political programs—by, say, political communication researchers—they would be more likely to be influenced by them because they generally know less about politics.

The Appeal of Conventional Wisdom on Partisan News

We admit that we find intuitive the idea that the hosts of shows on Fox News and MSNBC are influential enough to dramatically drive Americans apart. These shows seem like they should be persuasive, with hosts crying on cue, berating their opponents as "the worst persons in the world," and delivering impassioned appeals to the camera. It all makes for good television. How could this content not deeply affect viewers? Further, many of the people we know who watch these shows certainly have strong political views. Finally, it seems like the public is polarized, or at least that is what we hear on television.

The impression that partisan news talk shows are dramatically influential is consistent with our own anecdotal experiences—some of our friends and family members regularly repeat facts and arguments they seem to have gleaned from Fox and MSNBC shows. However, *we* recognize that these experiences are embedded in a social and political context that represents only a small fraction of viewers, the highly interested, politically minded ones. We have comparatively few close friends more interested in learning the latest gossip about a celebrity like Kim Kardashian than news about a high-profile legislative debate or political campaign. We hazard to guess that many of the pundits and scholars who are so certain that partisan news is rending the nation apart have a similarly circumscribed experience. When we consider the broader picture—viewers inattentive to public affairs and television programming beyond political shows—the evidence for large, direct, polarizing effects associated with partisan news is substantially attenuated.

This finding is important for two reasons. First, it should substantively affect how pundits and politicians criticize the contemporary news environment. From our perspective, the reason to be ill at ease with the state of partisan news on cable television is not because it polarizes the public or even because it misleads people. Rather, the reason to be concerned with these shows revolves around the content itself. These shows may not be corrupting to the polity—the people who watch them tend to know well enough what they want from politics—but this does not imply that we endorse or like the content partisan news outlets feature.

Often, hosts like Sean Hannity and Ed Schultz simply fail to realize their shows' full potential for informing the public. Their shows are not as edifying as the political discourse the members of the Sloan Commission envisioned for cable television. When Hannity associates President Obama with the North American Man/Boy Love Association (Frederick, Schulman, Schweber-Koren, and Weiland 2009) and Schultz calls another political commentator names, including a misogynist slur (Farhi 2011), they are letting themselves and their viewers down. These are dishonorable actions on their own terms, and we do not need to allege media effects in order to criticize them. The mere expression of opinion, in our view, is an entirely different matter. We tend to agree with Rachel Maddow's assessment, quoted in chapter 7: "Opinion has always been a kissing cousin to news, and one man's ideology is another man's objective passion." Our concern is over the undeniably underhanded tactics to which partisan news talk show hosts resort when articulating their opinions.

Second, our explanation for the limited effects of partisan cable programs—viewer choice—points to what we consider to be a far greater problem in contemporary political communication than ideological polarization or political distrust. The vast expansion of viewer choice seems likely to deepen the inequitable distribution of information among the mass public. Prior (2007) identifies this trend over time in the aggregate—access to cable television and the Internet exacerbates the political knowledge differences between people interested and those not interested in politics. Free societies may thrive on the presence of choices, but it must be said that, despite its faults, less choice draws more people into contact with political information. We observe this directly, as participants in our studies sort themselves into news and entertainment seekers.

This chapter summarizes our findings and explains the importance of our insights. We also tackle the bigger questions arising from the contemporary debate about mass polarization. Given that we find evidence that partisan cable news reflects, rather than creates, polarization, how polarized are Americans today, and why? We explore a variety of potential explanations and consider how changes in the structure of the media environment—the expansion of choice—may serve to increase the perception of partisan polarization even as that choice limits the media's influence over it.

What Have We Learned?

We offer evidence consistent with the motivational model of selective exposure that lies at the heart of our active audience theory. When viewers are allowed to choose among political and entertainment programming options, the apparent political effects of news-oriented talk shows are substantially blunted. We show this general phenomenon across a series of specific media effects, including evaluations of the president and issue opinions in chapter 4, responses to political arguments in chapter 5, issue salience and reactions to frames in chapter 6, and perceived media hostility and trust in government in chapter 7. In each case, we replicate the core finding that forcing people to watch partisan media affects the influence of those media. For example, we show that forcing people to watch attitude-consistent programming encourages them to have more attitude-consistent evaluations of the president (see fig. 4.1 above). In this sense, these programs polarize. When it cannot be avoided, a talk show from MSNBC pushes a liberal to have a more approving evaluation of a Democratic president, whereas a Fox News talk show has the opposite effect on a conservative. However, in the more naturalistic environment of choice among political and entertainment shows, this finding is substantially diminished.

Because we conducted a number of experimental studies, it is possible to conduct a meta-analysis to combine the results of these studies

TABLE 8.1. **Meta-Analysis of Partisan News Effects from Selective Exposure and Participant Preference Experiments**

| | Selective Exposure Experiments | | Participant Preference Experiments | | | |
| | | | Entertainment Seekers | | News Seekers | |
Treatment	Combined Effect	Range of Effects	Combined Effect	Range of Effects	Combined Effect	Range of Effects
Proattitudinal	.338 (.174)	[−.39, 1.17]	.543 (.071)	[.33, .65]	.018 (.076)	[−.15, .18]
Counterattitudinal	.499 (.255)	[−.27, 1.97]	.371 (.178)	[−.06, .81]	.149 (.153)	[−.28, .33]
Choice	.159 (.075)	[−.19, .46]				

Note: Standard errors are given in parentheses. For complete details on study effects, see tables A8.1 and A8.2.

and see what we have learned. Randomized experiments lend themselves nicely to meta-analysis since we can assume that each observed effect is a random draw from the distribution of all possible effects. Each additional experiment gives us a better idea about what the distribution of possible effects looks like.

We conducted separate meta-analyses for the selective exposure experiments and the participant preference experiments (for details, see the appendix). The results are reported in table 8.1. We calculated the combined effects of proattitudinal, counterattitudinal, and choice treatments by taking the average of the standardized effects for each analysis.[2] Positive effect sizes indicate that the treatment affected the dependent variable under investigation in the expected direction (e.g., polarizing attitudes or increasing hostile media perceptions), and negative effect sizes indicate that the treatment had an unexpected effect. An effect size equal to zero indicates that the treatment had no effect. We calculated the standard error of the combined effect by dividing the standard deviation of the effects by the square root of the number of studies, enabling us to test whether the combined effect is statistically significant.[3]

Across all five selective exposure experiments in which we estimated the effects of pro- and counterattitudinal shows, we observe a wide range of effects but find that, on average, partisan news shows have a substantial effect on political attitudes in the expected direction. Partisan news shows have the capacity to polarize, set the agenda, increase hostile media perceptions, and influence levels of political trust.[4] While counterattitudinal shows appear to have a stronger effect on attitudes than proattitudinal shows, we cannot rule out sampling variability as a possible explanation for the difference.[5]

Providing participants with the option to watch something other than partisan news shows significantly affects these inferences. On average, we observe smaller effects in the choice condition than in either the pro- or the counterattitudinal condition.[6] However, the small effect that we do observe in the choice condition is significantly different from no effect.[7] Of course, the size of the effect observed in the choice condition is undoubtedly affected by the number of choices available. Had we given people 130 channels from which to choose, we likely would have observed even smaller effects. Nonetheless, these results offer suggestive evidence that partisan news shows may have a very small overall effect in a media environment that includes a number of choices and reduces the size of the inadvertent partisan news audience in the process.

The meta-analysis of the participant preference experiments suggests that it is the reaction of the inadvertent audience that drives the magnitude of the effects of partisan news shows observed in the forced exposure conditions. In both participant preference experiments, pro- and counterattitudinal shows had substantial effects on entertainment seekers who had no other option but to watch a partisan news show.[8] Consistent with our expectations, these shows had modest effects on news seekers.[9] In stark contrast to entertainment seekers, news seekers were virtually unaffected by exposure to proattitudinal shows.[10] However, it does appear that counterattitudinal shows had a modest effect on news seekers, and, while the effect of counterattitudinal shows is quite a bit smaller among news seekers than it is among entertainment seekers, we cannot rule out sampling variability as a possible explanation for the difference.[11]

One implication of our experiments is that the only time partisan news shows should have large direct effects is when the inadvertent partisan news audience is large. Although people may be able to change the channel most of the time, we appreciate that there are instances in which political debate reaches even those who prefer to avoid it. Divisive elections, large protests, and times of war constitute examples of when the chronically inattentive may tune in—either by choice or by accident. It is during these times that politics becomes a regular topic of conversation, and public places that generally offer entertainment on television, such as bars and waiting rooms, may feature news instead. Because cable news programs are on the air twenty-four hours a day, they become the go-to source for current information, and the people who would normally turn away from partisan news have diminished choice in the matter. When they do occur, which is rare to begin with, these events are short-lived.

Both the individual studies and this meta-analysis support our contention that most of the time partisan news plays a relatively minor role in in directly shaping mass opinion. Note that we are asserting, not that it plays no role at all, but rather that self-selection and the ability of entertainment seekers to entirely remove themselves from political programming limit the direct effects of partisan news shows. Our results suggest that cable news is unlikely to be the driving force behind any potential secular increase in mass-level polarization. These findings are consistent with Garner and Palmer's (2011) work, which shows that Americans developed stronger patterns of attitudinal consistency across issues prior to the rise of cable news. Partisan news may be an aspect of political polarization in the United States—it certainly appears to be a venue for it—but it is unlikely the cause.

In this project, we are primarily interested in the mechanisms of media effects, but we recognize the importance of other questions, specifically whether members of the American public are ideologically polarized, the extent of polarization if it exists, and its root causes. Our research speaks to this important question, and we briefly turn to it before concluding with a final experimental study aimed at elucidating an aspect of this puzzle that is relevant to our project. We offer a perspective hinted at earlier in this chapter. It is possible that, while Americans may be more polarized today than at some other times in U.S. history, this sorting is not quite the dramatic problem—at the mass level—that some observers make it out to be. Elites are certainly more polarized today than they have been for the past several decades. That said, academics, political pundits, and other highly attentive viewers may overestimate the extent of mass polarization because they are more cognizant of the availability of partisan news than most people. We find evidence for this projection of polarization in the final study in this book, discussed below.

Partisan News and the Mass-Level Polarization Debate

Congressional coalitions within the Republican and Democratic Parties have become more ideologically coherent over the past 50 years. Particularly in roll call voting in the U.S. Congress, political parties have diverged dramatically (McCarty, Poole, and Rosenthal 2006; Layman, Carsey, and Horowitz 2006; Hetherington 2009). Members of the two major parties in both chambers during the 111th Congress (the most recent term at the time of writing) were more ideologically distinct and exhibited far greater party unity than they did in the mid-twentieth century (McCarty, Poole, and Rosenthal 2011). Thus, the question of polarized politics among officeholding *elites* is authoritatively addressed by political scientists. In contrast, a debate rages about whether members of the American public have themselves become more polarized.

Some scholars argue that Americans have become more polarized on political issues, with partisans espousing more coherent and more extreme views in recent years (Abramowitz and Saunders 2008). Voters appear to be better at sorting themselves ideologically into parties (Carsey and Layman 2006; Levendusky 2009) and finding neighbors who are like-minded (Bishop 2008; but see Abrams and Fiorina 2012). Others contend that political attitudes and ideological predispositions have not become more extreme over time. By and large, Americans remain middle-of-the-road and pragmatic on most issues (Fiorina, Abrams, and Pope 2006). It is also not clear that they are more polarized on issues (Fiorina and Abrams 2008; Hetherington 2009), but it may be the case that the most important issues of the day tend to be divisive (Hetherington and Weiler 2009). Because elites have become more polarized, political choices in elections and in policy debates have become more extreme. If public opinion operates like V. O. Key's (1966) echo chamber, Americans only seem more polarized because their choices have become polarized (Fiorina and Abrams 2008).

Consequently, this is an unsettled matter, complicating the search for causes of polarization in the mass public. But assume for the time being that members of the mass public are more polarized today than they were during the middle of the twentieth century. Why might this be the case if partisan media are not to blame? Trends in the public's identification with political parties point to several factors that may affect greater division in the mass public. These include the efforts of elites to cultivate support for their side, tendencies among more moderate voters to simply excuse themselves from politics, and the recent spike in income inequality (see Bartels 2008; Gelman, Shor, Bafumi, and Park 2007; Hayes 2012; McCarty, Poole, and Rosenthal 2006).

Clearly, voters are more likely to see differences between the political parties in contemporary politics (Hetherington 2001). Voters are also capable of responding to cues communicated by party leaders (Nicholson 2012). The greater clarity in distinguishing parties and leaders may affect mass polarization by making it easier for voters to craft a coherent political ideology (Levendusky 2009).[12] In addition to greater clarity of party brands and their complementary ideologies caused by elite polarization, it also appears that parties are working harder to communicate their differences directly to voters. Figure 8.1 shows the dramatic increase in party-contacting activities as those tracked by the venerable American National Election Studies (2010). Almost 45 percent of voters in the last several elections report having been directly contacted by at least one of the major political parties. The rate of reported direct contact has doubled since the 1950s, sharply rising since the 1980s (see Rosenstone and Hansen 1993). With bigger differences between party elites and more aggressive direct interaction with voters, we might expect increases in mass polarization.

Elite polarization might also create the appearance of mass polarization by causing citizens with less intense partisan commitments to exit the system rather than sort themselves into a team. Prior (2007) makes the point that people with lower levels of political interest increasingly select entertainment options over news and are less likely to vote. Because they also tend to be more moderate, their departure from the political stage heightens the contrast between the groups of more interested, more intense partisans that remain. Given the context of our findings, if the entertainment seekers we identify are less likely to vote, what re-

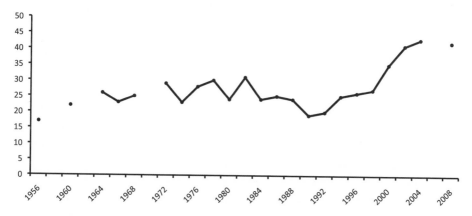

FIGURE 8.1. Trends in partisan contacting, 1956–2008.
Source: American National Election Studies (2010).

mains should be a more polarized electorate. The content of mass media may have something to do with these patterns of exit, but news media may be changing, not the minds of voters—only the composition of the electorate.

Does partisan news cause polarization by persuading people to adopt more extreme partisan or ideological viewpoints? Unlikely. It may cause viewers who are already strong partisans to sort themselves more effectively and thus appear to be more polarized. In addition to the behavioral results reported here, we also recognize that Fox News and MSNBC must know their viewers and are likely to cater to them, designing programs tailored to anticipated audience responses. The contemporary cable environment is polarizing in the same way elections are. These shows allow people to make choices and express their political orientations with their viewing habits.

We also find that people who choose to watch partisan cable shows in our studies tend to monitor both Fox News and MSNBC. We observe that the hosts on Fox News and MSNBC routinely reference the hosts and content of the other partisan news organization as well as mainstream and other more moderate media sources like CNN. Viewers of Fox News and MSNBC should be substantially more cognizant of the availability of partisan news, from both the Left and the Right. We hypothesize that this may affect beliefs about polarization, a possibility we consider next.

Partisan News and the Perception of Polarization

Could greater mass polarization be illusory and the perception of polarization rooted in a sort of media effect? Although we find little evidence that the fragmented media environment contributes to mass-level polarization, we are left with the reality that many Americans perceive the country to be more divided than ever before. We suspect that the rise of choice, and the ideologically variegated news environment it has wrought, may be at least partially responsible for the perception of polarization. Rather than causing polarization, partisan media may encourage viewers to think the country is more polarized.

We explore this possibility with data collected in the fall 2011 selective exposure experiment (SEE). Recall that participants were randomly assigned to watch a clip from a conservative show appearing on

Fox News (*The O'Reilly Factor*), a clip from a liberal show appearing on MSNBC (*Last Word with Lawrence O'Donnell*), a clip from an entertainment program appearing on basic cable (Animal Planet's *Pet Stars* or *For Rent* from HGTV), or a clip of their choice (the choice condition, in which they could change the channel among these shows). After watching the clip, participants answered questions about the fairness with which cable and broadcast news networks report the news as well as the effects that the news media have on the polity.

The numbers in the cells in table 8.2 are the mean responses to the question, "In presenting the news dealing with political and social issues, do you think [network] news deals fairly with all sides, or do they tend to favor one side?"[13] Participants gave their answers in terms of a four-point scale where 1 = always deals fairly with all sides, 2 = deals fairly with all sides most of the time, 3 = tends to favor one side most of the time, and 4 = always tends to favor one side. If we look at the responses in the control group, we get a sense of participants' baseline perceptions of network favoritism. Because perceptions of favoritism are likely influenced by the ideological lens through which people see the world, we display the mean responses broken down by conservatives, moderates, and liberals. The patterns that emerge are mostly unsurprising. Conservatives tended to perceive that Fox News is fair most of the time, while liberals tended to perceive that Fox News tends to favor one side. Likewise, liberals tended to believe that MSNBC is fair most of the time while thinking that Fox News tends to favor one side.[14] Moreover, on average, participants viewed both Fox News and MSNBC as expressing more favoritism to one side than do the broadcast news networks.[15] Even here, however, we observe a tinge of partisan reasoning. Liberals tended to think that MSNBC is as fair as they view broadcast news, and conservatives tended to think that Fox News is as fair as they view broadcast news.

Remarkably, exposure to the clips from Fox News or MSNBC did not substantially alter participants' perceptions of network favoritism. Liberals, moderates, and conservatives were no more likely to view either of the cable news or broadcast news networks as more or less one-sided after watching the Fox News clip, the MSNBC clip, or a clip of their choice.[16] Of course, a reasonable response is that our sample is too small to reliably detect the differences that do exist. It is certainly the case that a larger sample would allow us to estimate these means with greater precision, but, because these differences are so small, we are confident in concluding that, at most, these clips had a minor impact on people's per-

TABLE 8.2. **Perception of Network Favoritism by Treatment Assignment, Fall 2011 SEE**

	Network Favoritism Rating		
Network and Treatment	Liberals	Moderates	Conservatives
Fox News:			
Fox clip	2.4	2.2	2.3
MSNBC clip	2.6	2.3	2.5
Choice	2.8	2.3	2.0
Control	2.9	2.6	2.1
MSNBC:			
Fox clip	2.5	2.2	2.8
MSNBC clip	2.1	1.9	2.6
Choice	2.5	2.3	2.3
Control	2.1	2.6	2.8
Broadcast news (ABC, CBS, NBC):			
Fox clip	2.4	2.3	2.3
MSNBC clip	2.0	2.4	2.6
Choice	2.5	2.1	2.3
Control	2.1	2.0	2.2
N	55	36	36

Note: Higher numbers indicate that respondents in the subgroup perceive more favoritism toward one side of political issues most of the time in the rated networks. For full statistical model results, see table A8.3.

ceptions of a specific network's favoritism. These results are consistent with the work of Baum and Gussin (2008) and suggest that baseline perceptions of network favoritism are relatively fixed and unaffected by a single-shot exposure to network content.

Next, we turn our attention to participants' perceptions of the news media, broadly defined, and their impact. The items tapping these generalized perceptions use the standard semantic differential approach by placing opposing sentiments at the ends of a seven-point bipolar scale. Here, we are interested in whether watching proattitudinal or counterattitudinal shows affects participants' generalized perceptions. We calculated the mean score on each of the scales by treatment group and took the difference between each treatment group and the control group in order to estimate the effects of cable news shows on generalized media perceptions. The results are shown in figure 8.2. We find that watching cable news shows can influence viewers' perceptions of polarization. Moreover, an unexpected pattern emerges. We find a consistent effect emerging out of the choice group and less consistent effects emerging out of the forced treatment groups. Relative to participants in the control group, those assigned to watch either pro- or counterattitudinal clips

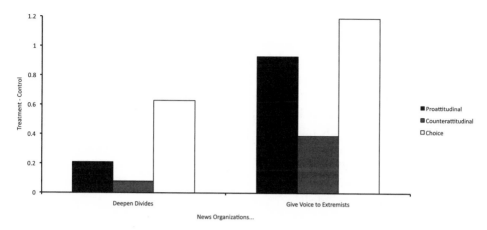

FIGURE 8.2. The effect of partisan news shows on evaluations on perceptions of the news media's effects, fall 2011 SEE.
Note: Bars represent difference in means between the treatment group and the control group. For the full statistical model results, see table A8.4.

were somewhat more likely to view news organizations as "deepen[ing] the country's political divides" and "giv[ing] too much voice to political extremists," but only in the latter case can we rule out chance as a possible explanation for the difference and only among forced exposure subjects assigned to the proattitudinal condition.[17] In contrast, subjects assigned to the choice group were considerably more likely than subjects in the control group to view the news media as a polarizing force.[18]

These results suggest that the presence of ideological news shows in the information environment may give rise to the perception of polarization. This is in stark contrast to evidence that allowing people to sort into their preferred content ameliorates the actual polarization we observe in the forced viewing conditions in chapters 4 and 5. The choice condition also allows people to directly observe the contrast between MSNBC and Fox News. Of course, one must keep in mind that in our experiment the choice condition is a stylized information environment in which political news predominates. Whether these effects would persist in a hyper-choice media environment is an open question.

It is worth noting that our stylized environment likely looks like the one in which many political observers immerse themselves. Politicians, pundits, and political communication researchers themselves keep tabs on the partisan media environment and are well aware of the contrasts it

offers. Stated bluntly, these politically informed groups most clearly ex-
emplify our news seekers, and they may be projecting broadly the polarization they see among friends and the elites to whom they pay close
attention. Much like these scholars and political observers, everyday citizens only naturally conclude that these shows must be having a polarizing effect when they are made aware that they are surrounded by news
shows promoting viewpoints at the extreme ends of the ideological spectrum. The politically interested viewers who attend to partisan media
may be particularly likely to perceive polarization. Compared to moderates, people with extreme political views are more likely to see the nation's politics as polarized (Judd, Van Boven, Huber, and Nunes 2012;
Van Boven, Judd, and Sherman 2012).

Limitations

Of course, our studies, like all studies, have limitations, and we would be
remiss to pass over them without comment. These include experimental
design issues as well as other theoretical considerations that fall outside
the scope of this project. It is impossible to cover everything interesting
about the contemporary media environment in a single book. As much
as anything else, recognizing the limitations of this work exposes several
areas for future research, discussed below.

With regard to the design of our experiments, some may wish to criticize the size of our studies. We have chosen to conduct many moderately
sized experiments and combine them in this chapter using the tools of
meta-analysis. Early on, we certainly considered conducting fewer, but
larger, studies. These are the trade-offs of experimental research given
constrained resources, and we opted for an incremental approach in
which we maximized the number of studies. At any rate, we are more
concerned about the scope and types of choices we offered participants.
As we have noted throughout, one of the principal limitations to our
studies is that, in our most expansive viewing environment, we offer our
participants a choice of only four television channels. We surmise that
this allows for substantial opportunity to detect media effects. In spite
of our expectations, it could be that, had we provided study participants
with an expanded array of choices, they would have found their brand of
political news and acted more clearly on their preferences. More choice

might even create more channel surfing and a bigger accidental audience for partisan news, boosting effects minimized here. We doubt these possibilities, but it is worth noting that they cannot be ruled out.

Perhaps the biggest limitation of our studies is that we implicitly assume that the effects of partisan news are primarily direct. Additional research could show, for example, that, even if the intense partisans who prefer ideologically consistent news are not themselves made more extreme, the content of partisan news makes it easier for them to communicate talking points or report bias to political discussants. Similarly, these shows could motivate partisans to talk to others and make them more confident and persuasive in doing so. The two-step flow of information (Lazarsfeld, Berelson, and Gaudet 1948) could extend the reach of partisan media to entertainment seekers.

In a similar vein, partisan news may reach farther as a function of its influence on precisely those elite political actors likely to pay most attention to it. Given their tendency to appear on Fox News and MSNBC, it seems that public officials attend to partisan media. President Obama's concern over Fox News (Menand 2009) and the potential problems of partisan media more generally (Obama 2010) reflect his administration's attention to it.

While it may be the case that partisan news media play some role in shaping political attitudes and outcomes, our research suggests that it is unlikely to be a driving force in the American polity. We should take seriously the subtle and indirect ways in which the partisan news media influence politics, but we should also not imagine the partisan news media to be an all-encompassing behemoth. If we conceptualize news viewers as an *active audience*, as interpreters of information who bring something of themselves to the news they watch (as opposed to passive tabulae rasae), then we should also consider the ways in which partisan news consumers shape the ways in which the partisan media cover the news. Chaffee and Metzger (2001, 375), writing just as the political news media were beginning to fragment, offer a prescient view of the future for media effect researchers: "The key problem for agenda setting theory will change from what issues the media tell people to think about to what issues people tell the media they want to think about." We take up the challenge Chaffee and Metzger present and outline the paths we could take in future research that would help bring our understanding of media effects in line with the reality of an altered and fragmented media landscape.

An Agenda for Future Research

We see this book as the beginning, rather than the conclusion, of our research on choice and media effects. Like any initial foray into a topic, we hope to have answered some questions while raising others. We consider it worthwhile to propose a few next steps, building on the limitations we recognize in what we have accomplished thus far. We focus on the potential indirect effects of political communication and the implications of expanding the choice set offered viewers in experiments, and we consider scenarios in which the news environment offers little in the way of choice, for example, in the case of major political events like wars, natural disasters, and political campaigns. Finally, we recognize the potential effects of less bombastic political programming, such as hard news and mainstream news. In each of these possible paths of research, we believe that the motivational framework underlying our theoretical model helps illuminate the way forward by making clear that people's choices are driven by their goals. These goals are likely shaped by individual preferences and contextual influences, and we see a fruitful agenda dedicated to understanding the sources and implications of goal-directed media consumption.

A New Two-Step Flow of Information

The original two-step flow model posits that active consumers of political media channel messages they receive from the media to people in their social network less interested in politics (Katz and Lazarsfeld 1955). Further, these more politically interested discussants are granted esteem by less active news consumers who value their opinion on political matters. In this way, active information consumers become opinion leaders and can have the power to shape the opinions of individuals who tend to tune out political media. Yet these opinion leaders do not behave as straightforward conduits, simply parroting the news they obtain from mass media. Instead, in the process of transmission they augment media messages with their own interpretations. The indirect effects of media are shaped by selection processes—self-exposure as well as personal biases—and may influence these secondary audiences in nuanced ways.

However, we also anticipate other kinds of information flow. In fact, scholars are already beginning to work on the interaction among news networks. A good example is a set of studies conducted by Matthew Levendusky (2012). He demonstrates that partisan news media have the power to influence the issues covered and frames used in mainstream media news coverage, which suggests that the partisan news media may be able to indirectly influence individuals who do not watch partisan news shows through mainstream news programs. If so, the mainstream news media may work as an amplifier that allows the partisan news to set the agenda without having a large audience. Levendusky also demonstrates that partisan news media may cause those who do watch to be less tolerant of compromise. Since partisan news audience members tend to be more involved politically, elected officials may be more responsive to them than they are to individuals who tend to tune out the news.

More Expansive Choices

The amount of choice available affects consumer decisions and the selection of information. Theoretically, complexity and uncertainty in a choice environment could increase the predictability of behavior (Heiner 1983). Decisionmakers cope with expansive choices by applying heuristics, such as satisficing by selecting the first option they come across that "exceeds their aspiration level" (Scheibehenne, Greifeneder, and Todd 2010, 420) or selecting a default option. Fischer, Schulz-Hardt, and Frey (2008) find that the choice criteria that consumers employ vary with the number of information options. When presented with more options, people are more likely to attend to decision-consistent information. Consequently, it could be the case that, in an environment with more choices and a political decision at hand, more people will pay more attention to political information than we observe in our current studies.

In response to the greater costs associated with channel surfing through expanded options, we expect to see both more satisficing among viewers and thus more selection of second- and third-choice viewing options. We also expect to see more employment of partisan heuristics among partisan viewers. Consequently, we anticipate that more extensive viewing options will result in more partisan selectivity and weaker media effects overall than we observed in our studies. However, an alternative expectation could easily be that, in this expanded choice environment, viewers may be more likely to land on news programming overall, to avoid more costly and exhaustive channel searching across entertainment options. Even weak partisans with more moderate political perspectives may be more likely in this environment to employ a partisan heuristic to sort themselves into proattitudinal programming—again, to avoid exhaustive searching. Accordingly, more persuadable people may end up viewing programming that affects their judgments, leading to stronger media effects. A set of experiments that compares the effects of minimal and expansive choice environments would distinguish these alternative expectations.

Focal News Events

In the research reported here, we considered only viewing scenarios featuring a generous set of choices. As noted above, on occasion, the cable environment provides viewers with very little choice, as in the case of such major events as the terrorist attacks on September 11, 2001, and the devastation of Hurricane Katrina in 2005. These tragedies drew the attention of far larger audiences than news programming usually receives. Our model suggests that much of that audience was likely more susceptible to the framing of those stories than the members of a conventional audience for news would be.

On a less tragic note, political campaigns vary in their loudness, intensity, and potential influence (Zaller 1996). Campaigns attract more attention as election day draws near (Campbell, Converse, Miller, and Stokes 1960). As a consequence, we expect that the size of the inadvertent audience fluctuates temporally and geographically, affecting the mix of news and entertainment seekers in the actual audience for news, and raising the possibility that in the aggregate the net influence of political communication changes as the volume and intensity of a news story vary, whether it is a national tragedy or a political campaign being covered. It is also worth exploring whether the cycles of news coverage set the conditions under which news seekers *are* influenced by exposure to political news. As we observed in chapter 6, it is undoubtedly the case that news seekers are episodically influenced by news coverage when the topic of conversation shifts. We believe that the model we presented in chapter 3 provides an organizing framework for understanding how and when variation in public interest and the cyclicity of news coverage matters.

Cable and Mainstream Hard News

We have focused on opinionated news talk shows here in part because we believe that these shows motivate the greatest normative concerns about media influence today—outside violent video games and pornography. We also expect that partisan news *talk* shows are more likely the types of shows that engender polarization and the other media effects we study here than are other types of partisan news shows. The next step is to bring mainstream news (e.g., *NBC Nightly News with Brian Williams*) and hard news programming from MSNBC and Fox News into the mix.

Mainstream news and its contrasts with partisan cable news are particularly interesting because this comparison invokes the differences between the news media of today and news at the inception of cable television in the 1980s. Thirty years ago, the news environment was effectively dominated by a common conversation informed by the priorities of the three major news networks. We hope to contrast the effects of a choice set dominated by the common conversation with a choice set dominated by the lack of consensus in contemporary cable news. We hope to study the expectation of many pundits that this common conversation promoted unity. However, there is an equally compelling alternative expectation that the choice among mainstream news will do little to mollify political disagreement because partisan viewers filter the news through their own ideological lenses (Vallone, Ross, and Lepper 1985). Mainstream news may be just as effective as partisan news at affecting polarization in the viewing and interpretation of political information. Hard news presented with less invective by hosts like Shepard Smith on Fox News and Tamron Hall on MSNBC is also somewhat different from the talk shows we use here. These shows are less direct in their presentation of the biases of their networks while still reading news that is colored by those biases. Their hosts may also be more credible to many viewers than the opinionated bombasts whose shows follow them on the air. These programming differences may trigger different kinds of effects. However, we remain guided by our general expectations that the news seekers who populate cable news audiences are generally less persuadable than the entertainment seekers who move past the news readers and talking heads on their way to reality all-stars and sitcom reruns.

There are a variety of potential directions for future research, and we have no doubt that there are many other viable questions. There is much to be gained, for instance, from departing from single-shot studies of media effects in order to understand the dynamics of media choice and influence (for an excellent and rare example, see Druckman, Fein, and Leeper [2012]). As we observed in our studies, people who regularly expose themselves to partisan news shows are less likely to be influenced by single-shot doses of partisan media. But why is this the case? Are these individuals simply less likely to be moved, or does previous exposure to partisan news shows have a cumulative effect? In sum, this is truly an exciting time for researchers interested in studying news media.

Conclusion

Our research makes at least two contributions to the understanding of media effects. Substantively, we extend and build on the growing understanding of the contemporary media environment. Political communication today is characterized by diversity and competition among cable news and opinion shows that give rise to an increasingly polarized presentation of political information and in-your-face, vituperative commentary. We simultaneously replicate classic and contemporary research on persuasion, priming, framing, and televised incivility and also extend each of these to consider the implications of selective exposure to ideologically polarized talk shows and entertainment options.

In addition, we advance a new kind of experimental investigation of political communication envisioned by Bennett and Iyengar (2008), providing research participants controlled opportunities to self-select into exposure to different stimuli with the aid of two novel experimental designs: the selective exposure experiment and the participant preference experiment. Experimentalists using classic experimental designs for political communication research usually do not provide their subjects with choice when it comes to their consumption of political information—and for very good reasons. Nevertheless, this decision potentially distorts findings about the effects of political information. Scholars have assumed that the reception of political communication has equivalent effects across viewers, including those who would select out of the audience if they were given a choice. We address this blind spot in previous research by building choice over stimuli into the experimental design. We believe that these basic experimental designs, and others like them, can shed light on the influence of selective reception on other noted media effects.

The studies we report in this book strongly suggest that individual choice affects the impact of political communication. Future research will allow us to more fully investigate the conditions under which self-selection into political stimuli matters. The age of the large, inadvertent news audience is gone. We live in a new era in which the structure of mass media enables, if not encourages, an active audience. While this fact alone does not render the mass media unimportant—people can still be influenced by what they choose to consume—it does potentially alter *how* news media influence as well as *whom* they influence. Before us lies the task of disentangling the complex relationship between the preferences of the consumer and the media content they *choose* to consume.

Appendices

Chapter Three Appendix

Formal Model of Selective Exposure

We are ultimately interested in the effect of watching partisan news shows. We consider the effect of watching ideologically oriented news shows that are consistent with the viewer's predispositions, or *proattitudinal* news shows, and the effect of watching ideologically oriented news shows that are inconsistent with the viewer's predispositions, or *counterattitudinal* news shows. Our model of selective exposure posits that we should consider the fact that people possess different propensities to watch partisan news programs. News seekers like watching political programming, including partisan news programs, while entertainment seekers prefer to watch nonnews programming. Given these definitions, we model the effect of partisan news shows on political attitudes as

(1) $$E[A] = E[(A_n + \alpha_n p_n + \gamma_n c_n) + (A_e + \alpha_e p_e + \gamma_e c_e)],$$

where

A = political attitude of interest;
A_n = baseline political attitude among news seekers;
A_e = baseline political attitude among entertainment seekers;
α_n = weight measuring the amount of exposure to proattitudinal news shows among news seekers;
α_e = weight measuring the amount of exposure to proattitudinal news shows among entertainment seekers;

γ_n = weight measuring the amount of exposure to counterattitudinal news shows among news seekers;

γ_e = weight measuring the amount of exposure to counterattitudinal news shows among entertainment seekers;

p_n = effect of exposure to proattitudinal shows among news seekers;

p_e = effect of exposure to proattitudinal shows among entertainment seekers;

c_n = effect of exposure to counterattitudinal shows among news seekers; and

c_e = effect of exposure to counterattitudinal shows among entertainment seekers.

In a media environment that provides easily available choices among entertainment and news programming, news seekers will voluntarily expose themselves to more news programming than will entertainment seekers: $\alpha_n > \alpha_e$, and $\gamma_n > \gamma_e$. Theoretical models that assume homogenous effects also assume that the effect of pro- and counterattitudinal news is the same for news and entertainment seekers: $p_n = p_e$, and $c_n = c_e$. Finally, hypodermic needle models assume that partisan news shows are persuasive regardless of their content. Consequently, if one defines larger values of A as possessing attitudes that are more consistent with one's predispositions, watching proattitudinal news should make one's attitude even more extreme ($p_n > 0$, and $p_e > 0$), while watching counterattitudinal news should make one's attitudes less extreme ($c_n < 0$, and $c_e < 0$). In contrast, motivated reasoning models predict that watching proattitudinal shows should either reinforce preexisting attitudes or make them more extreme ($p_n \geq 0$, and $p_e \geq 0$) and that watching counterattitudinal shows should cause people to either dismiss the arguments or possibly adopt more extreme attitudes in the process ($c_n \geq 0$, and $c_e \geq 0$). Finally, we also consider whether the effects of partisan news are stronger among entertainment seekers than among news seekers: $p_e > p_n$, and $c_e > c_n$.

Note that our model allows baseline attitudes to differ among news seekers and entertainment seekers, which demonstrates an important point. For the sake of argument, assume that news seekers have more intense preferences than do entertainment seekers: $A_n > A_e$. Further, assume that partisan news has no effect: $p_n = 0$, and $c_n = 0$; and $p_e = 0$, and $c_e = 0$. Now, imagine that we conduct a survey in which we measure A for people who say they watch partisan news shows, like Fox or MSNBC, and for people who say they do not. Even though, by definition, we know that these shows have no effect, we will observe stronger attitudes among partisan news watchers than among those who do not watch partisan news shows because $A_n > A_e$. In fact, unless we can credibly assume that $A_n = A_e$, it would be difficult to estimate the effect of partisan news shows by simply observing the difference in attitudes between news seekers and entertainment seekers.

We address this issue by randomly assigning individuals to experimental conditions in which we vary what kind of television show they watch. The selective exposure protocol includes forced exposure conditions in which individuals are allowed to watch only a pro- or counterattitudinal show, a control group in which participants are allowed to watch only an entertainment show, and a choice condition in which participants can freely choose among the available news and entertainment options. Decomposing the model in equation (1) within each of these experimental groups yields

(2) $$E[A_{\text{control}}] = E[A_n + A_e],$$

(3) $$E[A_{\text{proattitudinal}}] = E[(A_n + p_n) + (A_e + p_e)],$$

(4) $$E[A_{\text{counterattitudinal}}] = E\,[(A_n + c_n) + (A_e + c_e)],$$

(5) $$E[A_{\text{choice}}] = E[(A_n + \alpha_n p_n + \gamma_n c_n) + (A_e + \alpha_e p_e + \gamma_e c_e)].$$

In the control group, no one is exposed to partisan news shows: $\alpha_n = \alpha_e = \gamma_n = \gamma_e = 0$. In the proattitudinal group, both news seekers and entertainment seekers are exposed only to proattitudinal news shows: $\alpha_n = \alpha_e = 1$, and $\gamma_n = \gamma_e = 0$. In the counterattitudinal group, however, both news seekers and entertainment seekers are exposed only to proattitudinal news shows: $\alpha_n = \alpha_e = 0$, and $\gamma_n = \gamma_e = 1$. Finally, the choice condition allows participants to select what shows they want to watch and set their own exposure weight.

Because participants are randomly assigned to these groups, the baseline attitudes should be the same, on average, across these conditions. As a result, if proattitudinal shows cause individuals to possess more extreme attitudes (i.e., $p_n > 0$, and $p_e > 0$), then $E[A_{\text{proattitudinal}}] >$

$E[A_{\text{control}}]$. If the hypodermic model is correct (i.e., $c_n < 0$, and $c_e < 0$), exposure to counterattitudinal shows should moderate attitudes: $E[A_{\text{counterattitudinal}}] < E[A_{\text{control}}]$. If, on the other hand, the motivated reasoning model is correct, exposure to counterattitudinal shows may actually strengthen attitudes: $E[A_{\text{counterattitudinal}}] > E[A_{\text{control}}]$. Finally, we can also test whether allowing choice attenuates the effect of partisan news shows by demonstrating that those attitudes in the choice condition are smaller than they are in the forced conditions: $E[A_{\text{choice}}] < E[A_{\text{proattitudinal}}]$, and $E[A_{\text{choice}}] < E[A_{\text{counterattitudinal}}]$. And we can also test whether the choice group is not different from attitudes in the control condition: $E[A_{\text{choice}}] = E[A_{\text{control}}]$.

The participant preference design allows us to explain why choice attenuates the effects of partisan news by providing an a priori indicator of news seekers and entertainment seekers. As a result, we can directly estimate p_n, p_e, c_n, and c_e by comparing the forced exposure conditions to one another separately for news seekers and entertainment seekers. If our hypothesis is correct, then $p_n < p_e$, and $c_n < c_e$.

TABLE A3.1. **Average Time Spent Watching Political Shows in Choice Condition, Selective Exposure Experiments**

	Winter 2009 SEE	Spring 2009 SEE	Summer 2009 SEE	Fall 2009 SEE	Winter 2010 SEE	Fall 2011 SEE
Conservative show:						
Full sample	N.A.	N.A.	N.A.	325.083	164.842	83.444
				(51.009)	(34.395)	(17.888)
Conservatives	N.A.	N.A.	N.A.	152.175	282.789	112.546
				(66.784)	(92.838)	(42.947)
Moderates	N.A.	N.A.	N.A.	483.142	193.236	100.643
				(130.813)	(92.883)	(37.519)
Liberals	N.A.	N.A.	N.A.	309.038	108.209	55.400
				(62.254)	(32.342)	(19.553)
Liberal show:						
Full sample	269.592	382.413	237.396	319.340	230.246	144.578
	(36.030)	(47.966)	(35.751)	(48.989)	(40.001)	(23.690)
Conservatives	338.562	358.710	194.354	348.825	197.192	111.455
	(114.530)	(100.339)	(57.961)	(131.364)	(67.582)	(40.001)
Moderates	305.682	351.756	213.488	190.617	161.039	112.357
	(58.809)	(74.174)	(62.518)	(80.773)	(57.318)	(39.492)
Liberals	210.823	431.193	300.200	360.241	258.242	185.350
	(46.783)	(82.989)	(64.135)	(65.668)	(57.593)	(39.453)

Note: Numbers in cells are time spent watching shows measured in seconds; standard errors are given in parentheses. N.A. = not applicable.

Viewing Behavior in Choice Condition of Selective
Exposure Experiments

For a more detailed accounting of viewing patterns in the choice conditions of the selective exposure experiments, see table A3.1. We report average viewing times for the full sample, as well as for ideological subgroups.

Preface to the Chapters 4–8 Appendices

Common Elements for All Statistical Analyses

In the statistical analyses described below, the following measures are common across all studies:

> *Proattitudinal.* Indicator variable measuring exposure to proattitudinal news clips (1 = exposed).
> *Counterattitudinal.* Indicator variable measuring exposure to counterattitudinal news clips (1 = exposed).
> *Forced Moderates.* Indicator-variable moderates who were exposed to one of the news clips (1 = exposed).
> *Choice.* Indicator variable in selective exposure studies measuring assigned to choice condition (1 = exposed).
> *Ideology.* When it comes to your own politics, would you say that you are very conservative, somewhat conservative, moderate, somewhat liberal, or very liberal?

We report treatment effect estimates along with standard errors or test statistics in the chapter appendices. Using this information, we calculate exact p-values, which are reported in relevant notes within chapters. We report one-tailed p-values when we are testing a directional hypothesis and two-tailed p-values when either the hypothesis under scrutiny does not make a directional prediction or the observed effect is in the opposite direction. Interested readers can convert one-tailed p-values to two-tailed p-values by multiplying the p-value by 2. Conversely, two-tailed p-values can be converted to one-tailed p-values by dividing the p-value by 2.

Chapter Four Appendix

Question Wording, Coding, and Results

SPRING 2009 SEE

Economy. How do you feel about how Barack Obama is handling the economy? Do you strongly disapprove, somewhat disapprove, somewhat approve, or strongly approve? 1 = strongly disapprove, 2 = somewhat disapprove, 3 = somewhat approve, 4 = strongly approve.

Iraq. How do you feel about how Barack Obama is handling the situation in Iraq? Do you strongly disapprove, somewhat disapprove, somewhat approve, or strongly approve? 1 = strongly disapprove, 2 = somewhat disapprove, 3 = somewhat approve, 4 = strongly approve.

Health Care. How do you feel about how Barack Obama is handling health care policy? Do you strongly disapprove, somewhat disapprove, somewhat approve, or strongly approve? 1 = strongly disapprove, 2 = somewhat disapprove, 3 = somewhat approve, 4 = strongly approve.

Terrorism. How do you feel about how Barack Obama is handling terrorist threats? Do you strongly disapprove, somewhat disapprove, somewhat approve, or strongly approve? 1 = strongly disapprove, 2 = somewhat disapprove, 3 = somewhat approve, 4 = strongly approve.

Immigration. How do you feel about how Barack Obama is handling immigration? Do you strongly disapprove, somewhat disapprove, somewhat approve, or strongly approve? 1 = strongly disapprove, 2 = somewhat disapprove, 3 = somewhat approve, 4 = strongly approve.

Overall. How do you feel about the job that Barack Obama is doing as president? Do you strongly approve, somewhat approve, somewhat disapprove, or strongly disapprove? 1 = strongly disapprove, 2 = somewhat disapprove, 3 = somewhat approve, 4 = strongly approve.

For the analyses, these items were recoded such that higher values indicated predisposition-consistent attitudes: approval for liberals and disapproval for conservatives.

FALL 2009 SEE

Party Rating. Which party in Congress do you trust to do a better job with health care? 1 = strongly trust Democrats, 2 = trust Democrats more, 3 = slightly trust Democrats more, 4 = trust neither party, 5 = slightly trust Republicans more, 6 = trust Republicans more, 7 = strongly trust Republicans.

Personal Impact. From what you've heard or read, do you think the changes to the health care system under consideration in Congress will mostly help you personally, will mostly hurt you personally, or don't you think they will have much of an effect on you personally? 1 = health care changes will mostly help me personally, 2 = health care changes will mostly hurt me personally, 3 = health care changes will not have much of an effect on me personally.

Public Option. Would you favor or oppose the government offering everyone a government-administered health insurance plan—something like the Medicare coverage that people sixty-five and older get—that would compete with private health insurance plans? 1 = strongly oppose, 2 = oppose, 3 = slightly oppose, 4 = slightly favor, 5 = favor, 6 = strongly favor.

Individual Mandate. Do you support or oppose requiring people to have health insurance? 1 = strongly oppose, 2 = oppose, 3 = slightly oppose, 4 = slightly favor, 5 = favor, 6 = strongly favor.

Tax Wealthy. Do you support or oppose raising taxes on families with incomes of more than $350,000 as a way to pay for changes to the health care system? 1 = strongly oppose, 2 = oppose, 3 = slightly oppose, 4 = slightly favor, 5 = favor, 6 = strongly favor.

For the analyses, these items were recoded such that higher values indicated predisposition-consistent attitudes. For liberals, higher values = trust Democrats, see health care as helping, favor public option, favor individual mandate, favor taxing the wealthy. For conservatives, higher values = trust Republicans, see health care as hurting, oppose public option, oppose individual mandate, oppose taxing the wealthy.

WINTER 2010 SEE

We used the same presidential approval items employed in the fall 2009 SEE. Items were recoded in predisposition-consistent fashion and summed into an index (see explanation in chapter 4).

FALL 2011 PPE

Party Rating. Which party do you trust to do a better job with tax policy? 1 = strongly trust Democrats, 2 = trust Democrats more, 3 = slightly trust

Democrats more, 4 = trust neither party, 5 = slightly trust Republicans
more, 6 = trust Republicans more, 7 = strongly trust Republicans.

Tax the Rich. Households that earn over $250,000 a year should pay more in
taxes. 1 = strongly disagree, 2 = disagree, 3 = somewhat disagree, 4 =
somewhat agree, 5 = agree, 6 = strongly agree.

Lower Taxes. The economy would start growing again if we just lowered taxes
on corporations and businesses. 1 = strongly disagree, 2 = disagree, 3 =
somewhat disagree, 4 = somewhat agree, 5 = agree, 6 = strongly agree.

Tax System Unfair. The American tax system is unfair because the rich do
not pay their fair share in taxes. 1 = strongly disagree, 2 = disagree, 3 =
somewhat disagree, 4 = somewhat agree, 5 = agree, 6 = strongly agree.

For the analyses, these items were recoded such that higher values indicated predisposition-consistent attitudes. For liberals, higher values = trust Democrats, strongly agree with taxing the rich, strongly disagree with lowering taxes, and strongly agree with sentiment that tax system is tipped in favor of the rich. For conservatives, higher values = trust Republicans, strongly disagree with taxing the rich, strongly agree with lowering taxes, and strongly disagree with sentiment that tax system is tipped in favor of the rich.

The full model results for the analyses presented in chapter 4 can be found in tables A4.1–A4.4.

TABLE A4.1. **The Effects of Partisan News on Presidential Approval, Spring 2009 SEE**

	Economy	Iraq	Health Care	Terrorism	Immigration	Overall
Proattitudinal	.385	.149	.056	−.081	−.058	.091
	(.240)	(.215)	(.228)	(.216)	(.227)	(.218)
Counterattitudinal	−.244	−.241	−.185	−.213	.127	−.285
	(.266)	(.239)	(.255)	(.240)	(.252)	(.242)
Choice	.034	−.018	.056	.068	.174	.193
	(.150)	(.135)	(.144)	(.135)	(.143)	(.136)
Liberal	.845	1.010	1.224	1.363	.890	1.525
	(.178)	(.160)	(.168)	(.161)	(.169)	(.161)
Conservative	.269	−.007	.371	.246	.221	.271
	(.183)	(.165)	(.177)	(.165)	(.174)	(.167)
Forced moderates	−.224	−.205	.143	.100	.014	−.020
	(.298)	(.268)	(.283)	(.278)	(.291)	(.271)
Constant	2.042	2.115	1.948	1.900	1.986	1.747
	(.149)	(.136)	(.142)	(.134)	(.141)	(.136)
N	180	180	179	179	177	181
R^2	.23	.34	.31	.39	.19	.47

Note: OLS slope coefficients are given in cells; standard errors are given in parentheses.

TABLE A4.2. **The Effect of Partisan News Shows on Issue Attitudes, Fall 2009 SEE**

	Party Rating	Personal Impact	Public Option	Individual Mandate	Tax Wealthy
Proattitudinal	.768	.422	.660	−.161	.211
	(.361)	(.231)	(.391)	(.427)	(.471)
Counterattitudinal	.394	−.222	.908	.576	.388
	(.394)	(.253)	(.428)	(.467)	(.515)
Choice	.053	.169	.122	.193	−.285
	(.268)	(.172)	(.290)	(.317)	(.350)
Liberal	1.899	.343	1.030	.881	.550
	(.308)	(.197)	(.334)	(.364)	(.402)
Conservative	.224	−.171	−.453	−.349	−.202
	(.377)	(.242)	(.409)	(.446)	(.493)
Forced moderate	−.292	−.210	−.326	−.040	−1.690
	(.541)	(.347)	(.587)	(.641)	(.707)
Constant	3.292	−.076	3.183	3.183	3.833
	(.337)	(.216)	(.365)	(.398)	(.440)
N	117	117	117	117	117
R^2	.46	.16	.29	.15	.16

Note: OLS slope coefficients are given in cells; standard errors are given in parentheses.

TABLE A4.3. **The Effect of Partisan News Shows on Evaluations of Presidential Job Performance, Winter 2010 SEE**

	β
Proattitudinal	.236
	(.119)
Counterattitudinal	.113
	(.130)
Choice	.125
	(.105)
Liberal	−.856
	(.150)
Conservative	−.114
	(.158)
Forced moderate	−.112
	(.207)
Constant	3.546
	(.155)
N	132
R^2	.44

Note: OLS slope coefficients are given in cells; standard errors are given in parentheses. Dependent variable = approval of Obama index.

TABLE A4.4. **The Effects of Partisan News on Tax Policy Attitudes, among News Seekers and Entertainment Seekers, Fall 2011 PPE**

	Party Rating	Tax the Rich	Lower Taxes	Tax System Unfair
Proattitudinal	.753	.807	.789	.995
	(.201)	(.253)	(.242)	(.251)
Counterattitudinal	.424	.679	.763	.790
	(.196)	(.245)	(.236)	(.244)
Prefer news	.732	.244	.610	.486
	(.193)	(.243)	(.232)	(.241)
Proattitudinal × prefer news	−.845	−.604	−.818	−.953
	(.295)	(.371)	(.355)	(.368)
Counterattitudinal × prefer news	−.229	−.154	−.410	−.267
	(.288)	(.363)	(.348)	(.362)
Moderate assigned to *O'Reilly*	−.570	−1.216	−.857	−1.422
	(.291)	(.366)	(.351)	(.363)
O'Reilly moderate × prefer news	−.534	−.142	−1.189	−.612
	(.525)	(.661)	(.632)	(.655)
Moderate assigned to *Last Word*	−.768	−1.282	−1.056	−1.484
	(.270)	(.340)	(.325)	(.336)
Last Word moderate × prefer news	−.810	−.107	−1.324	−.408
	(.483)	(.607)	(.581)	(.601)
Constant	4.483	3.782	3.770	3.770
	(.133)	(.168)	(.160)	(.166)
N	498	498	497	495
R^2	.15	.15	.18	.21

Note: OLS slope coefficients are given in cells; standard errors are given in parentheses.

Chapter Five Appendix

Question Wording, Coding, and Results

FALL 2009 SEE

Political Arguments. For the wording of the arguments, see chapter 5. Before reading the arguments, subjects read the following question stem:

> Now we would like you to evaluate several arguments for and against the current health care legislation in Congress. We understand that you may already have an opinion about health care reform, but we would like you to set your feelings aside and consider the arguments fairly. Please be as objective as possible. The arguments we have selected were sampled from activists, political parties, and organizations on both sides of the issue.

Subjects gave their responses in terms of a nine-point scale ranging from 1 = very strong argument to 9 = very weak argument.

For the analysis, these responses were coded so that larger values are attitude consistent. For liberals, 9 = strong for liberal arguments, and 9 = weak for conservative arguments. For conservatives, 9 = weak for liberal arguments, and 9 = strong for conservative arguments.

> *Need for Cognition.* On the pretest, subjects completed the short form need for cognition battery developed by Cacioppo, Petty, and Kao (1984). The exact wording for the battery is as follows:
>
> > Below is a list of statements. You will find that some of these statements describe you, and some will not, to various degrees. For each of the statements below, please indicate how well each statement describes you on the following scale: 1 = extremely *un*characteristic of you (not at all like you), 2 = somewhat *un*characteristic of you, 3 = uncertain, 4 = somewhat characteristic of you, and 5 = extremely characteristic of you (very much like you).
> >
> > 1. I would prefer complex to simple problems.
> > 2. I like to have the responsibility of handling a situation that requires a lot of thinking.
> > 3. Thinking is not my idea of fun.
> > 4. I would rather do something that requires little thought than something that is sure to challenge my thinking abilities.
> > 5. I try to anticipate and avoid situations where there is a likely chance I will have to think in depth about something.
> > 6. I find satisfaction in deliberating hard and for long hours.
> > 7. I only think as hard as I have to.
> > 8. I prefer thinking about small, daily projects to thinking about long-term ones.
> > 9. I like tasks that require little thought once I've learned them.
> > 10. The idea of relying on thought to make my way to the top appeals to me.
> > 11. I really enjoy a task that involves coming up with new solutions to problems.
> > 12. Learning new ways to think doesn't excite me very much.
> > 13. I prefer a task that is intellectual, difficult, and important to one that is somewhat important but does not require much thought.
> > 14. I feel relief rather than satisfaction after completing a task that required a lot of mental effort.
> > 15. It's enough for me that something gets the job done; I don't care how or why it works.

16. I usually end up deliberating about issues even when they do not affect me personally.

FALL 2011 SEE

Political Arguments. For the wording of the arguments, see chapter 5. We preserved the response set and coding protocol from the fall 2009 SEE while using a more appropriate question stem:

Now we would like you to evaluate several arguments for and against aspects of U.S. tax policy. We understand that you may already have an opinion about tax policy, but we would like you to set your feelings aside and consider the arguments fairly. Please be as objective as possible. The arguments we have selected were sampled from activists, political parties, and organizations on both sides of the issue.

Need for Cognition. On the pretest, subjects completed the same battery used in the fall 2009 SEE.

FALL 2011 PPE

Political Arguments. We used the same arguments, questions, and coding protocol used in the fall 2011 SEE.

Need for Cognition. On the pretest, subjects completed a shorter version of the need for cognition battery used in previous studies. We used the same question stem and response set:

1. I like to have the responsibility of handling a situation that requires a lot of thinking.
2. I try to anticipate and avoid situations where there is a likely chance I will have to think in depth about something.
3. I really enjoy a task that involves coming up with new solutions to problems.
4. Learning new ways to think doesn't excite me very much.
5. It's enough for me that something gets the job done; I don't care how or why it works.

News Preference. Imagine you had a choice among the four television shows listed below. Please rank these shows on the basis of how much you would like to watch them, with your most-preferred show at the top and your least-preferred show at the bottom:

____ *The O'Reilly Factor* with Bill O'Reilly on the FOX News Channel

_____ *The Last Word with Lawrence O'Donnell* on the MSNBC News Channel

_____ *Pet Star* on the Animal Planet network

_____ *For Rent* on the HGTV network

Subjects who ranked either *The O'Reilly Factor* or *The Last Word* as their most-preferred show were coded as preferring news.

The full model results for the analyses presented in chapter 5 can be found in tables A5.1–A5.2.

TABLE A5.1. **The Effects of Partisan News on Resistance to Opposing Arguments, Fall 2009 and Fall 2011 SEEs**

	Fall 2009 SEE		Fall 2011 SEE	
Proattitudinal	−.127	−.304	.229	−.920
	(.529)	(.756)	(.540)	(.739)
Counterattitudinal	1.289	.214	.223	−.440
	(.578)	(.787)	(.483)	(.660)
Choice	.342	.265	−.187	−.914
	(.393)	(.625)	(.391)	(.572)
Liberal	.607	1.217	1.345	1.011
	(.451)	(.642)	(.456)	(.656)
Conservative	−.137	.224	.594	−.053
	(.553)	(.891)	(.488)	(.694)
Forced moderate	.937	1.913	−.182	−1.128
	(.794)	(1.113)	(.626)	(1.139)
High NFC		1.069		−1.395
		(1.009)		(.922)
Counterattitudinal × NFC		2.667		1.463
		(1.162)		(.961)
Proattitudinal × NFC		.392		2.596
		(1.048)		(1.069)
Choice × NFC		.286		1.339
		(.820)		(.774)
Liberal × NFC		−1.270		.699
		(.915)		(.899)
Conservative × NFC		−1.292		1.388
		(1.165)		(.956)
Forced moderate × NFC		−2.194		1.686
		(1.598)		(1.383)
Constant	3.206	2.712	1.974	2.683
	(.494)	(.761)	(.471)	(.658)
N	117	117	127	127
R^2	.09	.17	.14	.23

Note: NFC = need for cognition. OLS slope coefficients are given in cells; standard errors are given in parentheses.

TABLE A5.2. **The Effects of Partisan News on Resistance to Opposing Arguments by News Seeking and Need for Cognition, Fall 2011 PPE**

Proattitudinal	.912	.587
	(.227)	(.338)
Counterattitudinal	.416	.392
	(.223)	(.325)
Prefer news	.850	.754
	(.219)	(.354)
Proattitudinal × prefer news	−.961	−.698
	(.335)	(.517)
Counterattitudinal × prefer news	−.517	−.801
	(.328)	(.544)
Moderates assigned to *O'Reilly*	−.754	−.548
	(.329)	(.482)
O'Reilly moderates × prefer news	−1.280	−.057
	(.593)	(1.513)
Moderates assigned to *Last Word*	−.609	−.540
	(.305)	(.429)
Last Word moderates × prefer news	−.748	−1.176
	(.561)	(.959)
NFC		−.198
		(.304)
Proattitudinal × NFC		.603
		(.458)
Counterattitudinal × NFC		.019
		(.449)
O'Reilly moderates × NFC		−.411
		(.662)
Last Word moderates × NFC		−.190
		(.614)
NFC × prefer news		.175
		(.453)
Proattitudinal × NFC × prefer news		−.492
		(.682)
Counterattitudinal × NFC × prefer news		.412
		(.690)
O'Reilly moderates × NFC × prefer news		−1.191
		(1.668)
Last Word moderates × NFC × prefer news		.706
		(1.198)
Constant	3.073	3.184
	(.150)	(.228)
N	492	492
R^2	.14	.15

Note: NFC = need for cognition. OLS slope coefficients are given in cells; standard errors are given in parentheses.

Chapter Six Appendix

Question Wording, Coding, and Results

FALL 2009 SEE

Health Care Issue Salience. Regardless of whether you favor or oppose the health care legislation that is currently being discussed, do you personally care about this issue a great deal, a fair amount, just some, or very little? 1 = care about the issue very little, 2 = care about the issue just some, 3 = care about the issue a fair amount, 4 = care about the issue a great deal.

WINTER 2010 SEE

Health Care Issue Salience. Regardless of whether you favor or oppose the health care legislation that is currently being discussed, do you personally care about this issue a great deal, a fair amount, just some, or very little? 1 = care about the issue very little, 2 = care about the issue just some, 3 = care about the issue a fair amount, 4 = care about the issue a great deal.

Most Important Problem. What do you think is the most important problem facing this country? Open-ended response.

Obama Performance Evaluation. For a description of question wording and coding, see the chapter 4 appendix.

FALL 2011 SEE

Most Important Problem. What do you think is the most important problem facing this country? Open-ended response.

SUMMER 2010 PPE

Most Important Problem. What do you think is the most important problem facing this country? Open-ended response.

News Preference. In a moment, you will be assigned to watch a television program—one of four options we have for you today. If you were given the choice, which of these shows would you most want to watch?

1. *Dog Whisperer with Cesar Millan.* Canine behavioral problems are discussed, and courses of treatment are suggested. *Dog Whisperer* documents the remarkable transformations that take place under Cesar's calm-assertive guidance.

2. *O'Reilly Factor.* The best-selling author mixes news, interviews, and

analyses and some of his most passionate commentaries. The conservative "No Spin Zone" has been the major factor in Fox News's climb (past CNN) to the top of the cable-news chart.

3. *Countdown with Keith Olbermann.* The program ranks the day's top five stories by what will likely be the next morning's hottest topics. Olbermann frequently offers a progressive "Special Comment" on the news.

4. *Dhani Tackles the Globe.* NFL linebacker Dhani Jones attempts regional sports around the world. By trying his hand at beloved national pastimes from around the globe, Dhani explores the way sports help define culture.

Subjects who chose either the *O'Reilly Factor* or *Countdown with Keith Olbermann* as were coded as preferring news.

FALL 2011 PPE

Most Important Problem. What do you think is the most important problem facing this country? Open-ended response.

Problem Definition. Please indicate how important each of these ideas is to you when you think about the question of federal tax policy. Please rank them in order of importance from most important to least important:

____ High tax rates on the wealthy

____ Not enough people paying federal taxes

____ Out-of-control government spending

____ Rich people not paying their fair share

____ Big corporations not paying enough taxes

____ Too many deductions

News Preference. For description of question wording and coding, see the chapter 5 appendix.

The full model results for the analyses presented in chapter 6 can be found in tables A6.1–A6.7.

TABLE A6.1. **The Effect of Partisan News on the Salience of Health Care Issue**

	Fall 2009 SEE	Winter 2010 SEE
Proattitudinal	.417	.484
	(.262)	(.253)
Counterattitudinal	.656	.637
	(.286)	(.276)
Choice	.099	.301
	(.194)	(.225)
Liberal	−.046	.132
	(.223)	(.319)
Conservative	.043	−.064
	(.274)	(.337)
Forced moderates	.275	−.489
	(.393)	(.440)
Constant	1.868	1.489
	(.244)	(.330)
N	117	132
R^2	.06	.12

Note: OLS slope coefficients are given in cells; standard errors are given in parentheses.

TABLE A6.2. **The Effects of Partisan News on the Salience of Income Inequality or Tax Policy, Fall 2011 SEE**

Proattitudinal	1.333
	(.995)
Counterattitudinal	−.280
	(1.272)
Choice	.499
	(.883)
Liberal	.000
	(.932)
Conservative	−.155
	(1.020)
Forced moderates	−.119
	(1.465)
Constant	−2.589
	(1.039)
N	127
Pseudo-R^2	.04

Note: Logit coefficients are given in cells; standard errors are given in parentheses. Dependent variable = income inequality or tax policy named most important problem.

TABLE A6.3. **The Effects of Different Agendas on Perceptions of the Most Important Problem, Winter 2010 SEE**

O'Reilly	.259
	(.642)
Olbermann	−.617
	(.585)
Choice	−.029
	(.552)
Liberal	−.663
	(.622)
Conservative	−.692
	(.682)
Constant	1.606
	(.713)
N	132
Pseudo-*R*2	.02

Note: Logit coefficients are given in cells; standard errors are given in parentheses. Dependent variable = economy named most important problem.

TABLE A6.4. **Priming Health Care Evaluations, Winter 2010 SEE**

Obama health care evaluation	−.046
	(.179)
Proattitudinal	−.748
	(1.090)
Counterattitudinal	−2.138
	(1.272)
Choice	−.517
	(.840)
Proattitudinal × Obama health care evaluation	.344
	(.337)
Counterattitudinal × Obama health care evaluation	.742
	(.388)
Choice × Obama health care evaluation	.155
	(.262)
Constant	3.062
	(.587)
N	132
R^2	.06

Note: OLS coefficients are given in cells; standard errors are given in parentheses. Dependent variable = overall evaluation of President Obama's performance.

TABLE A6.5. **Effects of Partisan News on Perception of Most Important Problem among News Seekers and Entertainment Seekers, Summer 2010 PPE**

Proattitudinal	1.145
	(.656)
Counterattitudinal	−.154
	(.721)
Prefer news	.000
	(.825)
Proattitudinal × prefer news	−1.751
	(1.382)
Counterattitudinal × prefer news	−.944
	(1.402)
Constant	−1.792
	(.549)
N	152
Pseudo-R^2	.07

Note: Logit coefficients are given in cells; standard errors are given in parentheses. Dependent variable = environment named most important problem.

TABLE A6.6. **Effects of Partisan News on Perception of Most Important Problem among News Seekers and Entertainment Seekers, Fall 2011 PPE**

Proattitudinal	.879
	(.457)
Counterattitudinal	.581
	(.466)
Prefer news	−.339
	(.552)
Proattitudinal × prefer news	−.192
	(.731)
Counterattitudinal × prefer news	.163
	(.726)
Moderates assigned to *O'Reilly*	.262
	(.712)
O'Reilly moderates × prefer news	.157
	(1.346)
Moderates assigned to *Last Word*	−1.136
	(1.077)
Last Word moderates × prefer news	1.332
	(1.562)
Constant	−2.159
	(.352)
N	500
Pseudo-R^2	.03

Note: Logit coefficients are given in cells; standard errors are given in parentheses. Dependent variable = income inequality or tax policy named most important problem.

TABLE A6.7. **Effects of Partisan News on Problem Definition among News Seekers and Entertainment Seekers, Fall 2011 PPE**

	Entertainment Seekers	News Seekers
Attitude-consistent option	.593	.788
	(.129)	(.128)
Proattitudinal × attitude-consistent option	.143	−.263
	(.176)	(.183)
Counterattitudinal × attitude-consistent option	−.353	−.121
	(.169)	(.182)
N	205	183
LR χ^2	65.54	82.99

Note: Rank-ordered logit coefficients are given in cells; standard errors are given in parentheses. Dependent variable = rank of problem definitions.

Chapter Seven Appendix

Question Wording, Coding, and Results

SUMMER 2008 FEE

Semantic Differential Items. Below, you will find a list of pairs of words. You are to rate the television clip on each of the scales in order. Here is how you are to use these scales. If you feel that the television clip was very closely related to one of the words in the pair, you should place your check mark as follows:

good __✓_:___:___:___:___:___:___:___:____ bad *or*

good ____:___:___:___:___:___:___:___:_✓_ bad

If you feel that the television clip was quite closely related to one of the words in the pair (but not extremely), you should place your check mark as follows:

good ____:_✓_:___:___:___:___:___:___:____ bad *or*

good ____:___:___:___:___:___:___:_✓_:___ bad

If you feel that the television clip was related to one of the words in the pair (but even less closely related), you should place your check mark as follows:

good ____:____:_✓_:____:____:____:____:____ bad *or*

good ____:____:____:____ ____:____:____:_✓_:____:____ bad

If you feel that the television clip was only slightly related to one of the words in the pair (but is not really neutral), you should place your check mark as follows:

good ____:____:____:_✓_:____:____:____:____ bad *or*

good ____:____:____:____:____:_✓_:____:____ bad

The direction toward which you check, of course, depends on which of the two ends of the scale seem most characteristic of the television clip. If you consider the television clip to be neutral on the scale, both sides of the scale are equally associated with the television clip, or the scale is completely irrelevant, unrelated to the television clip, then you should place your check mark as follows:

good ____:____:____:____:_✓_:____:____:____ bad.

IMPORTANT: (1) Place your marks in the middle of spaces, not the boundaries. (2) Be sure you check every scale. Please do not omit any. (3) Never put more than one check mark on a single scale. Make each item a separate and independent judgment. Work at a fairly high speed through this test. Do not worry or puzzle over individual items. It is your first impressions, the immediate feelings about each television clip, for each of these scales that we want. On the other hand, please do not be careless because we want your true impressions.

Word Pairs. Fair/unfair, friendly/hostile, good/bad, quarrelsome/cooperative.
Uninformative. In general, I found the television programming to be informative. 1 = strongly agree, 2 = agree, 3 = slightly agree, 4 = slightly disagree, 5 = disagree, 6 = strongly disagree.
Not Stimulating. This television programming gave me food for thought. 1 = strongly agree, 2 = agree, 3 = slightly agree, 4 = slightly disagree, 5 = disagree, 6 = strongly disagree.

SUMMER 2009 FEE

> *Semantic Differential Items.* Same as the summer 2008 FEE.
>
> *Uninformative.* Same as the summer 2008 FEE.
>
> *Not Stimulating.* Same as the summer 2008 FEE.

FALL 2009 FEE

> *Semantic Differential Items.* Battery employed in the summer 2008 and summer 2009 FEEs with the following additional word pairs: *balanced/ skewed, one-sided/even-handed, American/un-American.*
>
> *Uninformative.* Same as the summer 2008 FEE.
>
> *Not Stimulating.* Same as the summer 2008 FEE.
>
> *Host Rating.* For the next few questions, I'd like to get your feelings toward some of our political leaders and other people who are in the news these days. I'll read the name of a person, and I'd like you to rate that person using something we call the *feeling thermometer.*
>
> Ratings between 50 degrees and 100 degrees mean that you feel favorable and warm toward the person. Ratings between 0 degrees and 50 degrees mean that you don't feel favorable toward the person and that you don't care too much for that person. You would rate the person at the 50 degree mark if you don't feel particularly warm or cold toward the person. If we come to a person whose name you don't recognize, you don't need to rate that person. How would you rate the host of the television show you just watched?
>
> *Hostile Media Perceptions.* This is a factor score based on four items:
>
> 1. *Newspaper reporters.* How much of the time do you think you can trust newspaper reporters to do what is right?
> 2. *Newspaper columnists.* How much of the time do you think you can trust newspaper columnists to do what is right?
> 3. *Television reporters.* How much of the time do you think you can trust television news reporters to do what is right?
> 4. *Television pundits.* How much of the time do you think you can trust television news commentators to do what is right?
>
> Response set for all four items: 1 = just about always, 2 = most of the time, 3 = only some of the time.

Hostile television Perception. This is a factor score based on two television items only in the *hostile media perceptions* measure.

WINTER 2009 SEE

Hostile Media Perceptions. Same as the fall 2009 FEE.

SUMMER 2009 SEE

Political Trust. Unless indicated, all items have the same response set: 1 = strongly agree, 2 = agree, 3 = slightly agree, 4 = slightly disagree, 5 = disagree, 6 = strongly disagree. The values of reverse-coded items were flipped before taking the average. Higher values on the scale indicate higher levels of trust: Politicians generally have good intentions. Politicians in the United States do not deserve much respect. When politicians make statements to the American people on television or in the newspapers, they are usually telling the truth. Most politicians can be trusted to do what is right. Despite what some people say, most politicians try to keep their campaign promises. Most politicians do a lot of talking, but they do little to solve the really important issues facing the country. Most politicians are dedicated people, and we should be grateful to them for the work they do. As far as the people running Congress are concerned, I have a great deal of confidence in them. At present, I feel very critical of our political system. Whatever its faults may be, the American form of government is still the best for us. There is not much about our form of government to be proud of. How much of the time do you think you can trust members of the U.S. Congress to do what is right (1 = only some of the time, 2 = most of the time, 3 = just about always)?

Conflict avoidance. All items have the same response set: 1 = strongly agree, 2 = agree, 3 = slightly agree, 4 = slightly disagree, 5 = disagree, 6 = strongly disagree. The values of reverse-coded items were flipped before taking the average. Higher values indicate higher levels of conflict avoidance: I hate arguments. I find conflicts exciting. I enjoy challenging the opinions of others. Arguments don't bother me. I feel upset after an argument.

FALL 2009 SEE

Hostile Media Perceptions. Same as fall 2009 FEE.

Political Trust. Same as the summer 2009 SEE, except the following statements were *not* included: Politicians in the United States do not deserve much respect. Most politicians do a lot of talking, but they do little to solve the really important issues facing the country. Most politicians are dedicated people, and we should be grateful to them for the work they do.

SUMMER 2010 PPE

Affective Reactions. Drawn from the thought-listing task (for a description, see chapter 7). Thought-listing instructions: We are interested in what you were thinking about during the television show you watched. You might have had ideas all favorable to the host of the show you watched, all opposed, all irrelevant to the host of the show, or a mixture of the three. Any case is fine; simply list what it was you were thinking during the television show. The next screen will present a form we have prepared for you to record your thoughts and ideas. Simply type the first idea you had in the first box, the second idea in the second box, etc. Please put only one

TABLE A7.1. **Effects of Partisan News on Oppositional Media Hostility (Figures 7.1–7.4)**

Variable	Summer 2008 FEE			Summer 2009 FEE			Fall 2009 FEE		
	Counter	Pro	t	Counter	Pro	t	Counter	Pro	t
Fair/unfair	5.38	4.36	1.85*	5.56	3.76	2.70**	6.14	4.15	3.00**
Friendly/hostile	6.18	5.05	2.16*	6.40	5.41	1.70*	6.50	4.94	2.22*
Good/bad	5.32	4.74	1.02	5.44	3.59	3.68***	5.21	3.59	2.36*
Quarrelsome/ cooperative	3.32	4.18	1.64†	3.32	4.53	1.79*	3.14	4.68	2.10*
Balanced/ skewed							6.71	4.94	2.41**
One-sided/ even-handed							2.79	4.18	1.99*
American/ un-American							3.93	2.68	2.04*
Uninformative	3.53	3.00	1.52†	3.32	2.47	1.52†	2.93	2.03	2.77**
Not stimulating	3.68	3.12	1.51†	3.32	2.71	1.18	3.29	2.65	1.54†
Host rating							44.71	73.76	2.90**
Hostile media perception							.35	.00	1.84*
Hostile television perception							.22	−.02	1.30†

* $p < .05$ (one-tailed test).
** $p < .01$ (one-tailed test).
*** $p < .001$ (one-tailed test).
† $p < .10$ (one-tailed test).

TABLE A7.2. **The Effects of Partisan News Shows and Selective Exposure on Hostile Media Perceptions in One-Sided (Winter 2009 SEE) and Two-Sided (Fall 2009 SEE) Information Environments**

	Winter 2009 SEE	Fall 2009 SEE
Proattitudinal	−.371	−.223
	(.245)	(.248)
Counterattitudinal	.974	.596
	(.529)	(.271)
Choice	−.069	.389
	(.177)	(.184)
Liberal	.042	.161
	(.184)	(.211)
Conservative	−.205	−.220
	(.264)	(.259)
Forced moderates	.085	.344
	(.312)	(.372)
Constant	.062	−.302
	(.187)	.231
N	166	117
R^2	.04	.12

Note: OLS coefficients are given in cells; standard errors are given in parentheses.

idea or thought in a box. You should try to record only those ideas you were thinking about *during* the television show. Please state your thoughts and ideas as concisely as possible . . . a phrase is sufficient. *Ignore spelling, grammar, and punctuation.* You will have two and a half minutes to write your thoughts. We have deliberately provided more space than we think most people will need to ensure that everyone will have plenty of room to write the ideas they had during the message. So don't worry if you don't fill every space. Just write down whatever your thoughts were during the message. Please be completely honest about the thoughts that you had.

Participants listed 729 thoughts. Two graduate student coders evaluated the valence of the responses using a content analysis rubric. We randomly selected 10 percent of the sample for both coders to evaluate and found 78 percent intercoder agreement. Imperfect intercoder agreement increases random measurement error and makes tests of statistical significance more conservative.

TABLE A7.3. **The Effects of Partisan News Shows on Affective Reactions, by Viewing Preferences, Summer 2010 PPE**

Proattitudinal	−1.096
	(.394)
Counterattitudinal	−1.301
	(.382)
Prefer news	−.481
	(.439)
Proattitudinal × prefer news	.945
	(.686)
Counterattitudinal × prefer news	.801
	(.617)
Constant	.815
	(.290)
N	146
R^2	.09

Note: OLS coefficients are given in cells; standard errors are given in parentheses.

TABLE A7.4. **The Effects of Uncivil Debate on Political Trust, Summer 2009 SEE**

	Figure 7.7a	Figure 7.8
Forced	−.206	−.240
	(.161)	(.228)
Choice	.012	−.250
	(.149)	(.212)
Conflict aversion		−.277
		(.219)
Forced × conflict aversion		.061
		(.321)
Choice × conflict aversion		.511
		(.296)
Constant	3.647	3.789
	(.110)	(.157)
N	120	120
R^2	.02	.05

Note: OLS coefficients are given in cells; standard errors are given in parentheses.

TABLE A7.5. **The Effects of Partisan News on Political Trust, Fall 2009 SEE**

	Figure 7.7*b*
Forced proattitudinal	.221
	(.197)
Forced counterattitudinal	−.160
	(.215)
Choice	.115
	(.146)
Liberal	.090
	(.168)
Conservative	.384
	(.206)
Forced moderates	.006
	(.295)
Constant	3.089
	(.183)
N	117
R^2	.06

Note: OLS coefficients are given in cells; standard errors are given in parentheses.

The full model results for the analyses presented in chapter 7 can be found in tables A7.1–A7.5.

Chapter Eight Appendix

Meta-Analysis

In conducting the meta-analysis, we followed these steps:

1. Identify treatment effects for inclusion in the analysis. Three considerations inform which effects we include:
   a. Because all but one experiment focuses on the effects of pro- and counter-attitudinal news shows, we included the results from five of the six selective exposure experiments (the summer 2009 SEE is excluded) and both participant preference experiments.
   b. In order to avoid double-counting effects drawn from sequential analyses of the same underlying dependent variable measured in a single study, we include only the effects for which we had strong a priori expectations. Thus, for the polarization analysis from the spring 2009 SEE (chap-

ter 4), we include only the effects of partisan news on President Obama's handling of the economy because the show explicitly discussed Obama's handling of the economy. And, for the analysis of resistance to opposing arguments (chapter 5, the fall 2009 and fall 2011 SEEs), we include only the effects among high need for cognition subjects.

   c. In order to maintain comparability, we include effects drawn from the comparison of means. Consequently, we convert the logistic models of issue salience (the winter 2010 and fall 2011 SEEs and the summer 2010 and fall 2011 PPEs) to linear probability models before standardizing the effects. Because the framing effect analysis relies on rank-ordered logit (the fall 2011 PPE), we exclude these effects rather than including incomparable effects.

2. Standardize treatment effects by converting them to d statistics (for a fuller discussion, see chapter 8).

3. Combine treatment effects by taking the average of the d statistics for each of the treatment conditions in the selective exposure and participant preference experiments.

4. Calculate standard errors using the most conservative definition of the number of observations: n = number of studies, not number of effects.

Tables A8.1–A8.2 display the standardized treatment effects included in the meta-analysis of the selective exposure and participant preference experiments.

Perceived Polarization: Question Wording, Coding, and Results

FALL 2011 SEE

   Fox Favoritism. In presenting the news dealing with political and social issues, do you think the Fox News Channel deals fairly with all sides, or does it tend to favor one side? 1 = always deals fairly with all sides, 2 = deals fairly with all sides most of the time, 3 = tends to favor one side most of the time, 4 = always tends to favor one side.

   MSNBC Favoritism. In presenting the news dealing with political and social issues, do you think the MSNBC cable news deals fairly with all sides, or does it tend to favor one side? 1 = always deals fairly with all sides, 2 = deals fairly with all sides most of the time, 3 = tends to favor one side most of the time, 4 = always tends to favor one side.

   Broadcast Favoritism. In presenting the news dealing with political and social issues, do you think the network television news, such as ABC, NBC,

TABLE A8.1. **Meta-Analysis of Selective Exposure Experiments**

Chapter	Dependent Variable	Study	Proattitudinal	Counterattitudinal	Choice
4	Polarization: economy	Spring 2009	.44	−.25	.03
4	Polarization: party rating	Fall 2009	.57	.28	.03
4	Polarization: personal impact	Fall 2009	.55	−.27	.23
4	Polarization: public option	Fall 2009	.56	.7	.09
4	Polarization: mandate	Fall 2009	−.12	.39	.14
4	Polarization: tax rich	Fall 2009	.15	.26	−.19
4	Polarization: Obama rating	Winter 2010	.42	.21	.27
5	Openness among high NFC	Fall 2009	.08	1.97	.33
5	Openness among high NFC	Fall 2011	1.17	.54	.26
6	Health care salience	Fall 2009	.51	.9	.13
6	Health care salience	Winter 2010	.56	.75	.33
6	Taxes/inequality MIP	Fall 2011	.48	−.04	.14
7	Hostile media	Winter 2009	−.39	1.08	−.07
7	Hostile media	Fall 2009	−.22	.74	.46
7	Political trust[a]	Fall 2009	.31	.22	.21

Note: NFC = need for cognition; MIP = most important problem.

[a] Negative effect in counterattitudinal condition is in the expected direction; consequently, $|d|$ is shown.

TABLE A8.2. **Meta-Analysis of Participant Preference Experiments**

			Entertainment Seekers		News Seekers	
Chapter	Dependent Variable	Study	Proattitudinal	Counter-attitudinal	Proattitudinal	Counter-attitudinal
4	Polarization: party trust	Fall 2011	.57	.32	−.07	.14
4	Polarization: tax rich	Fall 2011	.53	.42	.12	.33
4	Polarization: lower taxes	Fall 2011	.54	.49	−.02	.22
4	Polarization: unfair tax system	Fall 2011	.59	.49	.02	.32
5	Openness: full sample	Fall 2011	.63	.28	−.03	−.07
6	MIP	Summer 2010	.5	−.06	−.15	−.28
6	MIP	Fall 2011	.33	.22	.18	.22
7	Hostile thoughts[a]	Summer 2010	.65	.81	.09	.31

Note: MIP = most important problem.

[a] Negative effect is in the expected direction; consequently, $|d|$ is shown.

and CBS, deals fairly with all sides, or does it tend to favor one side? 1 = always deals fairly with all sides, 2 = deals fairly with all sides most of the time, 3 = tends to favor one side most of the time, 4 = always tends to favor one side.

Deepen Divides. Do you think news organizations deepen the country's political divides or have little effect on political divisions? 1 = deepen the country's political divides, 4 = neither applies, 7 = have little effect on political divisions. Recoded such that the scale is flipped—that is, 1 = have little effect on political divisions and 7 = deepen the country's political divides.

Give Voice to Extremist. Do you think news organizations give too much voice to political extremists or pay enough attention to moderates? 1 = give too much voice to political extremists, 4 = neither applies, 7 = pay

TABLE A8.3. **Perception of Network Favoritism by Treatment Assignment, Fall 2011 SEE**

	Fox News Favoritism	MSNBC Favoritism	Broadcast News Favoritism
Fox News clip	−.378	−.378	.333
	(.481)	(.429)	(.435)
MSNBC clip	−.314	−.742	.429
	(.505)	(.450)	(.457)
Choice	−.267	−.333	.133
	(.445)	(.397)	(.403)
Liberal	.267	−.467	.133
	(.445)	(.397)	(.403)
Conservative	−.500	.200	.200
	(.472)	(.421)	(.427)
Fox News clip × liberal	−.089	.744	−.067
	(.596)	(.532)	(.539)
MSNBC × liberal	.048	.709	−.562
	(.615)	(.549)	(.557)
Choice × liberal	−.267	.650	.233
	(.445)	(.476)	(.483)
Fox News clip × conservative	.528	.328	−.283
	(.701)	(.625)	(.634)
MSNBC × conservative	.714	.543	−.029
	(.634)	(.567)	(.575)
Choice × conservative	.167	−.133	.000
	(.578)	(.516)	(.523)
Constant	2.600	2.600	2.000
	(.385)	(.344)	(.349)
N	127	127	127
R^2	.11	.10	.06

Note: OLS coefficients are given in cells; standard errors are given in parentheses.

TABLE A8.4. **The Effect of Partisan News Shows on Evaluations of Perceptions of the News Media's Effects, Fall 2011 SEE**

	Deepen Divides	Give Voice to Extremist
Proattitudinal	.210	.928
	(.516)	(.477)
Counterattitudinal	.082	.391
	(.462)	(.426)
Choice	.632	1.190
	(.374)	(.345)
Liberal	.177	.347
	(.436)	(.402)
Conservative	−.294	.256
	(.466)	(.431)
Forced moderates	−.426	.955
	(.599)	(.553)
Constant	5.176	4.108
	(.451)	(.416)
N	127	127
R^2	.07	.10

Note: OLS slope coefficients are given in cells; standard errors are given in parentheses.

enough attention to moderates. Recoded such that the scale is flipped—that is, 1 = pay enough attention to moderates and 7 = give too much voice to political extremists.

The full model results for the analyses presented in chapter 8 can be found in tables A8.3–A8.4.

Notes

Chapter One

1. For simplicity's sake, when we refer to *cable television*, we implicitly include satellite television since the programming packages and multichannel offerings are similar across both platforms.

2. A similar expansion of choice has spawned tremendous interest in political communication and the Internet (e.g., Lawrence, Sides, and Farrell 2010; Nie, Miller, Golde, Butler, and Winneg 2010). We focus on television and the choices afforded by cable.

3. The sixteen-member commission was chaired by the economist Edward S. Mason, dean emeritus of Harvard University's Graduate School of Public Administration. The commission's membership was composed of political leaders such as the mayors of Atlanta and Boston, public policy experts from the Brookings Institution, the Urban Institute, and the Rand Corp., and other scholars, including James Q. Wilson of Harvard.

4. At first blush, it may seem like a contradiction to say that people make purposive viewing decisions and yet may be exposed to oppositional news programs. Although many people do prefer like-minded news shows over those with ideologically inconsistent views, some people appear to seek out opposing viewpoints or, at the very least, do not actively avoid them (Garrett 2009a, 2009b; Stroud 2011). Furthermore, we should also recognize that there are moments when people's ability to act on their preferences is constrained, such as when they endure a television show (perhaps on Fox News or MSNBC) while they wait to see their dentist, get their car serviced, or catch a plane.

Chapter Two

1. Authoritative reviews of research on the effects of mass media include Perse (2001), DeFleur and Ball-Rokeach (1989), and Kinder (1998).

2. Wei and Lo (2007) extend these basic findings to the perceived effects of negative campaign advertisements. Viewers tended to believe that an attack on a political opponent would be a more effective influence on others' opinions than on their own.

3. Interestingly, both Lippmann and Addison 130 years earlier use the word *liberty* in the titles of treatises calling for constraints on the content of news and publishing.

4. These tools are not as extreme as the Sedition Act, but public officials use them to punish political disagreement.

5. Satellite television is similar, except that the signal is sent wirelessly to a home and converted by a set-top box into a viewable signal on the television.

6. Related research shows that, as newspapers in the nineteenth century began relying on advertising revenue, they became more independent of political parties (Petrova 2011).

7. For instance, Melissa Harris-Perry, a Tulane University political scientist, has been a frequent guest of Maddow's and other hosts on MSNBC and developed her own weekend program for the network.

Chapter Three

1. We counted *CBS Evening News*, *ABC World News*, and *NBC Nightly News* as major broadcast news shows. Fox's opinionated talk shows included programs hosted by Sean Hannity and Glenn Beck as well as *The O'Reilly Factor* with Bill O'Reilly. MSNBC's talk shows included *Countdown with Keith Olbermann*, *Hardball with Chris Matthews*, and *The Rachel Maddow Show*. Pew interviewed 3,006 respondents and asked all of them about specific talk shows. We identified 446 respondents (14.8 percent) who regularly watch Fox News talk shows and 189 (6.3 percent) who regularly watch MSNBC talk shows. We used the full sample to identify inattentive people (203 [6.8 percent]). The survey restricted questions about broadcast newscasts to 1,509 respondents. Of these, 466 (30.9 percent) regularly watch broadcast news.

2. Our broad conceptualization of motivation mirrors work in psychology that has identified a set of motivations that commonly guide individual behavior—including the *epistemic* motivation to hold accurate beliefs (see Kruglanski 1989), the *defensive* motivation to uphold one's beliefs (see Kunda 1990), and the *hedonic* motivation to seek out pleasure and avoid pain (see Higgins 1997).

3. Even in authoritarian states, individual motivations to view types of programming (i.e., news vs. entertainment) on television affect the reach and influence of political messages (Kern and Hainmueller 2009).

4. There are a number of mechanisms through which individuals can discount counterattitudinal information. They could view the source as untrustworthy (Hovland and Weiss 1951). They could see the arguments themselves as weak and unpersuasive (Taber and Lodge 2006). They could also use different evaluative criteria than the one invoked by what they would concede is a strong counterattitudinal argument (Gerber and Green 1999)—a liberal who values fair treatment of the accused would be unmoved by the argument that harsh interrogation tactics are effective. Other possibilities surely remain. Nonetheless, we are less interested in identifying the mechanism by which people change or maintain attitudes than we are in establishing how people respond to partisan news shows.

5. It is important to note that differences across randomly constructed groups can happen by chance in any given sample. If we were to conduct an infinite number of experiments using an infinite number of random samples and took an average of the differences across treatment groups, we would be certain that any differences were caused in some way by the treatment. Of course, we cannot conduct an infinite number of experiments. Fortunately, we do not have to do so because it is possible to calculate the probability that we would have observed a difference among treatment groups even if there was none. As long as that probability is low, we can proceed as if the observed difference was caused in some way by the treatment (for a more extended discussion of the interpretation of treatment effects in the context of political communication research, see Arceneaux [2010]). We report these tests of statistical significance in relevant notes and in the appendix.

6. The media scholar Dolf Zillmann and his colleagues used a research design similar to this in the late 1970s to study how children are affected by educational television when they are provided viewing alternatives (see, e.g., Wakshlag, Reitz, and Zillmann 1982; Zillmann and Bryant 1985; Zillmann, Hezel, and Medoff 1980).

7. We thank David Nickerson for suggesting this experimental protocol.

8. Because the focal point of our research is the effects of partisan news in a media environment that includes entertainment options, we do not study the effects of mainstream news programs in the current project. We discuss future research exploring broadcast news in chapter 8.

Chapter Four

1. Several of the essays in Friedman (1998), a special issue of *Critical Review*, elucidate these concerns, as does a recent exchange among political scientists in

PS: Political Science and Politics regarding the challenge that incivility among elites, played out in the mass media, presents democracy, introduced by Strachan and Wolf (2012).

2. Hannity and Rove discussed former assistant deputy education secretary Kevin Jennings's expressed admiration for the gay rights pioneer Harry Hay. Hay was apparently friendly to NAMBLA, but this was not the aspect of his work of which Jennings expressed approval (see Frederick, Schulman, Schweber-Koren, and Weiland 2009). To be abundantly clear, Hannity and Rove demonstrated no authentic connection between President Obama and Hay or NAMBLA.

3. One early reader of this book called our attention to the fact that Lord, Ross, and Lepper (1979) use several imperfect measures of attitude polarization in their study, relying primarily on self-reported attitude change, casting some doubt on their conclusions. They argue that their multiple measures inform a "congruence of data . . . [that] . . . gives us some confidence concerning the results reported" (Lord, Ross, and Lepper 1979, 2101 n. 1). Despite this seminal study's shortcomings, we believe that subsequent research supports the contention that, in the context of political controversies, people are motivated to process information in a biased fashion in order to preserve their prior attitudes and may adopt more extreme attitudes in the process.

4. Political scientists have discovered circumstances, particularly anxiety-inducing situations, in which people are more open to counterattitudinal arguments (e.g., Brader 2006; Civettini and Redlawsk 2009; Marcus, Neuman, and MacKuen 2000).

5. In some sense, moderates do not have a team for which to root (or, if they do, they have not revealed it to us), so it is not possible to capture the kind of group-centric heuristics that many citizens use to make sense of political issues (Brady and Sniderman 1985; Sniderman 2000). Nevertheless, like the rest of their compatriots, moderates possess core values and predispositions that may help guide how they weigh political messages when forming issue attitudes (Feldman 1988; Goren 2005; Zaller 1992). To tap these predispositions, we asked participants in some of our studies questions on the pretest survey about the appropriate role of government in society and how satisfied people were with their health insurance. On each, the attitudes of moderates tended to be closer to those of self-identified conservatives than to those of liberals.

6. Liberals in the forced proattitudinal group rated Obama substantially higher than did liberals in the control group ($p = 0.055$, one-tailed).

7. Difference of means test: $p = 0.358$, two-tailed.

8. $p = 0.826$, two-tailed.

9. If we partition the choice condition by liberals, conservatives, and moderates, there are still no differences in effects across these groups within the choice condition ($F[2, 171] = 0.13, p = 0.87$).

10. Proattitudinal messages caused individuals to trust the party aligned with

their ideological faction to do a better job with the issue of health care ($p =$ 0.018, one-tailed), to view health care as having an impact on them personally ($p =$ 0.036, one-tailed), and to adopt more extreme positions on the question of whether a public option should be included in health care reform legislation ($p =$ 0.047, one-tailed).

11. The forced message had no statistically significant effect on attitudes about party competence and personal impact and led people to take attitude-consistent positions on the public option ($p =$ 0.018, one-tailed) and the individual mandate ($p =$ 0.11, one-tailed).

12. Subjects assigned to the choice condition do not express attitudes that are different from those of the control group with respect to which party they trust to handle health care reform ($p =$ 0.84, two-tailed), the perceived personal impact of the legislation ($p =$ 0.32, two-tailed), opinion about the public option ($p =$ 0.68, two-tailed), view of the individual mandate ($p =$ 0.54, two-tailed), or preferences regarding taxing the rich ($p =$ 0.42, two-tailed).

13. As with the previous studies, we coded moderates as conservatives for these measures, but our reported findings are substantively similar to those we obtain from coding moderates as liberals.

14. The combined measure is reliable as an indicator of President Obama's job performance evaluation (Cronbach's $\alpha =$ 0.69).

15. Proattitudinal messages caused individuals to rate the president more consistently with their ideological predispositions ($p =$ 0.025, one-tailed). In the counterattitudinal condition, participants' ratings of Obama are not significantly different from the control group ($p =$ 0.386, two-tailed). We also do not find statistically significant differences between the choice group and the control group ($p =$ 0.236, two-tailed).

16. As with previous studies, we coded moderates as if they were conservatives. Because the fall 2011 PPE is considerably larger than the other studies, it is possible to estimate the effects of the partisan news shows separately for moderates, making this an inconsequential decision. In this sample, it appears that moderates actually behave much like liberals as the conservative and liberal shows tended to cause them to adopt more liberal positions. For details, see the appendix.

17. Among entertainment seekers, proattitudinal effects were as follows: party trust, $p <$ 0.001; tax the rich, $p =$ 0.001; lower taxes, $p <$ 0.001; unfair tax system, $p <$ 0.001. Again among entertainment seekers, counterattitudinal effects were as follows: party trust, $p =$ 0.02; tax the rich, $p =$ 0.003; lower taxes, $p <$ 0.001; unfair tax system, $p <$ 0.001. All p-values are one-tailed.

18. Among news seekers, proattitudinal effects were as follows (all p-values are two-tailed): party trust, $p =$ 0.669; tax the rich, $p =$ 0.456; lower taxes, $p =$ 0.912; unfair tax system, $p =$ 0.877. Again among news seekers, counterattitudinal effects were as follows: party trust, $p =$ 0.359 (two-tailed); tax the rich, $p =$

0.03 (one-tailed); lower taxes, $p = 0.084$ (one-tailed); unfair tax system, $p = 0.03$ (one-tailed).

19. Differences between news seekers and entertainment seekers with respect to proattitudinal news are as follows (all p-values are one-tailed): party trust, $p = 0.002$; tax the rich, $p = 0.052$; lower taxes, $p = 0.011$; unfair tax system, $p = 0.005$. Differences between news seekers and entertainment seekers with respect to counterattitudinal news are as follows (all p-values are two-tailed): party trust, $p = 0.427$; tax the rich, $p = 0.671$; lower taxes, $p = 0.240$; unfair tax system, $p = 0.461$.

Chapter Five

1. The persuasiveness items scale together (fall 2009 SEE: $\alpha = 0.65$; fall 2011 SEE: $\alpha = 0.68$).

2. These items scale together (fall 2009 SEE: $\alpha = 0.84$; fall 2011 SEE: $\alpha = 0.83$).

3. Following the protocol we used in chapter 4, we treat moderates as conservatives for the sake of parsimony. However, if we code them as liberal, the results do not change substantively.

4. Fall 2009 SEE: $p = 0.811$, two-tailed; fall 2011 SEE: $p = 0.672$, two-tailed.

5. $p = 0.028$, two-tailed.

6. $p = 0.645$, two-tailed.

7. Fall 2009 SEE: $p = 0.689$ (proattitudinal), and $p = 0.786$ (counterattitudinal), two-tailed; fall 2011 SEE: $p = 0.216$ (proattitudinal), and $p = 0.507$ (counterattitudinal), two-tailed.

8. Fall 2009 SEE: $p = 0.001$, one-tailed; counterattitudinal $\times$ need for cognition: $p = 0.012$, one-tailed. Fall 2011 SEE: $p = 0.073$, one-tailed; counterattitudinal $\times$ need for cognition: $p = 0.066$, one-tailed.

9. $p = 0.016$, one-tailed; proattitudinal $\times$ need for cognition: $p = 0.009$, one-tailed.

10. Fall 2009 SEE: $p = 0.386$, two-tailed; fall 2011 SEE: $p = 0.415$, two-tailed.

11. $\alpha = 0.81$.

12. Difference between news seekers and entertainment seekers with respect to proattitudinal news, $p = 0.002$, and counterattitudinal news, $p = 0.058$, one-tailed.

13. $p < 0.001$.

14. $p = 0.062$, two-tailed.

15. Proattitudinal, $p = 0.845$, and counterattitudinal, $p = 0.676$, both two-tailed.

16. $p < 0.001$.

17. $p = 0.033$, one-tailed.

18. Difference between low and high need for cognition participants with respect to the effect of proattitudinal news: $p = 0.081$, one-tailed; effect of proattitudinal news among participants high in need for cognition: $p < 0.001$.

19. Need for cognition does not moderate the effects of proattitudinal news, $p = 0.839$, or counterattitudinal news, $p = 0.445$, both two-tailed.

Chapter Six

1. Effect of proattitudinal show: $p = 0.057$ (fall 2009 SEE), and $p = 0.029$ (winter 2010 SEE). Effect of counterattitudinal show: $p = 0.012$ (fall 2009 SEE) and $p = 0.012$ (winter 2010 SEE). All p-values are one-tailed.

2. Effect of proattitudinal show: $p = 0.09$, one-tailed; effect of counterattitudinal show: $p = 0.826$, two-tailed (the effect is in the unexpected direction, and, therefore, a one-tailed test is not appropriate).

3. $p = 0.073$, one-tailed.

4. Fall 2009 SEE: $p = 0.613$, two-tailed; winter 2010 SEE: $p = 0.183$, two-tailed.

5. $p = 0.572$, two-tailed.

6. $p = 0.958$, two-tailed.

7. Difference between slope coefficients in counterattitudinal and control groups: $p = 0.029$, one-tailed.

8. $p = 0.156$, one-tailed.

9. $p = 0.555$, two-tailed.

10. $p = 0.04$, one tailed.

11. $p = 0.831$, two-tailed; the effect is very close to zero and, nonetheless, in the opposite direction than was predicted.

12. $p = 0.618$; the agenda-setting effect is significantly smaller among news seekers than among entertainment seekers, $p = 0.10$, one-tailed.

13. $p = 0.361$, two-tailed.

14. Entertainment seekers, $p = 0.023$, and news seekers, $p = 0.11$, one-tailed. Difference in effects of proattitudinal news between entertainment seekers and news seekers, $p = 0.793$, two-tailed.

15. Entertainment seekers, $p = 0.11$, and news seekers, $p = 0.09$, one-tailed. Difference in effects of proattitudinal news between entertainment seekers and news seekers, $p = 0.822$, two-tailed.

16. Proattitudinal, $p = 0.151$, and counterattitudinal, $p = 0.506$, two-tailed.

17. A Hausman test rejects the null hypothesis that these rank-ordered logit models for news seekers are not different from the models for entertainment seekers, $\chi^2(3) = 83.72$, $p < 0.001$.

18. $p = 0.417$, two-tailed.

19. $p = 0.036$, two-tailed.

Chapter Seven

1. Also quoted in Cappella and Jamieson (1996). For an assessment of the declining trust in the media, see Gronke and Cook (2007).

2. $p < 0.05$, one-tailed for all the items except *good/bad* and *quarrelsome/cooperative* in the summer 2008 FEE, which are statistically significant at $p < 0.10$, one-tailed.

3. Summer 2008 FEE: $p < 0.10$, one-tailed for both the *uninformative* and the *not stimulating* items. Summer 2009 FEE: $p < 0.10$, one-tailed for only the *uninformative* item. Fall 2009 FEE: $p < 0.01$ for the *uninformative* item; $p < 0.10$ for the *not stimulating* item, one-tailed.

4. These batteries were combined into a single score using factor analysis.

5. $p < 0.01$, one-tailed.

6. $p < 0.05$ for overall perceptions, and $p < 0.10$ for television perceptions, both one-tailed.

7. Counterattitudinal: $p = 0.034$, one-tailed; proattitudinal: $p = 0.067$, one-tailed.

8. $p = 0.697$, two-tailed.

9. Counterattitudinal: $p = 0.015$, one-tailed; proattitudinal: $p = 0.185$, one-tailed; choice: $p = 0.037$, two-tailed.

10. Proattitudinal: $p = 0.003$, one-tailed; counterattitudinal: $p = 0.0005$, one-tailed.

11. Proattitudinal: $p = 0.788$, two-tailed; counterattitudinal: $p = 0.304$, two-tailed; difference in effects between those who preferred entertainment and those who preferred news: $p = 0.087$, one-tailed.

12. It is also possible that the negative reaction among entertainment seekers stems in part from the fact that we forced them to watch news even though they stated a preference for something else. Although this is plausible, we minimized this possibility in the summer 2011 PPE by placing distance between the viewing preference question and the assignment to treatment and still found a similar pattern.

13. $p = 0.10$, one-tailed.

14. $p = 0.935$, two-tailed.

15. $p = 0.053$, one-tailed.

16. $p = 0.432$, two-tailed.

17. $p = 0.084$, one-tailed.

18. $p = 0.294$, two-tailed.

19. $p = 0.044$, two-tailed.

Chapter Eight

1. The proliferation of options for political communication via the Internet also has implications for the role of self-selection into ideologically congenial information (e.g., Garrett 2009a; Lawrence, Sides, and Farrell 2010; Nie, Miller, Golde, Butler, and Winneg 2010; Valentino, Banks, Hutchings, and Davis 2009).

2. We standardized the treatment effects to adjust for the different metrics on which the various dependent variables were measured. We used the standard Cohen's d statistic, which divides the observed treatment effect by the pooled standard deviation,

$$d = \frac{\bar{y}_1 - \bar{y}_2}{\sqrt{\dfrac{(n_1 - 1)s_1^2 + (n_2 - 1)s_2^2}{n_1 + n_2}}}$$

where the numerator = the difference in means of two measures, y_1 and y_2 (e.g., mean attitude in the treatment group and mean attitude in the control group), n_1 = the number of observations in the first group, n_2 = the number of observations in the second group, s_1 = the standard deviation of y_1, and s_2 = the standard deviation of y_2.

3. Note that this is a more conservative approach than using the number of observed effects. We cannot assume that the observed effects for different dependent variables drawn from the same study are independent of one another. By using the number of studies, we inflate the size of the standard error. We also conducted a meta-analysis that essentially weighted the studies by sample size, with effect sizes coming from larger studies receiving more weight than effect sizes coming from smaller studies, and obtained the same results, but generally with smaller standard errors. Because this precision-weighted analysis makes the assumption that the treatment effects are independent of each other, it generates biased standard errors that are smaller than they should be. Consequently, we report the results from the more conservative (but less standard) approach here.

4. Cohen (1988) considers effects sizes between 0.2 and 0.8 to be medium. We can reject the null hypothesis that neither proattitudinal nor counterattitudinal shows had the expected effect, on average ($p = 0.055$, and $p = 0.054$, respectively, one-tailed).

5. $p = 0.344$, two-tailed.

6. Proattitudinal > choice: $p = 0.059$, one-tailed; counterattitudinal > choice: $p = 0.025$, one-tailed.

7. The overall standardized effect of the choice condition ($d = 0.16$) is considered small by conventional standards (Cohen 1988), but we can reject the null hypothesis that it is no different from $d = 0$ ($p = 0.044$, one-tailed).

8. Proattitudinal: $p = 0.008$, one-tailed; counterattitudinal: $p = 0.086$, one-tailed.

9. Proattitudinal: $p = 0.418$, one-tailed; counterattitudinal: $p = 0.217$, one-tailed.

10. Proattitudinal (entertainment seekers) > proattitudinal (news seekers): $p = 0.019$, one-tailed.

11. Counterattitudinal (entertainment seekers) > counterattitudinal (news seekers): $p = 0.222$, one-tailed.

12. Levendusky (2009) finds that participants in lab-based experiments respond to polarized cues from elites both by being more receptive to those cues and by developing greater ideological consistency. However, scholars analyzing patterns over time in observational data do not all agree that ideological clarity in elite cues has caused the political attitudes of partisans to become more ideologically constrained over time (Bafumi and Shapiro 2009; Baldassarri and Gelman 2008).

13. For the broadcast networks, the prompt read "do you think network television news such as ABC, NBC, and CBS."

14. The difference in means between liberals and conservatives in the control group is statistically significant for the perceptions for both Fox News ($p = 0.046$, two-tailed) and MSNBC ($p = 0.059$, two-tailed).

15. Fox News ($M = 2.6$) vs. broadcast news ($M = 2.1$, $p = 0.025$, two-tailed); MSNBC ($M = 2.4$) vs. broadcast news ($p = 0.095$, two-tailed).

16. A joint test of significance failed to reject the null hypothesis that the means were significantly different from each other among the three ideological groups (Fox: $F[11,115] = 1.24$, $p = 0.27$; MSNBC: $F[11,115] = 1.12$, $p = 0.35$; broadcast: $F[11,115] = 0.63$, $p = 0.799$).

17. For the "deepen the country's divides" item: counterattitudinal, $p = 0.859$, and proattitudinal, $p = 0.685$, both two-tailed. For the "give too much voice to political extremists" item: counterattitudinal, $p = 0.362$, and, proattitudinal, $p = 0.054$, both two-tailed.

18. For the "deepen the country's divides" item: $p = 0.094$, two-tailed. For the "give too much voice to political extremists" item: $p = 0.001$, two-tailed.

References

Abelson, Robert P. 1986. "Beliefs Are Like Possessions." *Journal for the Theory of Social Behavior* 16, no. 3:223–50.

Abelson, Robert P., and James C. Miller. 1967. "Negative Persuasion via Personal Insult." *Journal of Experimental Social Psychology* 3, no. 4:321–33.

Abramowitz, Alan I., and Kyle L. Saunders. 2008. "Is Polarization a Myth?" *Journal of Politics* 70, no. 2:542–55.

Abrams, Samuel J., and Morris P. Fiorina. 2012. "'The Big Sort' That Wasn't: A Skeptical Reexamination." *PS: Political Science and Politics* 45, no. 2: 203–10.

Achen, Christopher H. 1986. *The Statistical Analysis of Quasi-Experiments.* Berkeley and Los Angeles: University of California Press.

Addison, Alexander. 1798. *Liberty of Speech and of the Press: A Charge to the Grand Juries of the County Courts of the Fifth Circuit of the State of Pennsylvania.* Washington, PA: John Colerick.

Alterman, Eric. 2003. *What Liberal Media? The Truth about Bias and the News.* New York: Basic.

American National Election Studies. 2010. "Contacted by Either Major Party, 1956–2008." Table 6C.1a of *ANES Guide to Public Opinion and Electoral Behavior.* http://electionstudies.org/nesguide/toptable/tab6c_1a.htm.

Arceneaux, Kevin. 2010. "The Benefits of Experimental Methods for the Study of Campaign Effects." *Political Communication* 27, no. 2:199–215.

Arceneaux, Kevin, and Martin Johnson. 2007. "Channel Surfing: Does Choice Reduce Videomalaise?" Paper presented at the annual meeting of the Midwest Political Science Association, Chicago, April.

Arceneaux, Kevin, Martin Johnson, and John Cryderman. In press. "Communication, Persuasion, and the Conditioning Value of Selective Exposure: Like Minds Can Unite and Divide, but They Mostly Just Tune Out." *Political Communication.*

Arceneaux, Kevin, Martin Johnson, and Chad Murphy. 2012. "Polarized Politi-

cal Communication, Oppositional Media Hostility, and Selective Exposure."
  Journal of Politics 74, no. 1:174–86.
Arceneaux, Kevin, and Robin Kolodny. 2009. "The Effect of Grassroots Cam-
  paigning on Issue Preferences and Issue Salience." *Journal of Elections, Public Opinion, and Parties* 19, no. 3:235–49.
Arceneaux, Kevin, and Ryan Vander Wielen. In press. "The Effects of Need
  for Cognition and Need for Affect on Partisan Evaluations." *Political
  Psychology.*
Arpan, Laura M., and Arthur A. Raney. 2003. "An Experimental Investigation
  of News Source and the Hostile Media Effect." *Journalism and Mass Com-
  munication Quarterly* 80, no. 2:265–81.
Bafumi, Joseph, and Robert Y. Shapiro. 2009. "A New Partisan Voter." *Journal
  of Politics* 71, no. 1:1–24.
Baldassarri, Delia, and Andrew Gelman. 2008. "Partisans without Constraint:
  Political Polarization and Trends in American Public Opinion." *American
  Journal of Sociology* 114, no. 2:408–46.
Baron, Robert S., Sieg I. Hoppe, Chuan Feng Kao, Bethany Brunsman, Barbara
  Linneweh, and Diane Rogers. 1996. "Social Corroboration and Opinion Ex-
  tremity." *Journal of Experimental Social Psychology* 32, no. 6:537–60.
Bartels, Larry M. 2008. *Unequal Democracy: The Political Economy of the New
  Gilded Age.* New York: Sage.
Baum, Matthew A. 2003. "Soft News and Political Knowledge: Evidence of Ab-
  sence or Absence of Evidence?" *Political Communication* 20:173–90.
Baum, Matthew A., and Phil Gussin. 2008. "In the Eye of the Beholder: How
  Information Shortcuts Shape Individual Perceptions of Bias in the Media."
  Quarterly Journal of Political Science 3, no. 1:1–31.
Baum, Matthew A., and Samuel Kernell. 1999. "Has Cable Ended the Golden
  Age of Presidential Television?" *American Political Science Review* 93, no. 1:
  99–114.
Benen, Steve. 2011. *The "Other Side of the Story." Washington Monthly* blog,
  June 24. http://www.washingtonmonthly.com/political-animal/2011_06/the_
  other_side_of_the_story030476.php.
Bennett, W. Lance, and Shanto Iyengar. 2008. "A New Era of Minimal Effects?
  The Changing Foundations of Political Communication." *Journal of Communication* 58, no. 4:707–31.
———. 2010. "The Shifting Foundations of Political Communication: Responding to a Defense of the Media Effects Paradigm." *Journal of Communication*
  60, no. 1:35–39.
Bennett, W. Lance, and Jarol B. Manheim. 2006. "The One-Step Flow of Communication." *Annals of the American Academy of Political and Social Science* 608, no. 1:213–32.
Berelson, Bernard R., Paul F. Lazarsfeld, and William N. McPhee. 1954. *Voting:*

A Study of Opinion Formation in a Presidential Campaign. Chicago: University of Chicago Press.

Berinsky, Adam J., Gregory A. Huber, and Gabriel S. Lenz. 2012. "Evaluating Online Labor Markets for Experimental Research: Amazon.com's Mechanical Turk." *Political Analysis* 20, no. 3:351–68.

Biocca, Frank A. 1988. "Opposing Conceptions of the Audience: The Active and Passive Hemispheres of Mass Communication Theory." *Communication Yearbook* 11:51–80.

Bishop, Bill. 2008. *The Big Sort: Why the Clustering of Like-Minded America Is Tearing Us Apart.* Boston: Houghton Mifflin.

Blackstone, William. 1769. *Commentaries on the Laws of England; Book the Fourth.* Oxford: Clarendon.

Blumler, Jay G. 1979. "The Role of Theory in Uses and Gratifications Studies." *Communication Research* 6, no. 1:9–36.

Bowman, Gary. 1975. "Consumer Choice and Television." *Applied Economics* 7, no. 3:175–84.

Brader, Ted. 2006. *Campaigning for Hearts and Minds: How Emotional Appeals in Political Ads Work.* Chicago: University of Chicago Press.

Brady, Henry E., and Paul M. Sniderman. 1985. "Attitude Attribution: A Group Basis for Political Reasoning." *American Political Science Review* 79, no. 4: 1061–78.

Brewer, Marilynn. 2001. "The Many Faces of Social Identity: Implications for Political Psychology." *Political Psychology* 22, no. 1:115–25.

Brock, David, Ari Rabin-Havt, and Media Matters for America. 2012. *The Fox Effect: How Roger Ailes Turned a Network into a Propaganda Machine.* New York: Random House.

Buhrmester, Michael D., Tracy Kwang, and Samuel D. Gosling. 2011. "Amazon's Mechanical Turk: A New Source of Inexpensive, yet High-Quality, Data?" *Perspectives on Psychological Science* 6, no. 1:3–5.

Cacioppo, John T., and Richard E. Petty. 1981. *Attitudes and Persuasion: Classic and Contemporary Approaches.* Dubuque, IA: William C. Brown.

———. 1982. "The Need for Cognition." *Journal of Personality and Social Psychology* 42, no. 1:116–31.

Cacioppo, John T., Richard E. Petty, and Chuan Feng Kao. 1984. "The Efficient Assessment of Need for Cognition." *Journal of Personality Assessment* 48, no. 3:306–7.

Campbell, Angus, Philip Converse, Warren E. Miller, and Donald Stokes. 1960. *The American Voter.* New York: Wiley.

Cantril, Hadley. 1942. "Professor Quiz: A Gratifications Study." In *Radio Research 1941*, ed. Paul F. Lazarsfeld and Frank Stanton, 34–45. New York: Duell, Sloan & Pearce.

Cantril, Hadley, Hazel Gaudet, and Herta Herzog. 1940. *The Invasion from*

Mars: A Study in the Psychology of Panic. Princeton, NJ: Princeton University Press.

Cappella, Joseph N., and Kathleen Hall Jamieson. 1996. "News Frames, Political Cynicism, and Media Cynicism." *Annals of the American Academy of Political and Social Science* 546, no. 1:71–84.

———. 1997. *Spiral of Cynicism*. New York: Oxford University Press.

Carsey, Thomas M., and Geoffrey C. Layman. 2006. "Changing Sides or Changing Minds? Party Identification and Policy Preferences in the American Electorate." *American Journal of Political Science* 50, no. 2:464–77.

Center for Public Leadership. 2007. *Harvard University/U.S. News and World Report Poll #2007-NLI: National Leadership Index 2007—the National Study of Confidence in Leadership* (USYANK2007-NLI). Cambridge, MA: John F. Kennedy School of Government, Harvard University. Available at http://webapps.ropercenter.uconn.edu/CFIDE/cf/action/catalog/abstract.cfm?label=&keyword=USYANK2007-NLI&fromDate=&toDate=&organization=Any&type=&keywordOptions=1&start=1&id=&exclude=&excludeOptions=1&topic=Any&sortBy=DESC&archno=USYANK2007-NLI&abstract=abstract&x=32&y=9.

Chaffee, Steven H., and Miriam J. Metzger. 2001. "The End of Mass Communication?" *Mass Communication and Society* 4, no. 4:365–79.

Chan-Olmsted, Sylvia M., and Jiyoung Cha. 2007. "Branding Television News in a Multichannel Environment: An Exploratory Study of Network News Brand Personality." *International Journal on Media Management* 9, no. 4:135–50.

Chong, Dennis, and James N. Druckman. 2007. "Framing Theory." *Annual Review of Political Science* 10:103–26.

Ciciora, Walter S., James Farmer, David Large, and Michael Adams. 2004. *Modern Cable Television Technology: Video, Voice and Data Communications*. San Francisco: Morgan Kaufmann.

Civettini, Andrew J. W., and David P. Redlawsk. 2009. "Voters, Emotions, and Memory." *Political Psychology* 30, no. 1:125–51.

Coe, Kevin, David Tewksbury, Bradley J. Bond, Kristin L. Drogos, Robert W. Porter, Ashley Yahn, and Yuanyuan Zhang. 2008. "Hostile News: Partisan Use and Perceptions of Cable News Programming." *Journal of Communication* 58, no. 2:201–19.

Cohen, Bernard C. 1963. *The Press and Foreign Policy*. Princeton, NJ: Princeton University Press.

Cohen, Jacob. 1988. *Statistical Power Analysis for the Behavioral Sciences*. 2nd ed. Hillsdale, NJ: Erlbaum.

Cohen, Jeremy, Diana Mutz, Vincent Price, and Albert Gunther. 1988. "Perceived Impact of Defamation: An Experiment on Third-Person Effects." *Public Opinion Quarterly* 52, no. 2:161–73.

Cooper, Christopher A., and Anthony J. Nownes. 2005. "Media Coverage of

Scandal and Declining Trust in Government: An Experimental Analysis of 9/11 Commission Testimony." Paper presented at the annual meeting of the Midwest Political Science Association, Chicago, April.

Dagnes, Alison. 2010. *Politics on Demand: The Effects of 24-Hour News on American Politics*. Santa Barbara, CA: Praeger.

Dalton, Russell J., Paul A. Beck, and Robert Huckfeldt. 1998. "Partisan Cues and the Media: Information Flows in the 1992 Presidential Election." *American Political Science Review* 92, no. 1:111–26.

Davison, W. Phillips. 1983. "The Third-Person Effect in Communication." *Public Opinion Quarterly* 47, no. 1:1–15.

DeFleur, Melvin L., and Sandra Ball-Rokeach. 1989. *Theories of Mass Communication*. 5th ed. White Plains, NY: Longman.

Donaldson, Sam. 1982. "After Massacre, US Considering Sending US Troops Back to Beirut." *World News Tonight Sunday*, ABC, September 19. Transcript, LexisNexis Academic.

Druckman, James N. 2001. "Using Credible Advice to Overcome Framing Effects." *Journal of Law, Economics, and Organization* 17, no. 1:62–82.

Druckman, James N., Jordan Fein, and Thomas J. Leeper. 2012. "A Source of Bias in Public Opinion Stability." *American Political Science Review* 106, no. 2: 430–54.

Druckman, James N., and Kjersten R. Nelson. 2003. "Framing and Deliberation: How Citizens' Conversations Limit Elite Influence." *American Journal of Political Science* 47, no. 4:729–45.

Entman, Robert M. 1993. "Framing: Toward Clarification of a Fractured Paradigm." *Journal of Communication* 43, no. 4:51–58.

Farhi, Paul. 2011. "Schultz Suspended After Using Slur to Refer to Ingraham." *Washington Post*, May 26. http://www.washingtonpost.com/lifestyle/style/schultz-suspended-after-using-slur-to-refer-to-ingraham/2011/05/26/AGbbozBH_story.html.

Fairleigh Dickinson University. 2011. "Some News Leaves People Knowing Less." Press release, November 21. Madison, NJ: PublicMind Poll. http://publicmind.fdu.edu/2011/knowless/.

Feldman, Lauren. 2011. "The Opinion Factor: The Effects of Opinionated News on Information Processing and Attitude Change." *Political Communication* 28, no. 2:163–81.

Feldman, Stanley. 1988. "Structure and Consistency in Public Opinion: The Role of Core Beliefs and Values." *American Journal of Political Science* 32, no. 2:416–40.

Festinger, Leon. 1957. *A Theory of Cognitive Dissonance*. Evanston, IL: Row, Peterson.

Fiorina, Morris P., and Samuel J. Abrams. 2008. "Political Polarization in the American Public." *Annual Review of Political Science* 11:563–88.

Fiorina, Morris P., Samuel J. Abrams, and Jeremy C. Pope. 2006. *Culture War? The Myth of a Polarized America.* 2nd ed. New York: Pearson Longman.

Fischer, Peter, Eva Jonas, Dieter Frey, and Stefan Schulz-Hardt. 2005. "Selective Exposure to Information: The Impact of Information Limits." *European Journal of Social Psychology* 35, no. 4:469–92.

Fischer, Peter, Stefan Schulz-Hardt, and Dieter Frey. 2008. "Selective Exposure and Information Quantity: How Different Information Quantities Moderate Decision Makers' Preference for Consistent and Inconsistent Information." *Journal of Personality and Social Psychology* 94, no. 2:231–44.

Fischle, Mark. 2000. "Mass Response to the Lewinsky Scandal: Motivated Reasoning or Bayesian Updating?" *Political Psychology* 21, no. 1:135–59.

Forgette, Richard, and Jonathan S. Morris. 2006. "High-Conflict Television News and Public Opinion." *Political Research Quarterly* 59, no. 3:447–56.

Frederick, Brian, Jeremy Schulman, Raphael Schweber-Koren, and Morgan Weiland. 2009. "In Vicious New Smear, Rove Falsely Claims Jennings Advocated for NAMBLA." Media Matters, October 7. http://mediamatters.org/research/200910070044.

Frey, Dieter. 1986. "Recent Research on Selective Exposure to Information." In *Advances in Experimental Social Psychology* (vol. 19), ed. Leonard Berkowitz, 41–80. New York: Academic.

Friedman, Jeffrey, ed. 1998. "Public Ignorance and Democratic Theory." Special issue, *Critical Review,* vol. 12, no. 4.

Gaines, Brian J., and James H. Kuklinski. 2011. "Experimental Estimation of Heterogeneous Treatment Effects Related to Self-Selection." *American Journal of Political Science* 55, no. 3:724–36.

Gaines, Brian J., James H. Kuklinski, Paul J. Quirk, Buddy Peyton, and Jay Verkuilen. 2007. "Same Facts, Different Interpretations: Partisan Motivation and Opinion on Iraq." *Journal of Politics* 69, no. 4:957–74.

Gamson, William. 1992. *Talking Politics.* New York: Cambridge University Press.

Garner, Andrew, and Harvey Palmer. 2011. "Polarization and Issue Consistency over Time." *Political Behavior* 33, no. 2:225–46.

Garrett, R. Kelly. 2009a. "Echo Chambers Online? Politically Motivated Selective Exposure among Internet News Users." *Journal of Computer-Mediated Communication* 14, no. 2:265–85.

———. 2009b. "Politically Motivated Reinforcement Seeking: Reframing the Selective Exposure Debate." *Journal of Communication* 59, no. 4:676–99.

Garrett, R. Kelly, Dustin Carnahan, and Emily K. Lynch. In press. "A Turn toward Avoidance? Selective Exposure to Online Political Information, 2004–2008." *Political Behavior.* Advance online publication. doi:10.1007/s11109-011-9185-6.

Gelman, Andrew, Boris Shor, Joseph Bafumi, and David Park. 2007. "Rich

State, Poor State, Red State, Blue State: What's the Matter with Connecticut?" *Quarterly Journal of Political Science* 2, no. 4:345–67.

Gentzkow, Matthew, and Jesse M. Shapiro. 2006. "Media Bias and Representation." *Journal of Political Economy* 114, no. 2:280–316.

Gerber, Alan, and Donald P. Green. 1999. "Misperceptions about Perceptual Bias." *Annual Review of Political Science* 2:189–210.

Gilens, Martin. 2003. "How the Poor Became Black: The Racialization of American Poverty in the Mass Media." In *Race and the Politics of Welfare Reform*, ed. Sanford F. Schram, Joe Soss, and Richard C. Fording, 101–30. Ann Arbor: University of Michigan Press.

Goldberg, Bernard. 2002. *Bias: A CBS Insider Exposes How the Media Distort the News*. 2nd ed. New York: Perennial/HarperCollins.

Goldman, Seth K., and Diana C. Mutz. 2011. "The Friendly Media Phenomenon: A Cross-National Analysis of Cross-Cutting Exposure." *Political Communication* 28, no. 1:42–66.

Goren, Paul. 2005. "Party Identification and Core Political Values." *American Journal of Political Science* 49:881–96.

Green, Donald, Bradley Palmquist, and Eric Schickler. 2002. *Partisan Hearts and Minds: Political Parties and the Social Identities of Voters*. New Haven, CT: Yale University Press.

Gronke, Paul, and Timothy E. Cook. 2007. "Disdaining the Media: The American Public's Changing Attitudes toward the News." *Political Communication* 24, no. 3:259–81.

Gunther, Albert C., Cindy T. Christen, Janice L. Liebhart, and Stella Chih-Yun Chia. 2001. "Congenial Public, Contrary Press, and Biased Estimates of the Climate of Opinion." *Public Opinion Quarterly* 65, no. 3:295–320.

Hamilton, James T. 2005. "The Market and the Media." In *The Press*, ed. Geneva Overholser and Kathleen Hall Jamieson, 351–70. Oxford: Oxford University Press.

Hannity, Sean. 2009. "White House Manipulates Doctor Photo Op." *Hannity*, Fox News, October 7. Transcript, LexisNexis Academic.

———. 2011. "Usama Bin Laden Killed by U.S. Operation Inside Pakistan." *Hannity*, Fox News, May 2. Transcript, LexisNexis Academic.

Hayes, Thomas J. 2012. "The Representational Sources of Political Inequality." Ph.D. diss., University of California, Riverside.

Heiner, Ronald A. 1983. "The Origin of Predictable Behavior." *American Economic Review* 73, no. 4:560–95.

Hetherington, Marc J. 2001. "Resurgent Mass Partisanship: The Role of Elite Polarization." *American Political Science Review* 95, no. 3:619–31.

———. 2009. "Review Article: Putting Polarization in Perspective." *British Journal of Political Science* 39, no. 2:413–48.

Hetherington, Marc J., and Jonathan Daniel Weiler. 2009. *Authoritarianism and Polarization in American Politics.* New York: Cambridge University Press.

Hibbing, John R., and Elizabeth Theiss-Morse. 1995. *Congress as Public Enemy: Public Attitudes toward American Political Institutions.* New York: Cambridge University Press.

Higgins, E. Tory. 1997. "Beyond Pleasure and Pain." *American Psychologist* 52, no. 12:1280–1300.

Holbert, R. Lance, R. Kelly Garrett, and Laurel S. Gleason. 2010. "A New Era of Minimal Effects? A Response to Bennett and Iyengar." *Journal of Communication* 60, no. 1:15–34.

Hovland, Carl. 1954. "Effects of Mass Media of Communication." In *Handbook of Social Psychology,* ed. Gardner Lindzey, 244–52. Cambridge, MA: Addison-Wesley.

———. 1959. "Reconciling Conflicting Results Derived from Experimental and Survey Studies of Attitude Change." *American Psychologist* 14, no. 1:8–17.

Hovland, Carl I., and Walter Weiss. 1951. "The Influence of Source Credibility on Communication Effectiveness." *Public Opinion Quarterly* 15, no. 4: 635–50.

Iyengar, Shanto. 1991. *Is Anyone Responsible? How Television Frames Political Issues.* Chicago: University of Chicago Press.

Iyengar, Shanto, and Kyu S. Hahn. 2009. "Red Media, Blue Media: Evidence of Ideological Selectivity in Media Use." *Journal of Communication* 59, no. 1:19–39.

Iyengar, Shanto, Kyu S. Hahn, Jon A. Krosnick, and John Walker. 2008. "Selective Exposure to Campaign Communication: The Role of Anticipated Agreement and Issue Public Membership." *Journal of Politics* 70:186–200.

Iyengar, Shanto, and Donald R. Kinder. 1987. *News That Matters: Television and American Opinion.* Chicago: University of Chicago Press.

———. 2010. *News That Matters: Television and American Opinion.* Updated ed. Chicago: University of Chicago Press.

Jamieson, Kathleen Hall, and Joseph N. Cappella. 2008. *Echo Chamber: Rush Limbaugh and the Conservative Media Establishment.* New York: Oxford University Press.

Jennings, Peter. 1982a. "Israel Completes Conquest of Beirut." *World News Tonight,* ABC, September 17. Transcript, LexisNexis Academic.

———. 1982b. *World News Tonight,* ABC, September 24. Transcript, LexisNexis Academic.

Johnson, Martin, and Kevin Arceneaux. 2010. "Who Watches Political Talk? Revisiting Political Television Reception with Behavioral Measures." Paper presented at the annual meeting of the Southwestern Political Science Association, Houston, March–April.

Judd, Charles M., Leaf Van Boven, Michaela Huber, and Ana P. Nunes. 2012.

"Measuring Everyday Perceptions of the Distribution of the American Electorate." In *Improving Public Opinion Surveys: Interdisciplinary Innovation
and the American National Election Studies*, ed. John Aldrich and Kathleen
McGraw, 220–37. Princeton, NJ: Princeton University Press.

Katz, Elihu, Jay G. Blumler, and Michael Gurevitch. 1973–74. "Uses and Gratifications Research." *Public Opinion Quarterly* 37, no. 4:509–23.

———. 1974. "Utilization of Mass Communication by the Individual." In *The
Uses of Mass Communication: Current Perspectives on Gratifications Research*, ed. Jay Blumler and Elihu Katz, 19–34. Beverly Hills, CA: Sage.

Katz, Elihu, and Paul F. Lazarsfeld. 1955. *Personal Influence*. New York: Free
Press.

Kern, Holger Lutz, and Jens Hainmueller. 2009. "Opium for the Masses: How
Foreign Media Can Stabilize Authoritarian Regimes." *Political Analysis* 71,
no. 4:377–99.

Key, V. O. 1966. *The Responsible Electorate*. Cambridge, MA: Belknap Press of
Harvard University Press.

Kinder, Donald R. 1998. "Communication and Opinion." *Annual Review of Political Science* 1:167–97.

Kirzinger, Ashley E., Christopher Weber, and Martin Johnson. 2012. "Genetic
and Environmental Influences on Media Use and Communication Behaviors." *Human Communication Research* 38, no. 2:144–71.

Klapper, Joseph. 1960. *The Effects of Mass Communication*. Glencoe, IL: Free
Press.

Kolbert, Elizabeth. 1993. "Media Business: Television; to Pay or Not to Pay?
A War of Words Heats Up between Cable Systems and Broadcasters."
New York Times, August 23. http://www.nytimes.com/1993/08/23/business/
media-business-television-pay-not-pay-war-words-heats-up-between-cable
-systems.

Koppel, Ted. 2010. "Ted Koppel: Olbermann, O'Reilly and the Death of Real
News." *Washington Post*, November 14.

Kruglanski, Arie W. 1980. "Lay Epistemo-Logic—Process and Contents: Another Look at Attribution Theory." *Psychological Review* 87, no. 1:70–87.

———. 1989. *Lay Epistemics and Human Knowledge: Cognitive and Motivational Bases*. New York: Plenum.

Kruglanski, A. W., D. M. Webster, and A. Klem. 1993. "Motivated Resistance
and Openness to Persuasion in the Presence or Absence of Prior Information." *Journal of Personality and Social Psychology* 65, no. 5:861–76.

Kuhn, Deanna, and Joseph Lao. 1996. "Effects of Evidence on Attitudes: Is Polarization the Norm?" *Psychological Science* 7, no. 2:115–20.

Kunda, Ziva. 1990. "The Case for Motivated Reasoning." *Psychological Bulle-
tin* 108, no. 3:480–98.

Ladd, Jonathan M. 2010. "The Neglected Power of Elite Opinion Leadership to

Produce Antipathy toward the News Media: Evidence from a Survey Experiment." *Political Behavior* 32, no. 1:29–50.

———. 2012. *Why Americans Hate the Media and How It Matters.* Princeton, NJ: Princeton University Press.

Lakoff, George, and Mark Johnson. 1980. *Metaphors We Live By.* Chicago: University of Chicago Press.

Lasswell, Harold D. 1938/1972. *Propaganda Technique in the World War.* Reprint, New York: Garland. The 1938 edition is a reprint of the first, 1927 edition.

Lawrence, Eric, John Sides, and Henry Farrell. 2010. "Self-Segregation or Deliberation? Blog Readership, Participation, and Polarization in American Politics." *Perspectives on Politics* 8, no. 1:141–57.

Layman, Geoffrey C., Thomas M. Carsey, and Juliana Menasce Horowitz. 2006. "Party Polarization in American Politics: Characteristics, Causes, and Consequences." *Annual Review of Political Science* 9:83–110.

Lazarsfeld, Paul F., Bernard Berelson, and Hazel Gaudet. 1948. *The People's Choice: How the Voter Makes Up His Mind in a Presidential Campaign.* New York: Columbia University Press.

Lee, Tien-Tsung. 2005. "The Liberal Media Myth Revisited: An Examination of Factors Influencing Perceptions of Media Bias." *Journal of Broadcasting and Electronic Media* 49, no. 1:43–64.

Lerner, Jennifer, and Dacher Keltner. 2000. "Beyond Valence: Toward a Model of Emotion-Specific Influences on Judgment and Choice." *Cognition and Emotion* 14, no. 4:473–93.

Levendusky, Matthew S. 2009. *The Partisan Sort: How Liberals Became Democrats and Conservatives Became Republicans.* Chicago: University of Chicago Press.

———. In press. *Partisan News That Matters: How Partisan News Impacts American Politics.* Chicago: University of Chicago Press.

Lippmann, Walter. 1920. *Liberty and the News.* New York: Harcourt, Brace & Howe.

———. 1922/1965. *Public Opinion.* Reprint, New York: Free Press.

Lord, C. G., L. Ross, and M. R. Lepper. 1979. "Biased Assimilation and Attitude Polarization: The Effects of Prior Theories on Subsequently Considered Evidence." *Journal of Personality and Social Psychology* 27, no. 11: 2098–109.

Lubinsky, Charles. 1996. "Reconsidering Retransmission Consent: An Examination of the Retransmission Consent Provision (47 U.S.C. § 325(b)) of the 1992 Cable Act." *Federal Communications Law Journal* 49, no. 1:99–165.

Macias, Cathaleene, Paul B. Gold, William A. Hargreaves, Elliot Aronson, Leonard Bickman, Paul J. Barreira, Danson R. Jones, Charles F. Rodican, and William H. Fisher. 2009. "Preference in Random Assignment: Implications for the Interpretation of Randomized Trials." *Administration and Policy in Mental Health and Mental Health Services Research* 36, no. 5:331–42.

Maddow, Rachel. 2009. "Rachel Re." *The Rachael Maddow Show*, MSNBC, October 23. Transcript, MSNBC.

Mandese, Joe. 2009. "T.V. Universe Expands, Share of Channels Tuned Does Not." *Media Daily News*, July 21. http://www.mediapost.com/publications/article/110159/.

Manjoo, Farhad. 2008. *True Enough: Learning to Live in a Post-Fact Society*. New York: Wiley.

Mann, Thomas E., and Norman J. Ornstein. 1994. Introduction to *Congress, the Press, and the Public*, ed. Thomas E. Mann and Norman J. Ornstein, 1–14. Washington, DC: American Enterprise Institute/Brookings Institution.

Marcus, George E., W. Russell Neuman, and Michael B. MacKuen. 2000. *Affective Intelligence and Political Judgment*. Chicago: University of Chicago Press.

McCarty, Nolan, Keith T. Poole, and Howard Rosenthal. 2006. *Polarized America: The Dance of Ideology and Unequal Riches*. Cambridge, MA: MIT Press.

———. 2011. "Party Polarization: 1879–2010." January 11. http://voteview.com/polarized_america.htm#POLITICALPOLARIZATION.

McCombs, Maxwell E. 2004. *Setting the Agenda: The Mass Media and Public Opinion*. Malden, MA: Blackwell.

McCombs, Maxwell E., and Donald L. Shaw. 1972. "The Agenda-Setting Function of Mass Media." *Public Opinion Quarterly* 36, no. 2:176–87.

McCourt, Mike. 1982. "Begin Refuses Responsibility for Beirut Massacre and US Considers." *Weekend News Sunday Late*, ABC, September 19. Transcript, LexisNexis Academic.

McGuire, William J. 1968. "Personality and Susceptibility to Social Influence." In *Handbook of Personality Theory and Research*, ed. Edgar F. Borgatta and William W. Lambert, 13–87. Chicago: Rand McNally.

McGuire, William J., and Demetrios Papageorgis. 1962. "Effectiveness of Forewarning in Developing Resistance to Persuasion." *Public Opinion Quarterly* 26, no. 1:24–34.

Menand, Louis. 2009. "Chin Music." *New Yorker*, November 2.

Miller, Joanne M., and Jon A. Krosnick. 2000. "News Media Impact on the Ingredients of Presidential Evaluations: Politically Knowledgeable Citizens Are Guided by a Trusted Source." *American Journal of Political Science* 44, no. 2:301–15.

Morley, David. 1993. "Active Audience Theory: Pendulums and Pitfalls." *Journal of Communication* 43, no. 4:13–19.

Morris, Jonathan S. 2005. "The Fox News Factor." *International Journal of Press/Politics* 10, no. 3:56–79.

Morris, Jonathan S., and Peter L. Francia. 2010. "Cable News, Public Opinion, and the 2004 Party Conventions." *Political Research Quarterly* 63, no. 4: 834–49.

Moskalenko, Sophia, Clark McCauley, and Paul Rozin. 2006. "Group Identification under Conditions of Threat: College Students' Attachment to Country, Family, Ethnicity, Religion, and University Before and After September 11, 2001." *Political Psychology* 27, no. 1:77–97.

Moy, Patricia, and Michael Pfau. 2000. *With Malice toward All? The Media and Public Confidence in Democratic Institutions.* Westport, CT: Praeger.

Mullen, Megan. 2003. *The Rise of Cable Programming in the United States: Revolution or Evolution?* Austin: University of Texas Press.

Mutz, Diana C. 1989. "The Influence of Perceptions of Media Influence: Third Person Effects and the Public Expression of Opinions." *International Journal of Public Opinion Research* 1, no. 1:3–23.

———. 1998. *Impersonal Influence: How Perceptions of Mass Collectives Affect Political Attitudes.* New York: Cambridge University Press.

———. 2006a. *Hearing the Other Side: Deliberative versus Participatory Democracy.* Cambridge, MA: Cambridge University Press.

———. 2006b. "How the Mass Media Divide Us." In *Red and Blue Nation? Characteristics and Causes of America's Polarized Politics* (2 vols.), ed. Pietro S. Nivola and David W. Brady, 1:223–62. Washington, DC: Brookings Institution Press.

———. 2007. "Effects of 'In-Your-Face' Television Discourse on Perceptions of a Legitimate Opposition." *American Political Science Review* 101, no. 4: 621–35.

Mutz, Diana C., and Paul M. Martin. 2001. "Facilitating Communication across Lines of Political Difference: The Role of Mass Media." *American Political Science Review* 95, no. 1:97–114.

Mutz, Diana C., and Byron Reeves. 2005. "The New Videomalaise: Effects of Televised Incivility on Political Trust." *American Political Science Review* 99, no. 1:1–16.

Nicholson, Stephen P. 2012. "Polarizing Cues." *American Journal of Political Science* 56, no. 1:52–66.

Nie, Norman H., Darwin W. Miller III, Saar Golde, Daniel M. Butler, and Kenneth Winneg. 2010. "The World Wide Web and the U.S. Political News Market." *American Journal of Political Science* 54, no. 2:428–39.

Nielsen Co. 2008. "Average U.S. Home Now Receives a Record 118.6 TV Channels, According to Nielsen." Press release, June 6. http://www.nielsen.com/us/en/insights/press-room/2008/average_u_s__home.html.

Nielsen Media Research Group. 1981. *Nielsen Report on Television.* New York.

Norris, Pippa. 2000. *A Virtuous Circle: Political Communication in Postindustrial Societies.* New York: Cambridge University Press.

Obama, Barack. 2010. "Remarks by the President at University of Michigan Spring Commencement." White House, May 1. http://www.whitehouse.gov/the-press-office/remarks-president-university-michigan-spring-commencement.

Olbermann, Keith. 2010a. "gobp." *Countdown with Keith Olbermann*, MSNBC, June 17. Transcript, MSNBC.

———. 2010b. "Special Comment: Olbermann: The Witch-Hunt vs. Sherrod, and Those Who Made It Possible." *Countdown with Keith Olbermann*, MSNBC, July 21. Transcript, MSNBC.

O'Reilly, Bill. 2009. "Talking Points Memo and Top Story." *The O'Reilly Factor*, Fox News, April 23. Transcript, LexisNexis Academic.

———. 2010. "Moderate Liberals against Obama on Oil Spill; BP CEO a Sock Puppet in Washington; L.A. School District and Illegal Immigration." *The O'Reilly Factor*, Fox News, June 17. Transcript, LexisNexis Academic.

Paolacci, Gabriele, Jesse Chandler, and Panagiotis G. Ipeirotis. 2010. "Running Experiments on Amazon Mechanical Turk." *Judgment and Decision Making* 5, no. 5:411–19.

Parsons, Patrick R. 2008. *Blue Skies: A History of Cable Television*. Philadelphia: Temple University Press.

Pasley, Jeffrey L. 2001. *"The Tyranny of Printers": Newspaper Politics in the Early American Republic*. Charlottesville: University Press of Virginia.

Patterson, Thomas E. 2000. "Doing Well and Doing Good: How Soft News and Critical Journalism Are Shrinking the News Audience and Weakening Democracy—and What News Outlets Can Do about It." Faculty Research Working Paper no. RWP01-001. Cambridge, MA: Harvard University, John F. Kennedy School of Government.

Perloff, Richard M. 1989. "Ego-Involvement and the Third Person Effect of Televised News Coverage." *Communication Research* 16, no. 2:236–62.

Perse, Elizabeth M. 2001. *Media Effects and Society*. Mahwah, NJ: Erlbaum.

Peters, Chris. 2010. "No Spin Zones: The Rise of the American Cable News Magazine and Bill O'Reilly." *Journalism Studies* 11, no. 6:832–51.

Petersen, Michael Bang. 2010. "Distinct Emotions, Distinct Domains: Anger, Anxiety and Perceptions of Intentionality." *Journal of Politics* 72, no. 2: 357–65.

Petrova, Maria. 2011. "Newspapers and Parties: How Advertising Revenues Created the Independent Press." *American Political Science Review* 105, no. 4: 790–808.

Petty, Richard E., and Pablo Briñol. 2002. "Attitude Change: The Elaboration Likelihood Model of Persuasion." In *Marketing for Sustainability: Towards Transactional Policy Making*, ed. Gerard Bartels and Wil Nielissen, 176–90. Amsterdam: IOS.

Petty, Richard E., and John T. Cacioppo. 1986a. *Communication and Persua-*

sion: Central Route and Peripheral Routes to Attitude Change. New York: Springer.

———. 1986b. "The Elaboration Likelihood Model of Persuasion." In *Advances in Experimental Social Psychology* (vol. 19), ed. Leonard Berkowitz, 124–205. New York: Academic.

Petty, Richard E., and Duane T. Wegener. 1998. "Attitude Change: Multiple Roles for Persuasion Variables." In *The Handbook for Social Psychology* (4th ed.), ed. Daniel T. Gilbert, Susan T. Fiske, and Gardner Lindzey, 323–90. New York: McGraw-Hill.

Pew Research Center for the People and the Press. 2010. *June 2010 Media Consumption Survey* (data file and code book). Available at http://www.people-press.org/2010/09/12/june-2010-media-consumption-survey/.

———. 2011. "Press Widely Criticized, But Trusted More than Other Information Sources." Views of the News Media: 1985–2011. Washington, DC: Pew ResearchCenter.http://www.people-press.org/2011/09/22/press-widely-criticized-but-trusted-more-than-other-institutions/. Media%20Attitudes%20Release.pdf. Accessed November 22, 2011.

Pomerantz, Eva M., Shelly Chaiken, and Rosalind S. Tordesillas. 1995. "Attitude Strength and Resistance Processes." *Journal of Personality and Social Psychology* 69, no. 3:408–19.

Poole, Keith. 2012. "The Polarization of Congressional Parties." May 10. http://voteview.com/political_polarization.asp.

Priester, Joseph R., and Richard E. Petty. 2003. "The Influence of Spokesperson Trustworthiness on Message Elaboration, Attitude Strength, and Advertising Effectiveness." *Journal of Consumer Psychology*, 13, no. 4:408–21.

Prior, Markus. 2003. "Any Good News in Soft News? The Impact of Soft News Preference on Political Knowledge." *Political Communication* 20, no. 2: 149–71.

———. 2005. "News vs. Entertainment: How Increasing Media Choice Widens Gaps in Political Knowledge and Turnout." *American Journal of Political Science* 49, no. 3:577–92.

———. 2007. *Post-Broadcast Democracy: How Media Choice Increases Inequality in Political Involvement and Polarizes Elections.* New York: Cambridge University Press.

———. 2009. "The Immensely Inflated News Audience: Assessing Bias in Self-Reported News Exposure." *Public Opinion Quarterly* 73, no. 1:130–43.

PRNewswire. 2006. "Average U.S. Home Now Receives a Record 104.2 TV Channels, According to Nielsen." Press release, March 19. http://www.prnewswire.com/news-releases/average-us-home-now-receives-a-record-1042-tv-channels-according-to-nielsen-52170292.html.

Ramsay, Clay, Steven Kull, Evan Lewis, and Stefan Subias. 2010. "Misinformation and the 2010 Election: A Study of the US Electorate." Typescript, WorldPublicOpinion.org, Program on International Policy Attitudes, University of Maryland. Available at http://drum.lib.umd.edu/handle/1903/11375?mode=full.

Reynolds, Frank. 1982. "Gemayel Is Buried in Lebanon and Israel Moves against Army in Beirut." *World News Tonight*, ABC, September 15. Transcript, LexisNexis Academic.

Robinson, Michael J. 1975. "American Political Legitimacy in an Era of Electronic Journalism: Reflections on the Evening News." In *Television as a Social Force: New Approaches to TV Criticism*, ed. Douglass Cater and Richard Adler, 97–139. New York: Praeger.

Rosenberg, Norman L. 1984. "Alexander Addison and the Pennsylvania Origins of Federalist First-Amendment Thought." *Pennsylvania Magazine of History and Biography* 108, no. 4:399–417.

———. 1986. *Protecting the Best Men: An Interpretive History of the Law of Libel.* Chapel Hill: University of North Carolina Press.

Rosenstone, Steven J., and John Mark Hansen. 1993. *Mobilization, Participation, and Democracy in America.* New York: Macmillan.

Rudolph, Thomas J. 2006. "Triangulating Political Responsibility: The Motivated Formation of Responsibility Judgments." *Political Psychology* 27, no. 1: 99–122.

Rudolph, Thomas J., and Elizabeth Popp. 2007. "An Information Processing Theory of Ambivalence." *Political Psychology* 28, no. 5:563–85.

Ruggiero, Thomas E. 2000. "Uses and Gratifications Theory in the 21st Century." *Mass Communication and Society* 3, no. 1:3–37.

Scheibehenne, Benjamin, Rainer Greifeneder, and Peter M. Todd. 2010. "Can There Ever Be Too Many Options? A Meta-Analytic Review of Choice Overload." *Journal of Consumer Research* 37, no. 3:409–25.

Schmuhl, Robert, and Robert G. Picard. 2005. "The Marketplace of Ideas." In *The Press*, ed. Geneva Overholser and Kathleen Hall Jamieson, 141–55. New York: Oxford University Press.

Schultz, Ed. 2011. *The Ed Show*, MSNBC, May 2. Transcript, MSNBC.

Seaman, William R. 1992. "Active Audience Theory: Pointless Populism." *Media, Culture and Society* 14, no. 2:301–11.

Sears, David O., and Jonathan L. Freedman. 1967. "Selective Exposure to Information: A Critical Review." *Public Opinion Quarterly* 31, no. 2:194–213.

Slate.com. 2011. "Why MSNBC Is Not Fox News for Liberals: Rachel Maddow on How the Republican Party Stands and Salutes Roger Ailes and Fox News." December 21. http://www.slate.com/articles/video/conversations_with_slate/2011/12/rachel_maddow_takes_on_fox_news_in_interview_with_jacob_weisberg.html.

Slater, Michael D. 2007. "Reinforcing Spirals: The Mutual Influence of Media Selectivity and Media Effects and Their Impact on Individual Behavior and Social Identity." *Communication Theory* 17, no. 3:281–303.

Sloan Commission on Cable Communications. 1971. *On the Cable: The Television of Abundance*. New York: McGraw-Hill.

Smerconish, Michael. 2010. "The Media's Black and White World." *Washington Post*, June 11, A17.

Sniderman, Paul M. 2000. "Taking Sides: A Fixed Choice Theory of Political Reasoning." In *Elements of Reason: Cognition, Choice, and the Bounds of Rationality*, ed. Arthur Lupia, Mathew D. McCubbins, and Samuel L. Popkin, 67–84. New York: Cambridge University Press.

Sobieraj, Sarah, and Jeffrey M. Berry. 2011. "From Incivility to Outrage: Political Discourse in Blogs, Talk Radio, and Cable News." *Political Communication* 28, no. 1:19–41.

Spears, Russell, Martin Lee, and Stephen Lee. 1990. "De-Individuation and Group Polarization in Computer-Mediated Discussion." *British Journal of Social Psychology* 29, no. 2:121–34.

Stewart, Jon. 2011. "Fox News Channel—Fair and Balanced" (video). *The Daily Show*, Comedy Central, June 20. http://www.thedailyshow.com/watch/mon-june-20-2011/fox-news-channel---fair---balanced.

Strachan, J. Cherie, and Michael R. Wolf. 2012. "Political Civility." *PS: Political Science and Politics* 45, no. 3:401–4.

Stroud, Natalie J. 2008. "Media Use and Political Predispositions: Revisiting the Concept of Selective Exposure." *Political Behavior* 30, no. 3:341–66.

———. 2010. "Polarization and Partisan Selective Exposure." *Journal of Communication* 60, no. 3:556–76.

———. 2011. *Niche News: The Politics of News Choice*. New York: Oxford University Press.

Sung, Yongjun, and Namkee Park. 2011. "The Dimensions of Cable Television Network Personality: Implications for Media Brand Management." *International Journal on Media Management* 13, no. 1:87–105.

Sunstein, Cass R. 2007. *Republic.com 2.0*. Princeton, NJ: Princeton University Press.

———. 2009. *Going to Extremes: How Like Minds Unite and Divide*. New York: Oxford University Press.

Taber, Charles S., and Milton Lodge. 2006. "Motivated Skepticism in the Evaluation of Political Beliefs." *American Journal of Political Science* 50, no. 3: 755–69.

Thompson, Richard F. 2009. "Habituation: A History." *Neurobiology of Learning and Memory* 92, no. 2:127–34.

Torgerson, David, and Bonnie Sibbald. 1998. "Understanding Controlled Trials: What Is a Patient Preference Trial." *British Medical Journal* 316, no. 7128:360.

TV by the Numbers. 2012a. "'ABC World News with Diane Sawyer' Cuts Gaps with NBC by Double Digits." Press release, January 24. http://tvbythe numbers.zap2it.com/2012/01/24/abc-world-news-with-diane-sawyer-cuts -gaps-with-nbc-by-double-digits/117435.

———. 2012b. "Cable News Ratings for Friday, January 20, 2012." Press release, January 23. http://tvbythenumbers.zap2it.com/2012/01/23/cable-news -ratings-for-friday-january-20-2012/117311/.

TVB. 2011. "National ADS, Wired-Cable Penetration and Over-the_Air Trends." http://www.tvb.org/planning_buying/4722/4729/72512.

Valentino, Nicholas A., Antoine J. Banks, Vincent L. Hutchings, and Anne K. Davis. 2009. "Selective Exposure in the Internet Age: The Interaction between Anxiety and Information Utility." *Political Psychology* 30, no. 4: 591–613.

Valentino, Nicholas A., Ted Brader, Eric W. Groenendyk, Krysha Gregorowicz, and Vincent L. Hutchings. 2011. "Election Night's Alright for Fighting: The Role of Emotions in Political Participation." *Journal of Politics* 73, no. 1: 156–70.

Vallone, Robert P., Lee Ross, and Mark R. Lepper. 1985. "The Hostile Media Phenomenon: Biased Perception and Perceptions of Media Bias in Coverage of the 'Beirut Massacre.'" *Journal of Personality and Social Psychology* 49, no. 3:577–85.

Van Boven, Leaf, Charles M. Judd, and David K. Sherman. 2012. "Political Polarization Projection: Social Projection of Partisan Attitude Extremity and Attitudinal Processes." *Journal of Personality and Social Psychology* 103, no. 1:84–100.

Wakshlag, Jacob J., Raymond J. Reitz, and Dolf Zillmann. 1982. "Selective Exposure to and Acquisition of Information from Educational Television as a Function of Appeal and Tempo of Background Music." *Journal of Educational Psychology* 74, no. 5:666–77.

Wartella, Ellen, and Byron Reeves. 1985. "Historical Trends in Research on Children and the Media: 1900–1960." *Journal of Communication* 35, no. 2: 118–33.

Webster, James G. 2005. "Beneath the Veneer of Fragmentation: Television Audience Polarization in a Multichannel World." *Journal of Communication* 55, no. 2:366–82.

Wei, Ran, and Ven-Hwei Lo. 2007. "The Third-Person Effect of Political Attack Ads in the 2004 U.S. Presidential Election." *Media Psychology* 9, no. 2: 367–88.

Whitlock, Scott. 2011. "Matthews Apologizes for MSNBC's KKK Smear of

Romney: 'Appalling Lack of Judgment.'" December 14. http://newsbusters
.org/blogs/scott-whitlock/2011/12/14/matthews-apologizes-msnbcs-kkk
-smear-romney-appalling-lack-judgment.

Zaller, John. 1992. *The Nature and Origins of Mass Opinion*. New York: Cambridge University Press.

———. 1996. "The Myth of Massive Media Impact Revived: New Support for a
Discredited Idea." In *Political Persuasion and Attitude Change*, ed. Diana
Mutz, Richard Brody, and Paul Sniderman, 17–79. Ann Arbor: University of
Michigan Press.

Zillmann, Dolf, and Jennings Bryant. 1985. "Selective-Exposure Phenomena."
In *Selective Exposure to Communication*, ed. Dolf Zillmann and Jennings
Bryant, 1–10. Hillsdale, NJ: Erlbaum.

Zillmann, Dolf, Richard T. Hezel, and Norman J. Medoff. 1980. "The Effect
of Affective States on Selective Exposure to Televised Entertainment Fare."
Journal of Applied Social Psychology 10, no. 4:323–39.

Index

A page number followed by the letter *f* refers to a figure, and a page number followed by the letter *t* indicates a table.

CHICAGO STUDIES IN AMERICAN POLITICS

A series edited by Benjamin I. Page, Susan Herbst, Lawrence R. Jacobs, and James Druckman